MY DADDY IS A HERO

MY DADDY IS A HERO

How Chris Watts Went from Family Man
to Family Killer

LENA DERHALLY

"As a child I never imagined that all of the real monsters in the world would be human" —Mobeen Hakeem

FIRST EDITION

www.lenaderhally.com

Cover by Caroline Teagle Johnson

ISBN: 978-17342977-0-6 (Hardback)
ISBN: 978-1-7342977-1-3 (Paperback)

CONTENTS

DISCLAIMER

The information in this book has mostly been taken from the Frederick Colorado Police Department and the Colorado Bureau of Investigation (CBI) Discovery documents from the investigation of the disappearance of Shanann Watts and her daughters. The story and analysis in this book are based on numerous interviews, text messages, e-mails, internet searches, and body cam footage from the police and CBI documents, as well as Shanann Watts' social media videos and posts. Other sources, including academic journals, books, and interviews that were not part of the discovery documents are included in the footnotes and Bibliography.

The thoughts, views, and opinions are solely the author's and not necessarily the author's employer or any groups or individuals affiliated with the author. The psychoanalysis in this book is not intended as definitive truth, as it is speculation and opinion based on the author's professional opinion and expertise. The author has never personally met Chris Watts or anyone affiliated with this crime and is not officially diagnosing any individual with a mental illness.

Most important, the blame for this tragedy lies entirely

upon Chris Watts. It is important to remember that there are many victims in this tragedy, not limited to the families, friends, and law enforcement. The author wrote this book with the objective of understanding tragedies like this one, in hopes of preventing them in the future.

INTRODUCTION

When I saw Chris Watts's television interview when Shanann and her daughters first went missing, I was struck by how indifferent he was to their disappearance. Like many others who watched that interview, I was drawn into the case immediately and followed it obsessively from that moment on.

As a mental health professional who works with couples and specializes in relationships, I couldn't quite wrap my head around how someone so seemingly normal his entire life, with no warning signs or red flags, could do something so heinous and evil. In my opinion, there was no way Shanann would have been able to tell she was married to someone who was capable of something this atrocious. In fact, I believe she thought Chris was completely incapable of something like this. For most of her marriage, up until she left for North Carolina for her summer vacation, she felt safe with Chris. She trusted him implicitly.

I know that many people who followed this case have had so many questions: *Was Chris a nice guy who had a break from reality? Was he an evil psychopath? A narcissist? Something else?*

3

If he is a psychopath, how did he hide it for so long? How did Chris become like this? Was he born like this, or did he become this way over time? Were there any warning signs? Are there warning signs that I can look out for, so this doesn't happen to me?

These are all questions I have attempted to answer in this book, using my professional expertise in Imago Relationship Therapy and psychotherapy, and with the help of a criminal psychologist, a neuroscientist, and a journalist. I am aware that people following this case have many diverse beliefs, opinions, and views, and I respect and honor them all. I share my opinions in this book, not because I believe it is the gospel, but because I wanted to contribute something meaningful and substantive to the discussion, and hopefully help bring some knowledge or closure to those who still struggle to move on.

While retelling this story, I recognize that it would be impossible to report the full truth. There are different sides and perspectives to many of the stories in this book, and we probably will never know exactly what happened. All I can do is report the different perspectives that I am aware of, and let the reader make their own judgments of what they believe to be true. The only account we have of what really happened to Shanann, Nico, Bella, and CeCe the morning they died is what Chris has said in several confessions he has given. There is no way to know what parts of his accounts are true, but I told his version of events in this book because that was the only account I had.

Many of the people who are familiar with this case will

already know some of the information presented in the book because they have poured over the discovery documents countless times themselves. I felt it was important to retell the story for those who were not familiar with the case and for everyone reading the book to use as reference when they read the psychological exploration of Chris and the story of the Watts family murders.

There was no way anyone involved in this tragedy could have seen it coming. The only thing we can do is try to learn from situations like this going forward. My hope is that we can prevent abuse and violence if we have more of an understanding and know what signs to look out for. By understanding important relational dynamics, attachment theory, and the traits and characteristics of Chris Watts and people like him, people can either leave a bad situation before it's too late, or they can get the help they need before things reach a point of catastrophe that they can never come back from.

Ultimately, this book was born out of a desire to understand how something like these murders could happen and to explore ideas of how, individually and collectively, we can try to prevent similar tragedies in the future. Although we cannot bring back Shanann, Bella, CeCe, and Nico, we can honor the beautiful legacy they have left behind.

CHAPTER 1

"Is Shanann ok?"

Monday August 13, 2018

Nicki Atkinson had a sinking feeling she couldn't explain when she woke up on the morning of August 13. Only five hours earlier, she had returned home to Frederick, Colorado, from a quick weekend business trip in Scottsdale, Arizona, with her best friend, Shanann Watts, but she couldn't shake the feeling that something was amiss.

Shanann and Nicki, both promoters of lifestyle products called Thrive by the up-and-coming Le-Vel company, were always in contact. Shanann in particular was incredibly motivated after these trips. Without fail, after a Le-Vel getaway, she would contact Nicki first thing in the morning. Shanann would jump on social media as soon as she woke up and would post on Facebook, sometimes earlier than seven o'clock.

This morning, something was different. When Nicki rolled over to check her phone, expecting her usual bombardment of text messages from her friend, nothing was there. Shanann's three- and four-year-old daughters, Celeste (known to all as CeCe) and Bella, were early risers. Shanann also had an appointment with her OB-GYN that morning to check on the status of her third pregnancy, and she had a busy day ahead of her. No way would she still be sleeping.

Besides the fact that Shanann was fifteen weeks pregnant and had a high-risk pregnancy because of several auto-immune diseases with which she struggled, she had been uncharacteristically emotionally distraught over the last several weeks. Her marriage, which she had thought was close to perfect, had been crumbling before her eyes, and the sudden change in her husband, Chris, was completely out of left field.

In a matter of only weeks, Shanann's normally doting, loving, and attentive spouse of six years had gone completely cold and unresponsive with no rational explanation. Shanann, Bella, and CeCe had been away from him five weeks, visiting family in North Carolina while he stayed behind in Colorado for work. Chris had joined his family the sixth week of the trip, and they all returned home to Colorado together.

Chris had recently told Shanann he no longer wanted the baby she was carrying, even though he was the one who pushed for the third child. Chris had always wanted a boy, and the couple was hoping that the third time would be the charm. Instead, Chris now said they were no longer com-patible, and he wanted a separation. When Shanann pushed him for definitive answers, he would vacillate between aloof and distant and giving her false hope that he might be open to working things out.

Right before Shanann and Nicki left for Arizona for their business trip, Chris had seemed more open to working on their marriage; he had even kissed Shanann once or twice, and he hadn't touched her in months. She was finally starting to feel that for the first time in the last six weeks of a hellish nightmare, perhaps her marriage could be saved. However, her anxiety was still heightened and palpable. Her friends with her in Arizona were worried because she wasn't eating or drinking much water. The normally unflappable and vivacious Shanann was withdrawn, depressed, and anxious.

It was unsettling for Nicki to see her normally optimistic, upbeat, and vibrant friend so despondent. Shanann was always the most dynamic person in the room. With porcelain, flawless skin, sparkling hazel eyes, glossy dark hair, and a dazzling smile that lit up her whole face, she was stunning. Her rebellious side was reflected on her face with a tiny nose ring stud she never took out. She was always impeccably put together. She loved bright colors, and her nails were always done in bold tones to match her stylish outfits.

Her outer beauty, however, was no match for her inner beauty. If you were lucky enough to be in Shanann's inner circle, you were blessed with the most warm, loyal, loving, and generous friend one could ever hope to have. Shanann doted on her loved ones and would do anything for them. She had tons of friends, and despite being as busy as she was, kept in constant contact with her friends and family. Being connected to people was her lifeblood.

On their flight back home to Colorado the night before, Nicki noticed that Shanann was physically uncomfortable and in pain. Her migraines had been debilitating, and the pregnancy and recent emotional distress were starting to take their toll. The flight had been delayed a few hours, so they didn't arrive home to Frederick until the early morning hours of August 13. Despite all the recent problems in her marriage, Shanann had been reading books on how to fix relationship troubles and had even sent a copy of *Hold Me Tight: Seven Conversations for a Lifetime of Love* to Chris while she had been in North Carolina.

Before she boarded her flight, she posted on Facebook, *"Ready to be home with Chris and the girls."* She hadn't really wanted to go to Arizona, but Chris had pushed her to go, reassuring her that they would talk when she got back.

Nicki had left her car at the airport over the weekend and drove them back home in her car after the flight landed. When they pulled up to the Watts home, it was around 1:45 am.

"Sucks that I'll be awake in three hours," Shanann said, turning to Nicki, exasperated.

"Why?" Nicki asked, not comprehending how Shanann would be able to function on so little sleep.

"CeCe gets up at 5:30 because she's still on North Carolina time," Shanann said, shaking her head.

Nicki gave her a hug. "Let me know if you need anything tomorrow or if you want me to go to your doctor's appointment with you," she said. She knew Shanann really needed support right now and wanted to help in whatever way she could.

Nicki did her due diligence as a good friend and watched Shanann drag her suitcase by the handle up the walkway, punch her entry code into the front door keypad, and disappear into the darkness of her picturesque mocha-colored home. When she safely made it inside, Nicki pulled away and drove back to her house.

No one would have ever predicted Shanann wasn't safe in her home, and nowhere in the darkest, most sinister corners of Nicki's mind, would she ever have imagined the horrors that would follow in the mere hours afterward.

Shanann locked the door behind her and used a security system to keep evil away from her and her family. She had no idea that the evil she needed to protect themselves from was the person she trusted the most.

· · ·

Kodi Roberts, a burly man in his early twenties, with kind brown eyes and shaggy hair, worked with Chris Watts, Shanann's husband. Chris and Kodi both worked in the fields for Anadarko Petroleum, cleaning up crude oil spills and leaks and making sure the sites were running efficiently. Kodi was at work early in the morning when he noticed three unanswered calls from Chris.

The night before, Chris had texted and told him not to bother going to Cervi 319, the site where Kodi was supposed to check out an oil leak. Chris mentioned in his text that there was no sense in both of them going out to Cervi. It wasn't typical for him to text on a Sunday like that, but Chris was always helping other people, so Kodi didn't think too much about it.

After the missed calls, Kodi noticed an incoming text from Chris.

"Where you at?" Chris asked.

"Just got fuel in Kersey" Kodi replied.

Chris attempted another call, but Kodi didn't pick up.

"Ok. I'm in Cervi. Where you going first?" Chris texted after not getting through to Kodi on the phone.

"DPC State," Kodi responded.

Chris responded with a thumbs-up emoji.

At 6:35 am, Kodi texted Chris, *"I need to call Chad and see if he plans on still stroking the 10-29 out there to see if it'll pump up….If so, I'll have to meet him, or he will have to get the cannon plugs from Tony, ok?"*

"Ok. Let me know before I leave here," Chris responded.

"I think he might be heading out there today. Phone was breaking up pretty bad," Kodi added.

Chad McNeil, another co-worker, also received a call from Chris at 6:45 am. Chad didn't pick up but shortly after, saw a text from Chris:

"You headed out to Cervi? I'm out here. Kodi said something about pumping up the 10-29."

Chad responded, *"Well since you're out there, you want to fix it up? Having Kodi bring his cables. I'll head that way in a bit."*

At 7:30 am, yet another co-worker, Troy McCoy, grabbed a

burrito from a mobile vendor and got into his truck to head over to Cervi 319. As he was driving, a call came in from Chris. Troy maneuvered the steering wheel and pulled over to the side of the road to take the call. Chris told him he was testing the bypass line that was leaking. Troy was headed over that way and told Chris he would see him soon.

Chris had been at Cervi 319 by himself for almost an hour when he texted his wife Shanann at 7:40 am, "*If you take the kids somewhere, please let me know where they are at!*"

• • •

"Primrose School of Erie. This is Shannan. How can I help you?" Shannan Meyer, who coincidentally spelled her name the same as Shannan Watts, was one of the owners of The Primrose School, a childcare facility Bella and CeCe Watts attended. Meyer answered the phone at 8:15 am. The girls hadn't been there in weeks because they had been vacationing with family in North Carolina, and they were scheduled to start school again that morning.

"Hi, this is Chris Watts," Chris said, "Bella and CeCe's dad."

"Oh hi!" Meyer replied. "We're excited to see the girls today."

"Well, that's why I'm calling. The girls won't be coming back to school," Chris said.

There was an awkward silence, and then he continued. "I'm not really sure what's going on yet, but we are putting the house up for sale and moving and not sure where we're going to be yet."

"That's pretty crazy," Meyer said hesitantly.

"The girls aren't there…are they?" Chris asked.

"I haven't seen them, but I can check to see if they've clocked in yet."

Meyer put Chris on hold and found out the girls had not arrived at school that day. She picked up the phone again to tell Chris.

"Ok, put them down as not coming in then," he said.

"Do you want me to put them on the waitlist in case anything changes?" Meyer asked.

"Sure. Might as well. But we don't know what's going on right now."

"Ok…well, the teachers will be sad not to see them… please keep us updated."

"Will do. Thanks," Chris said, and hung up.

He then called Ann Meadows, his real estate agent. Ann picked up, surprised to hear from him because she usually dealt only with Shanann. Years ago, she had helped the Watts family buy the house they were living in, and Shanann had contacted her recently about putting their current house up for sale and looking for something new.

After she greeted him, Chris replied, "Hi Ann. Has Shanann called you yet?"

"I talked to her through Facebook messenger and suggested you guys get preapproved for a loan," Ann said.

"Listen. No one knows this yet. Not even our family," Chris

said bluntly, "but Shanann and I are getting divorced. We haven't been getting along in over a year."

Ann was silent for a moment, completely shocked. Shanann and Chris seemed like the happiest couple on earth to her. They appeared to be truly in love and fond of each other. Their affection didn't feel fake or forced either. They genuinely seemed to enjoy each other's company and were a great team in so many ways. Shanann was so lovely, sweet, and ambitious, and Chris was quiet and a great father to the girls.

"Wow. I'm sorry," Ann said, completely confused about how to respond to the news.

Chris told her he would be in touch later and proceeded to call Shanann's cell. There was no answer.

• • •

Melissa Parrish, another Anadarko employee, worked closely with Chris Watts, Troy McCoy, Chad McNeil, and Kodi Roberts. They were all planning to head to the Cervi 319 site to check on the leak that Chris had been working on. Parrish was new to Anadarko, and this was her first time at the site. At 8:25 am, she and McNeil arrived there. Chris would usually text the group when he was at a site, but he hadn't that morning.

Parrish liked Chris a lot. He was always quiet, yet calm and easy to be around. In her eyes, he was a true family man, and his daughters were his world. He gushed about them all the time. When Parrish saw Chris for the first time, she noticed a shovel and a hole in the ground next to where he was standing. The hole was about one foot wide and six- to eight-inches deep.

Troy McCoy arrived at Cervi 319 next, at 8:51am. Troy's gaze immediately landed on Chris' work truck that was parked right next to the well head. It was odd, considering that spot was far away from the oil leak that he was supposed to be fixing. Instead of wearing his usual tight-fitting, fire-resistant clothing, Chris was wearing a baggy navy-blue shirt. He was also wearing his older pair of boots, and he'd tucked only one side of his pants into one of them.

Chris greeted the group as they approached him.

"What, are you slumming it today?" Troy asked, as he eyed Chris up and down.

Chris laughed. "Been worried about snakes and legless lizards," Chris retorted.

The group began to make small talk about their weekends as they normally would. Chris told Parrish that he had gotten a babysitter Saturday night and gone to the Colorado Rockies game.

Parrish noted while they were all chatting that Chris hadn't cleaned up the oil spill as he usually did. He was meticulous with clean up, but this time, he wasn't. Other than that, it was a totally normal Monday morning for the team.

Shortly afterward, the group went in their separate vehicles to another site, Cervi 1029. Chris arrived at Cervi 1029 at 9:49 am.

At 10:10 am, Chris searched the lyrics for the song, "Battery" by Metallica on his phone. A die-hard Metallica fan, he even had a Metallica tattoo on his back.

The lyrics included lines about hypnotizing power, lunacy, and aggression. There was even a line about not killing the family.

At 10:28 am, Sandi Rzucek, Shanann's mother, texted Chris.

"Is Shanann ok?"

Chris picked up the phone and called Sandi immediately. After getting off the phone, he searched the internet for "hotels in Aspen" and then placed a short call to the Westin Snowmass Resort.

Sandi called Chris again. He continued his web searching and looked up the contact information for "Groupon." Shanann had made reservations through Groupon for them in Aspen for the upcoming weekend so they could work on their marriage, and he needed to call and cancel.

After sorting out some of his business, Chris noticed sunflowers in the open prairie of the oil fields. He took out his cellphone and snapped a photo of them. He wanted to send the picture to someone special in his life.

CHAPTER 2

"Don't call the police."

At 11:45 that morning, Nicki Atkinson still hadn't received a response or any communication from Shanann. She looked at her phone and at the screen of texts she had been sending Shanann since early morning:

"How are you?"

"Just wanted to see if you're okay. I know you were hurting a lot last night. I hope you're okay."

"Let me know how your appointment goes."

Nicki started to feel panicked, so she asked her teenage son, Matt,[1] if he would drive over to Shanann's house. With no make-up, a T-shirt, black leggings. and her auburn hair shoved into a messy bun, she grabbed a pair of oversized white-rimmed sunglasses and made her way to her car with Matt. A spitting image of her except for the hair shaved on both sides of his head, he wore a T-shirt and shorts. Nicki would be returning exactly where she had safely dropped Shanann off just hours earlier.

---

1. This person is a minor, and his name has been changed for his protection.

"I'm very worried about you. I'm coming to your house," she texted Shanann before leaving.

As Nicki and Matt made the drive over to Shanann's, Nicki texted other mutual friends, telling them she was on her way to the house and would keep them updated. Worst-case scenario, she thought, maybe Shanann had just passed out, and Nicki would let herself in and get her the help she needed.

Nicki had the door code to the Watts house because when they were away, she and Matt would watch over the family dachshund, Dieter, and take care of things around the house.

When they pulled up to the Watts house, Nicki went straight to the front door and punched in the code. Her heart sank into her stomach. The chain was latched to the door from the inside. Normally, Shanann and Chris would do this so three-year-old CeCe, a known toddler escape artist, wouldn't let herself out of the house. Now, there was no way they could get in the house to see if Shanann was okay. Nicki peered in through the glass into the front entry way of the home. Right by the door, she spotted the flip-flops that Shanann wore everywhere. Clearly this would indicate she was still home. She never went anywhere without them. Near the flip-flops, sat her suitcase from the trip to Arizona.

Nicki's next idea was to see if Shanann's car was still there. If she had gone somewhere with the children, the car would be gone as well.

"If we move the car up to the garage, you can stand on it

and look in the window to see if her car is still there," she told Matt.

They moved the car adjacent to the garage, and Matt hoisted himself up on top of it, peering through the window into the garage. Shanann's white Lexus SUV was still in the garage. The car seats were clearly visible, and Nicki knew her friend never would have left the house without the girls in car seats. Chris' pickup truck was their only other vehicle, and he had taken it to work that day.

Internally, Nicki started to panic. Cassie, another close friend of Shanann's, had been in close communication with Nicki throughout the morning hours. Cassie and her husband Josh had a good relationship with Chris. While Nicki was at the Watts house, trying to get in, Cassie was contacting Chris and was stunned at how nonchalant he seemed. Nicki was getting really frustrated that Chris didn't seem worried at all, and she conveyed her dismay to Cassie.

Cassie, extremely concerned and baffled as well, decided to send Chris a series of text messages in hopes that he would take the situation more seriously if they ganged up on him.

"Shanann is in a very bad way emotionally, and I'm worried about her. I know you are having issues, and I don't know to what extent, but I do know I have never seen her so broken to an extent I am worried."

Chris replied, *"She went to a friend's house with the kids. She won't tell me where though. When I get home, I will update you."*

"Sweetie, nobody knows about you and her other than Nicki and me, so where would she go if not with Nicki and not to Arizona

where I'm at? Her car and shoes and everything are at the house. What the heck is going on with you guys that she would totally shut out everything? It's not like her."

"I told Nicki about it so she won't freak out about it anymore at the house," he texted back. *"I think Cristina knows as well. We talked last night, and I told her I wanted to sell the house, get something smaller. Separation would be best right now if we can work thru the issues. I really don't want you to think I'm a bad person Cassie."* Chris was oddly more concerned about how others were perceiving him than his missing pregnant wife and daughters.

Amid his text messages with Cassie, Chris resumed his text conversation with the real estate agent, Ann Meadows. Ann had been texting both Shanann and Chris that morning, completely oblivious to what was going on.

"Hi. I'm working on your market analysis. I would like to bring my listing coordinator with me when I bring it. Did you finish the basement? Any other upgrades?" Ann asked.

"Basement is still unfinished. No other upgrades," Chris quickly typed back.

He then went back to check his new messages from Cassie. His phone was blowing up with messages.

"Right now, I don't care about you or your relationship or what type of person you are or not or what I think of you and I'm not trying to be rude when I say that," Cassie texted back, infuriated. *"Right now, I'm worried about your damn wife and her well-being. Nicki is calling the police. (Shanann) is broken emotionally. Her blood sugar dropped due to not eating and it could*

cause her to pass out. So, unless you want the police to bust your damn door down, you get home and check on your family. I'm sorry if I'm being rude but I'm seriously concerned."

"I'm going home Cassie. On my way. Don't call the police. I will be there in 45 minutes."

While Cassie was hammering Chris with questions, Nicki called 911 to do a wellness check on Shanann and the girls. Officer Coonrod, a man with a slender build and short dark hair, arrived at the Watts house and introduced himself to Nicki and Matt. He walked up to the front door and started pounding on it several times. Dieter, the dog, was inside, barking furiously. Other than that, the house seemed empty and silent.

Officer Coonrod walked around the back exterior of the house, peering inside to see if he could find a way inside without breaking in. He loudly called Shanann's name several times, but only echoes and silence filled the air. As he made his way back to the front of the house, Nicki was on the phone with Sandi, Shanann's mother.

"I don't think Chris is coming," Officer Coonrod told Nicki.

At that exact moment, Chris pulled up to the house in his work truck. He jumped out and ran toward Officer Coonrod.

Standing relatively tall at 5'10," Chris was muscular and tan. That day, he was wearing a long-sleeved gray shirt, jeans, and tinted sunglasses. Even though he was only thirty-three-years-old, his hair was streaked all over with gray and buzzed in a close shave.

Officer Coonrod made note of these details and then

asked, "Chris?"

He nodded.

"Scott. How you doing?" Officer Coonrod said, introducing himself by first name and extending his hand to Chris. "This is the only vehicle that she would have? That she would drive?" he asked Chris, pointing toward the garage.

"Yeah," Chris said.

Chris opened the garage and ducked in. Then, he quickly opened the front passenger door of Shanann's car and appeared to pick something up from the floorboard before he closed the car door. He slipped something in his pocket before rushing into the house.

A neighbor, Nate Trinastich, noticing the commotion, lumbered over to the Watts' front yard. Trinastich was tall and husky, wearing a T-shirt, shorts, and a backward baseball cap. He told Nicki he had a security camera that had a view of the Watts' driveway, and he was willing to share the footage if it would help.

"The neighbor checked his camera and said he saw a white car drive away around one. That was me, though," Nicki said out loud on her cellphone, talking to Sandi, Shanann's mother.

"That's the only movement the whole day," Nate replied.

"Besides Chris leaving?" Nicki asked.

"Yeah," Nate said, nodding.

"The girls' car seats are in the car too, so if she left with a friend, she would've taken the girls' car seats," Nicki said to Sandi, still on the phone with her.

"Can we go in the house?" Nicki asked, pulling the phone away from her face and looking at Coonrod.

"I mean that's up to him. It's his house." The officer gestured to Chris as he opened the front door to let them in.

"You mind if I come in, Chris?" he asked.

Chris nodded, opened the door, and let Coonrod, Nicki, and Matt inside the home.

The house was eerily quiet except for the sounds of Dieter still frantically barking. It appeared neat and well kept. The ceilings were high. Black leather sofas and patterned chairs with blue pillows filled the family living area at the entrance of the home. A staircase in the front entry way led up to the bedroom area. Officer Coonrod walked through the first floor and into a bathroom with bright aqua walls. He pulled open a shower curtain covered in palm trees. There was nothing in the bathtub.

Upstairs, Chris was wandering around when Officer Coonrod made his way up to the second floor. Coonrod noticed a common area on the second-floor landing with another black leather couch and a television. He went into the girls' bedrooms first. Bella's room was a lilac purple with black accents, and CeCe's was bright blue like the bathroom on the first floor. Chris commented to Coonrod that the girls' blankets seemed to be missing, and that they wouldn't go anywhere without them. Was this implying that Shanann took them somewhere?

In an interesting and important development, Matt told the group he just found Shanann's iPhone buried in the cushions of the couch in the upstairs common area.

"Her phone's here?" Nicki shrieked in a panicky voice, nervously shaking her hand. She knew Shanann never went anywhere without her phone.

"Can we unlock the phone?" Officer Coonrod asked Chris.

"I don't know the code," he said, shrugging.

"It's the baby's due date!" Nicki muttered, exasperated.

Chris seemed calm to Coonrod as he explained that Shanann's flight was supposed to land at eleven the night before but was delayed. She got home at two in the morning instead. Chris said he left the house around 5:15 to 5:30 am.

"You told me she went on a playdate with the girls," Nicki said.

"That's what she told me. She left go to a friend's house with the kids," he told her. "That's why they weren't at school."

"You guys having any marital issues?" Officer Coonrod asked.

"We're going through a separation," he replied, as Nicki stood by silently.

"You guys filed yet or anything?" Officer Coonrod inquired.

"No, we're going to sell the house," Chris said.

"And how's that going? Civil, for the most part?"

"Yeah, civil," Chris said with a nervous laugh.

He then walked into the master bedroom, and after a few minutes, emerged holding Shanann's wedding ring gingerly on the tip of his index finger. He told them he found the ring Shanann never took off on the bedside table.

Officer Coonrod walked into the master bedroom,

noticing a four-poster mahogany bed, stripped of its sheets. A wedding photo of Shanann and Chris was on the dressing table.

"And there was no note or anything by the wedding ring?" Coonrod asked Chris.

"Nope."

"Any clothes, anything like that missing?" Coonrod asked. "She tell you anything about leaving, moving out?"

"Not moving out...I mean, last time I talked to her was this morning. She said she was gonna take the kids to a friend's house, and that's where she was gonna be. I've texted her today and never heard anything...but the car is here. Unless somebody came and picked her up, but the people that I know...nobody's seen her."

Chris and Coonrod walked through a large master bathroom with bright orange towels that led to a walk-in closet. Shanann's closet was purple with the letters "GORGEOUS" spelled out in black on the top of one wall. Clothes were hung on racks throughout the entire closet, and Chris mentioned it would be hard to know if she took anything because of the amount of clothing she owned.

"Definitely an odd one..." Coonrod said out loud as he walked back through the master bathroom to the main area.

Shanann's mother, Sandi, called Officer Coonrod directly while he was at the house and adamantly pleaded with him to check the GPS on Chris's truck. Up until this point, Sandi would never have imagined that Chris could be capable of harming her daughter or granddaughters, but she had an overwhelming feeling that Chris had something to do with whatever was going on.

Officer Coonrod observed that the only thing that seemed slightly amiss at the house was that the sheets, comforter, and pillows had been removed from the master bed. There was no top sheet to be found. Other than that, there was no suggestion of foul play, an altercation, or robbery in the home. However, Shanann's purse, medications, ID, credit cards, wallet, phone, keys, and the girls' medications, including CeCe's Epi-pen for a life-threatening nut allergy, were all still in the house. Anyone who knew Shanann knew that she was incredibly responsible and organized and never would have left the house without any of these things. Officer Coonrod felt he needed back up and called Detective Baumhover of the Frederick Police Department to come to the house.

• • •

Eager to help the police, neighbor Nate Trinastich knew right away he would be able to. He thought it was unusual that Chris had backed his truck into the garage in the early morning hours. He had never seen him do that before, and he had been reviewing the footage of his security camera that faced the front of the Watts house. Trinastich invited the group to his home to watch the security footage he had recorded. Nate's camera faced the Watts' garage directly, and he could see any vehicle that would be arriving in and around the home. While staring at his phone, Chris started nervously mumbling what he was loading in his truck that morning. "My water jugs, my bookbags, my computer."

"This is him at 5:17," Nate said, staring intensely at the television screen.

Chris started fumbling his words again. He looked away from the television screen and put both his hands on top of his head, rocking back and forth anxiously. He stared directly at Officer Coonrod.

"My detective just showed up," Coonrod said. "He'll probably want to talk to you. He said he might have you call the bank and see if there's any kind of activity."

Chris started rambling again. "The other week, people were caught for like stealing stuff out of people's garages and stuff like that."

Nate, still in a backward orange baseball cap and gray t-shirt, and towering over Chris, pointed his remote at the television. "I have your car right here. Any action that would have happened, any cars that would have left your house, I would have got it."

Nate turned off the security footage, and an image of a fetus in an hourglass flashed across the screen in front of Chris's face. It was an advertisement for the television show, *American Horror Story*. In the ad, the fetus in the hourglass turns into an explosion, and a skull emerges from a puddle of black goo resembling crude oil.

"She's pregnant as well," Chris blurted out to Coonrod, turning away from the grotesque images on the television screen.

"Oh yeah, how far along?"

"Fifteen weeks."

"All right, I appreciate your time," Officer Coonrod said.

Chris and Nate shook hands, and Chris turned around, brusquely walking toward the front door as if he couldn't get out of there fast enough.

"He's not acting right at all," Nate said, shaking his head vigorously as soon as the door shut behind Chris.

"No?" Coonrod asked.

Nate imitated Chris's exaggerated body movements.

"Rocking back and forth," he said, as he continued to mimic Chris's movements.

Then Nate sharply turned and walked back to the television, flicking it on. "He never loads his stuff in and out of the garage. It just seems kind of odd to me. Why would he pull the truck up?" Nate's voice trailed off

"Yeah," Matt chimed in. "I've never seen him pull it back."

"If he loads his stuff, he normally walks back and forth. I get him on camera walking back and forth," Nate said, gesturing.

"What is he normally loading up?" Officer Coonrod asked.

"Looks like a computer and a water jug, and that's it. But the fact that he was in here explaining to you over and over…"

"A little odd," Coonrod said.

"He doesn't look worried," Nate insisted. "He looks like he's trying to cover his tracks. And if he's loading his stuff, why is he walking back and forth? But I can't see what he's doing in the back of the truck because he's pulled into the garage, and he knows my camera is there."

Nicki walked into Nate's house, sharing that she had just been texting with Shanann's mother.

"Don't you think it's kind of odd?" Nate said, looking at Nicki.

"I know."

"I'm just saying, it's kind of odd. He pulls his truck back behind my camera, and he never backs his truck into the driveway."

"That's what her friend Cristina was saying," Nicki exclaimed. "He never backs up. He carries his stuff to the house!"

"This is suspicious," Nate said. "He's normally quiet. Subdued. He's telling you three times what he took out...what he did."

"He's very reserved," Nicki agreed.

"He never talks! So, the fact that he's over here blabbing his mouth makes me kind of suspicious," Nate told them.

"Yeah," Coonrod said. "But I mean put yourself in his situation. Anyone's going to be nervous on what to do," Officer Coonrod told them.

"No, I agree," Nate said, "but I'm just saying, the way he told you three times what he brought with him...why is he telling you exactly what he brought with him...why is he worried about you knowing what he's carrying out? That's all I'm saying."

• • •

Officer James, Detective Baumhover, and Sergeant Bakes, all from the Frederick Police Department, went over to the Watts home to help Coonrod with this odd case that was growing stranger by the minute. Officer James went through the house again, and Detective Baumhover talked to Chris in the kitchen. Baumhover, a thin man with a moustache, wore a purple, long-sleeved button-down and tie. He had seen his fair share of domestic violence cases and knew that outward surfaces of even the most perfect homes and families could be deceiving. From an outward appearance, this family seemed perfect from what he could tell. Everything about the house alluded to a happy home, from the bright and festive colors peppered throughout the house, to the photos of the attractive and smiling couple with their adorable toddler daughters. Baumhover had been alerted to the fact that Chris was telling people that he and Shanann were in the process of a separation and about to sell the house, but you wouldn't have guessed it being inside a home that seemed so full of love.

Officer James went down to check out the unfinished basement area and noticed the basement was extremely well organized. Shanann was self-professed OCD and prided herself on being a stellar organizer. Everything had its place, and if something was even slightly out of place, it would drive her crazy. Although the basement was mainly used for storage, there was an unmade bed in the corner. Apparently,

Chris had been staying there because of the "separation."

Upstairs, Officer James saw children's clothing swishing in the washing machine and dryer as if this were a normal day. In the bathroom adjacent to the loft area and playroom, children's toys were in the bathtub.

Chris's version of the chain of events was that the family had returned home to Frederick from North Carolina on August 7. Shanann had been there for five weeks with the girls, visiting both her Chris's families from June 26 through August 7. Chris joined them for the final week of the trip, and they all flew home together. A few days after that, on Friday August 10, Shanann left with Nicki for her business trip to Arizona. The flight home, scheduled to land on Sunday night, August 12, around eleven o'clock, was delayed to Monday at around 1:45 am. Chris said he stayed in the master bedroom with Shanann that night and woke up around 4 am. He then woke Shanann to have a conversation about selling the house and separating. According to him, the conversation lasted about forty-five minutes, it was emotional, and they were both crying. He then loaded up his truck and left for work around 5:15 to 5:30 am. Shanann said she was taking the girls to a friend's house for a playdate, even though they were scheduled to be in school that day. Chris said he didn't know which friend.

Officer James also spoke with Chris about the separation. Chris maintained that while Shanann was gone for those five weeks, there was a "disconnect," and they had fallen out of love. When he went to North Carolina for the sixth week

31

of the trip, he felt "it" wasn't there anymore, and the relationship wasn't the same. He also mentioned he felt like he could never be himself around Shanann. The entire situation was very odd considering Shanann was pregnant with a third baby. Also strange was that after being with Shanann for eight years, and with a third child on the way, Chris claimed he just fell out of love in a mere five weeks and was willing to throw in the towel on his marriage and family. Officer James left Chris with his card and told him to call if he had heard anything. Detective Baumhover took Shanann's phone and other evidence back to the police station to be analyzed.

CHAPTER 3

"I'm in."

Amanda Thayer had just arrived home to Colorado after an emotionally exhausting trip to Kentucky. Amanda's brother had just passed away, and she and her husband Nick had gone there to attend the funeral. Amanda had befriended Shanann in 2016 when Amanda was the director at the Primrose School in Erie, Colorado, where Bella and CeCe were enrolled.

Their friendship quickly progressed from chatting at school drop-offs and pick-ups to spending time together on weekends with their husbands and daughters. The Thayers' daughter also formed a close friendship with Bella and CeCe. Nick and Chris had a relatively casual friendship and got along well, and when Chris developed an interest in physical fitness, they became running buddies. Although Nick considered Chris a friend, he admittedly didn't know much about him. He thought of Chris as "self-contained" and thought he was a nice guy but hard to get to know on a deeper level.

Amanda was no longer the director at Primrose, and she and her family had moved from Frederick to Thornton, so they didn't see the Watts family as much as they used to. However, Shanann had convinced Amanda to sell Thrive products, and she had recently joined the Le-Vel company as a promoter and salesperson on Shanann's team.

Only a few days had passed since Shanann had dropped a bombshell that her marriage, which was once so strong, was deteriorating rapidly. Today, Amanda had received a barrage of messages from Cassie and Nicki, asking if she had heard anything. Nicki told Amanda that Chris had been changing his version of events about what had happened in the early morning hours. He had told Cassie one story and Nicki another.

Confused and concerned, Nick and Amanda decided to go check on Chris at the Watts home around six o'clock that evening.

Right before they arrived, Chris responded to an email about a Fantasy Football league: *"I'm in,"* he responded, alarming a few people on the email chain who were aware his wife and daughters were missing.

When Amanda and Nick arrived at the house, they stood in the entry way, firing questions at Chris. As he recounted his version of the story, they made their way into the kitchen. Amanda observed Chris pacing and thought he looked numb and lost. His behavior reminded her of the shock and disbelief she felt after losing her brother. Probably grief, she told herself, imagining that Chris must be completely paralyzed with fear and dread, considering what was happening.

Amanda, Nick, and Chris sat at the kitchen table together.

"Shanann and I have been having issues in our marriage," Chris said.

"I know. She told me," Amanda said.

"This morning, I woke up around 4 am and told her I wanted to sell the house and separate," Chris said. "We need something smaller. Things have been tight financially, and we only built this house because it made Shanann happy and reminded her of our other house back in North Carolina. I wanted to tell Shanann in person that it was over. I didn't want to do it over phone or text. When I left around five, she was emotional and crying. I was at work, and Nicki Atkinson was texting me, telling me she couldn't get a hold of anyone. So, I rushed home. On my way home, I called the school to see if they showed up there."

"Have they found any leads?" Nick asked. "Do the police have any idea as to where they could have gone?"

"They took Shanann's phone," Chris replied. "Our doorbell camera has footage of Shanann getting home last night, and the neighbor has a security camera that shows me loading up my truck for work and leaving, but that's it. The cops got a warrant to search the house. I found a charge on our credit card for a taxi, but that's it. I have no idea what to do."

"I'm sorry," Amanda said.

"It's too quiet and empty in this house." Chris's tone was flat and devoid of emotion. "I just want them back and to hug them again."

"What are you going to do about all the media attention?" Nick asked.

"I don't want to talk to them. They're going to pry and twist my words around, and I'll look like public enemy number one."

"Are you going to be okay?" Amanda asked. "Do you want to stay at our house tonight?"

"Not tonight. I want to stay home in case they come home, and I want to clean up for them."

The doorbell rang, and Chris excused himself to go answer it.

Lauren Arnold stood at the door, anxious and worried about how Chris was doing considering the bizarre news. Lauren was Shanann's good friend who had attended high school with her in North Carolina and who now lived in Colorado. She saw Shanann and Chris at least once a month and considered herself close friends with both. Lauren knew Chris well, and she knew how much he adored Shanann and the girls. She figured he must be losing his mind and going crazy with worry. Lauren was hoping she could do something to help. Maybe she could be a shoulder to cry on or get Chris some dinner because he would obviously be too distraught to think about eating.

Chris answered the door and immediately swept Lauren in an embrace.

"Are you OK?" she asked.

"No," he replied.

Lauren stepped inside, and her gaze landed on the large staircase that was a focal point in the main family room.

As if reading her mind, Chris said, "I had to close the doors, the doors upstairs. I had to close all of the doors because I can't handle going up there and seeing everything, like the toys and stuff." He motioned to the second floor.

Lauren hadn't even noticed the closed doors. Why would he make a comment like that?

As they walked through the house toward the kitchen, Lauren noticed the girls' toys scattered about the living room, a snapshot in time of a house once filled with playing and laughter.

Why is it okay for him to see the toys down here but not upstairs? Lauren wondered, and an ominous feeling washed over her.

As they entered the kitchen, Lauren saw a petite woman with short, bleached hair and a rail-thin bald man. The couple appeared to be in their early thirties. Lauren had never seen them before and was surprised because she had pretty much met all Shanann's and Chris's friends in Colorado over the years.

Chris introduced them as Nick and Amanda Thayer.

"Have you gone out looking for them yet?" Lauren asked Chris.

"The police told us not to go anywhere," Nick said.

"Well, I'm going to drive around and look as soon as I leave," Lauren told them. Then she looked at Chris. "What did she say to you this morning? What was the last thing she said?"

As if unable to meet her eyes, he stared down at the floor, acting very odd. Lauren had known about the sudden shift in his behavior the last two months. She was just as perplexed as Shanann had been. Lauren had first met Chris after he married Shanann in 2012 and immediately loved him. She always observed Chris and Shanann as equal partners, loving and attentive toward one another and the girls.

That's why it was so shocking when Lauren felt the shift in Chris sometime in June. Lauren would be over at the Watts house spending time with Shanann, and Chris would come home from work, acting distant, which was very unlike him. In the past, he would immediately kiss Shanann, say hi to the girls, go upstairs to shower, and then come back down to hang out with Lauren and Shanann.

In June, that all changed. With the other pregnancies, Chris had been caring and attentive. With the third pregnancy, he completely ignored Shanann and couldn't care less about how sick she was feeling.

On her way out of the house, she pulled the Thayers aside and asked them not to leave Chris alone in the house that night. Lauren wasn't concerned about Chris anymore. She was now worried he would try to clear his tracks if he had done something, which seemed to feel more and more like an actual possibility. Chris was wearing a tank top, and Lauren quietly scanned his bare arms, looking for signs of scratches or injuries.

She left the house feeling very suspicious of Chris. She

decided to drive around the neighborhood to look for Shanann and the girls before heading home.

After Lauren and the Thayers left around 9:30 that night, Chris's friend David Colon showed up at the house to check on him. David had previously lived in the same sub-development as the Watts and had met Shanann and Chris seven years before when they had first moved to Colorado. They had all worked together at the Longmont Ford Dealership where Chris had been a mechanic and Shanann worked in sales.

Although Colon considered both Shanann and Chris friends, he had unfriended Shanann on Facebook because of her incessant posting, promoting, and selling Thrive. Chris had also recently told him that Shanann wrote his Facebook posts for him. This made sense to Colon because he always found Chris's posts odd and "not guy-ish," in the sense that they were all about how great his wife and family were. This didn't seem to line up with Colon's perception of Chris, who did not gush or talk about feelings.

Colon was also surprised to hear that there had been difficulties in the marriage. Although he considered Shanann overbearing, he thought she was a good mother and person and that Chris and Shanann complemented each other well. They were a classic case of "opposites attract." Shanann was dominant and knew exactly what she wanted, and Chris was laid back and a "go with the flow" kind of guy. He always seemed completely comfortable with Shanann making all the decisions in the relationship.

Chris had told David over the phone that he had gone to work that morning, and sometime after that, Shanann had disappeared, leaving behind her keys and other personal belongings.

When David stepped in the house, he noticed Chris had been doing housework. The carpet appeared as it had just been vacuumed, and Chris was in the middle of making himself a protein shake. Jeremy Lindstrom, a mutual friend, showed up shortly after. Chris had just been at Jeremy's house with his daughters the day before, on Sunday, for Jeremy's son's birthday party.

Chris told his friends that he and Shanann were having marital difficulties and that the reason for Shanann's trip to North Carolina was a trial separation to see how they would be when they were apart. This morning, he had told her that he wanted an official separation. Colon asked Chris about the potential of foul play, but Chris confided that he thought Shanann had taken the girls and was hiding out somewhere. He also mentioned that he was worried that the girls didn't have any of their medications with them.

Colon thought Chris seemed emotionally blank considering everything that was happening, but it wasn't like him to show emotion anyway. He seemed stunned, almost in disbelief this was happening to him. Colon thought of Chris as the most low-key guy he had ever met and firmly believed he had nothing to do with their disappearance. In fact, he believed that if there was anything like infidelity going on in the relationship, Shanann would be the one to cheat, not Chris.

• • •

Back at the Frederick Police Station, Officer James was making calls to Shanann's and Chris's friends to see if they had any information pertaining to the whereabouts of Shanann, Bella, and CeCe.

He picked up the phone and called Addy, one of Shanann's closest friends. Even though Addy lived in Maryland, she was in constant contact with Shanann. On the same Thrive sales team, they spoke frequently about work, and their friendship had also become extremely close to the point that they confided in each other about personal matters.

When Officer James reached Addy on the phone, she was very worried about Shanann. She had just been in Arizona with her, Nicki, Cassie, and some other friends for the Le-Vel business trip. She told Officer James that on Sunday evening, right before Shanann boarded her flight home to Colorado, she had expressed concern to Addy that she thought Chris might be having an affair. His change in behavior and wanting a separation had been so sudden that the thought had crossed Shanann's mind that he could have met someone else. Still, she had brushed that thought aside, mentioning that Chris had "no game."

Besides, that also would have been completely out of character for him. Addy and the other girls had reassured her there was no way Chris would do that. They all knew him and the way he looked at Shanann. He was not one of "those guys," and in fact, he was the opposite of a smooth-talking adulterer.

However, that Saturday night Shanann was in Arizona, she noticed a strange charge come through on her credit card alert. Shanann handled the Watts family finances, and every charge made on their card came directly to her phone. Chris had asked Jeremy Lindstrom's daughter to babysit that evening so he could go to the Colorado Rockies baseball game with co-workers. Later that evening, a charge had come through on the credit card for $62 from the Lazy Dog Restaurant. That was quite hefty for the Lazy Dog, let alone for one person. When Shanann quizzed him on the charge over a text, Chris said he had only had a beer and salmon. Shanann went online, looked at the menu, and saw that $62 was double the cost of a beer and salmon.

Shanann had also been in communication over text with the babysitter Chris had hired, so she knew he had been out until 10:30, which was well past the time the Rockies game had ended.

Addy told Officer James that it was a "huge, huge shock" when she heard Chris and Shanann were having problems. She also mentioned that Shanann had been trying to save the marriage for the past couple of weeks, and there had been several "red flags."

Chris didn't want the baby anymore and had been deleting messages from his phone. Shanann even saw Chris deleting text messages from his father, which she thought was incredibly bizarre. He had changed the wallpaper on his phone from a photo of Shanann and the girls to a landscape of the

Sand Dunes National Park. It was as if his family, once the center of his world, now meant nothing to him.

Chris had told Shanann that it was nothing she did wrong, and it was all him. Shanann didn't want to go to Arizona, especially because he seemed to be coming around, but Chris told her they would talk when she got back. They were supposed to go to Aspen upon her return to try to salvage the marriage, and she was looking forward to the upcoming weekend getaway with him. Addy was feeling hopeful that Shanann and Chris would work things out.

Around two o'clock in the morning, Officer Goodman, who was also working on the case, tried calling Chris numerous times with no answer. When Chris called back five minutes later, Goodman immediately thought to himself that it was peculiar Chris did not ask if there was any new information on the whereabouts of his family. His voice and demeanor were totally calm and disaffected. Officer Goodman was calling to get specific information about Shanann and the girls so he could file them as missing persons. After he filed the missing person's report, he received a call from Sandi, Shanann's mother.

"My husband and I believe Chris is involved, and this is a matter of foul play," she said, her raspy voice distraught. "Chris is acting weird. He's telling people he has to go to work and isn't right. I think he's going to pour oil on their bodies and dispose of them somewhere."

Sandi had always viewed Chris as the perfect husband and father. Although she was somewhat aware of the marital troubles and knew that Chris had recently been agitated and annoyed with Shanann and the girls, she never would have suspected anything like this.

"If Chris did something to her after the emotional conversation he said they had, she wouldn't be able to fight because of her lupus," Sandi told Officer Goodman.

After they got off the phone, Sandi called back one more time. "Officer, I just got off the phone with Chris and didn't feel any genuine emotion or concern from him. He's not shedding any tears. He also called a neighbor to tell them he thinks the police are watching him."

"Thank you. We are looking into all of it and will keep you posted," Officer Goodman assured her.

The next day, everything would blow up into a media circus.

CHAPTER 4

"I'd do anything for those girls."

On the morning of Tuesday August 14, a search and rescue team with K9s was deployed to look for Shanann and the girls. The more time passed, the more concerning the situation became.

Officer Katherine Lines showed up at the house first thing in the morning, noting the strong odor of cleaning chemicals. The house was spotless, and fresh lines on the carpet suggested someone had just been vacuuming. Chris had done the laundry and made the girls' beds. He explained to the officers that he had a hard time sleeping because he was used to the girls throwing chicken nuggets at him, and he missed that.

Officer Lines also made sure to note Chris's behavior, which she considered incredibly bizarre. Lines overheard Officer Perez, another officer at the Watts home, commenting to Chris that he couldn't imagine what he was going through. Later, when Officer Lines documented her visit to the house, she wrote: "While speaking with Chris, he showed no emotion and did not seem to respond appropriately to the situation. Chris did not ask any questions or offer to help at any time. Chris's facial expressions rarely changed. However, when they did, he seemed to smile/smirk inappropriately, displaying a lack of empathy, specifically when speaking about his children; his voice remained low and even toned. His nonverbal cues were very apparent. Chris had very erect and almost tense posture, and his arms crossed most of the time. Chris lacked eye contact and appeared to be nervous, looking around constantly."

Reporters and media had started to gather at the Watts home. The story was exactly the type of compelling content the media loved. The local news channel, Denver 7, had asked Chris to do an interview with them, and to everyone's surprise, he agreed.[2] Chris was known to be socially awkward and quiet, so doing a televised interview was out of character for him. Sandi advised Chris not to do any media interviews because he was the last person to see Shanann and the girls alive, and he would look suspicious. He didn't listen.

Standing outside on the porch of his large suburban home, wearing a North Carolina Tar Heels shirt, he folded his arms tightly across his chest, his eyes looking vacant and far off, and explained his version of the events to the interviewer and the camera man. Shanann had arrived home in the early hours of the morning, he had left for work around 5:15am,

---

2. Watts, Chris. Interview with Tomas Hoppough. Denver 7 ABC. August 15, 2018.

and the call from Nicki prompted him to become concerned and return home. As the camera zoomed in on his face, the interviewer, Tomas Hoppough, asked him the names of his daughters, and he gulped, looking nervous. He said their names slowly. Hoppough asked him to spell Celeste's name. He gulped again and, in a soft tone, spelled her name. "Do you think she just took off? Hoppough asked him. "Right now, I don't want to like, throw anything out there. Like I hope she's somewhere safe right now and with the kids. But I mean, could she have just taken off? I don't know. But if somebody has her, and they're not safe, I want them back. Now. Like, that's what's in my head. If they're safe right now, they're going to come back. But if they're not safe right now...that's the not knowing part...Like if they're not safe...Last night I had every light on in the house on. I was hoping I would get just ran over by the kids running in the door, like barrel rushing me, but it didn't happen, and it was a traumatic night trying to be here." His voice was a complete monotone, and the corners of his mouth turned up in the slightest smile.

Hoppough asked Chris about his relationship with his kids. "The kids are my life. Those smiles light up my life. Last night when they usually eat dinner, I miss them, I miss telling them, 'Hey if you're not going to eat that, you're not going to get your dessert. You're not going to get your snack after." Chris laughed and continued, "You know, I miss that. I miss them cuddling up on their couches. They have a Minnie Mouse couch and a Sofia couch that they cuddle up on and watch Bubble Guppies or something."

He smiled again. "It was tearing me apart last night. I needed that. I needed that last night, and for nobody to be here last night and to go into their rooms and know that I wasn't going to turn their rain machines on. To know I wasn't going to turn their monitor on. To know that I wasn't going to kiss them to bed….it was…that's why last night was horrible. I couldn't do it. I just want everybody to come home. Wherever they're at, come home. That's what I want." His voice remained monotone, mixed with smiles, little laughs, and suppressed smirks.

There was a moment of silence, and all that could be heard was the sound of barking K9 dogs around the empty house.

When Hoppough asked about Shanann and the night she came home, Chris held his arms tighter across his chest, continuously smacking his lips. He swayed back and forth, ever so slightly.

"I know this must be a tough question, but did you guys get into an argument before?" Hoppough asked.

"It wasn't like an argument. It was an emotional conversation. I'll leave it at that. I just want them back." He laughed again. "I just want them back, and if they're not safe right now, that's what's tearing me apart. If they are safe, they're coming back, but if they're not, this has got to stop. Like, somebody has to come forward." Again, he smirked.

Hoppough was shocked Chris answered the question candidly, admitting they had a marital spat before his wife disappeared into thin air. It didn't make him look good; that was for sure. Hoppough followed up with another question. "My last question. If your wife can see this, if your wife is watching, what would you like to tell your wife and kids?"

Chris gulped again. His eyes seemed blank, almost soulless. He shifted his gaze away and back toward the camera. "Shanann, Bella, Celeste. If you're out there, just come back. If somebody has her, please bring her back. I need to see everybody again. This house is not complete without anybody here. Please bring them back."

The camera turned off.

Later that evening, around eight o'clock, Chris went to the police department to do an in-person interview with Special Agent Grahm Coder of the FBI. Around forty years old, Coder was a skilled interviewer and was ready to get Chris to crack. He knew that if Shanann and the girls were dead, they needed to find out what happened to them and where they were right away in order to have forensic evidence to prosecute Chris.

Coder told Chris his suspicions about him and pointed out that it looked odd that the day he and his wife had a fight was the same day she went missing.

"Uh, I - makes me sick to my stomach, honestly. Like I know I talked to a few of my friends like, you know, this does not look good on you, I'm like, I know." If people knew that we were having marital issues, they're gonna look at me. Especially with the way everything looks. And it honestly just makes me sick to my stomach because this is something that I would never do. Ever. And I know you have to look at every vantage point. This is something I would never do to my kids or my wife. At all. I'm not sure what I could do to make people believe that. Just because they knew we were having marital discord, they automatically look at me. But there's no way I would harm anybody in my family. At all. I know we were having marital discord, and we had that conversation that morning, and we have no idea where she is. Or the kids. I promise you, I had nothing to do with any of that," Chris said.

"Are you telling me the truth?" Coder responded.

"I am telling you the absolute truth."

"Why should I believe you?"

"Because I'm a very trustworthy person, and people that do know me, they know how I am a calm person. I am not an argumentative person. I am a person who is - that's never gonna be abusive or physical in any kind of relationship. I would never harm my kids. I would never harm my wife. And you can talk to any of my friends. Any of her friends. They know me. They know I'm a low-key guy that's quiet, I'm - I'm not about confrontation. I'm not about anything that elevates to that level. Like, if someone yells at me, screams at me, I just take it, and I just try to get by the wayside and get it back to where it's cool and just a cool conversation to where like none of that - nothing that gets to that height. Because I am not that person. I've never been that person."

"Okay. You can imagine my job, okay?" Coder said. "And I told you that tonight we talk about things that might offend you. You know that we have to get to the bottom of this.

Would you take a polygraph?"

"Sure," Chris said.

Coder needed to keep Chris talking and say something that he could use to get him to confess.

"So, we have your daughters going missing, we have your wife who's missing, okay? And that's the most important thing right now. Okay? Do you agree with that?" Coder asked.

"Yes" Chris said.

"Okay. So, you've done very good in talking to me about this really hard conversation you guys had. Very good. That's sometimes hard. And I understand why sometimes someone in your position doesn't want to tell me about that because 'please go and help me find my kids and you don't need to know about my marriage argument,' okay? I gotta say, you've done very good at that, and I need you to keep doing that. So, I need to ask you about your marriage and infidelity," Coder said, wanting to see if Chris would take his bait.

"I have never cheated on my wife. And I fully suspect she has never done that to me. Like, she has always been a trustworthy person, I've always been a trustworthy person. I fully expect if we ever thought about straying another way... that we would tell each other before it happened," Chris said.

"I think that sounds ridiculous!" Coder retorted.

"Okay."

"Because in the history of the earth, nobody ever does that," Coder said bluntly.

"Okay. That's what I would like to think. I know mistakes

happen. But that's what I would think in my head, I would hope would happen."

"Now, even though I think that sounds ridiculous, if I was in your shoes, I'd say the exact same thing and - and I believe that. Okay? But I kind of don't, and you can imagine, in my job, I meet all kinds of people. And you can imagine that there are people who have Saturdays with their girlfriends and Sundays with their wives, right? And they consider themselves to be very virtuous people, okay? So, with that in mind, I don't care if there's been anything in your relationship. I just don't. And I'm not going to tell the news. I'm not going to tell anyone. But I do need to know. So, is there anyone that you think that maybe your wife got close with?" Coder said intently. He knew that it was highly unlikely Shanann was cheating on Chris, but he used this tactic to ease his way into asking Chris about his own infidelity.

"If she did, it was very like secret then, if that was the case. Because I had no inkling," Chris said.

Coder asked Chris some more questions about Shanann and possible infidelity on her end and then went after what it seemed he really wanted to know.

Okay. On your end. I gotta ask," Coder said. "What's her name?"

"I don't have another one," Chris stated flatly.

"Okay. So again, highly trained investigator over here, right? I see pictures of you from a few years ago. And I see you standing before me now. You've gotten pretty fit," Coder said, referencing the changes in Chris' physical appearance over the years.

When Chris and Shanann had started dating, Chris was overweight, pale, and socially awkward. When he started doing Thrive, per Shanann's suggestion, he began to lose weight rapidly. He also started working out religiously and watching his calories. The transformation had been remarkable. As Chris sat before Coder, he was an objectively lean, muscular, tan, and handsome man.

"You can imagine when guys start cheating or want to cheat, that's what happens" Coder said.

"Yes."

"So. Tell me about it," Coder said.

"I did not cheat on my wife. Now, Thrive helped me. I went from 245 pounds to about..." Chris trailed off.

"You were 245?" Coder said in disbelief.

"I was 245 pounds. And I'm 185...180 right now. And I've been eating cleaner. Thrive has helped me a lot, but to maintain it, eating cleaner has really helped me as well," Chris told him.

"Okay. And I've got to imagine that maybe there was a girl that inspired that?"

"No."

"Okay. Why are you falling out of love?" Coder said, referencing conversations he knew Chris had had with other law enforcement officers.

"Over the last five weeks, like being by myself and being able to be myself again, I couldn't be myself around Shanann anymore."

"Why not?" Coder said, pressing further.

"It was like I was walking on eggshells type of thing. It's kind of like, you feel like you're always doing something that's wrong."

"The timing doesn't make sense to me" Coder said, calling Chris out on his lies again.

"Okay. But like, if you can't be yourself around your wife, who can you be yourself around?" Chris asked.

"Why couldn't you be yourself around your wife?" Coder asked.

"I just felt like I'd always have to change who I was. Because I was always about - I mean I was doing the laundry- I do everything that I could for her. Everything. And then I was just, you know, just being myself, just doing me. And I just thought to myself, like one of my buddies Mark. He lives out in San Diego. It's like one big test that he learned. He was the worst at one point, and it was like, 'So if you could picture your wife, and she was with someone else, would you get jealous?' I was like, 'At this point, I'd have to say no.' And he was like, 'Well, there's your answer. Like, if you love her, it would be a different answer.'"

"When did you start falling out of love?" Coder asked.

"It wasn't in the last five weeks. It's been ongoing process for probably about a year," Chris said.

"Why?" Coder asked.

"I just felt like everything that we had when we first started dating and met -like we met in 2010, everything, a new relationship spark, everything we had was great. Get married, everything's still great. And then, you know, people just fall out of love. And that's where I was. I felt over the last year, I thought that maybe this is just a phase. Maybe this is what happens if you've been with somebody so long. Maybe if the spark isn't there, you just reignite it somehow, some way. But, you know, our conversations weren't the same. Like when we were apart, everything was short, and nothing felt right anymore," he explained. "The disconnection was there."

"But why?" Coder said, continuing to press.

"It wasn't there. I didn't feel it. It was like I didn't have that passion anymore."

"Why not?" Coder asked again.

"Honestly, I really couldn't tell you. It's the passion. I didn't feel it in my heart anymore. I really can't give you a definitive answer other than that. It's like my heart wasn't in it."

"I gotta tell you, it sounds like a load of horseshit to me," Coder said. When Chris didn't reply Coder switched topics. "What about the girls?"

"Bella and Celeste are the light of my life. I'd do anything for those girls. I'd step in front of a bullet, stand in front of a train for those girls."

Chris continued to use one phony cliché after another. Although his words sounded good, he didn't sound as if he meant any of it.

"It doesn't add up to me," Coder said, going back to the marriage. "Then why did the spark die?"

"The relationship between me and Shanann has nothing to do with the love I have for these girls. I mean, you love the girls, they're the light of my life. I would do anything for them. But me and Shanann talked about if we separated or if we stayed together, what's best for the kids? Like, do we stay together for the kids? It might cause more issues for the kids later down the road, their psyche, their personality, or something. They know when they get older, they can see Mom and Dad don't sleep in the same room anymore, like what's going on? I mean, you can't take the kids into the factor because the love you have for your kids is gonna be like, exponential. No matter what, that would never die. Because they're your kids. That would never die. Between you and your wife, the love that you have for each other from the start to finish, like, from right when you started to where your relationship ends. When you're in that type of relationship, you're with somebody that long, something happens. It's just a connection that isn't there… like you know when you can look at someone and put your forehead to their forehead and you hold them, you know what each other's thinking? That's a connection. I didn't have that connection anymore."

Chris sounded as if he was reciting an over-the-top romance novel. Does anyone put their foreheads together and know what the other is thinking? It was obvious Chris was being insincere.

"Okay," Coder said, trying another angle. "What do I do to help you walk out of this room and not look like the person who is responsible?"

Chris pointed to a photograph of his daughters on the table in front of Coder and him. "You have to trust me that when I tell you that these two beautiful girls right here, I did nothing to them and to my beautiful wife. I did nothing to her. You have to trust me and believe me. I know you don't know me. You've known me for two and a half, three hours. And I don't know what your opinion is, but you have to realize that these two beautiful girls right here, and my wife... I had nothing to do with the disappearance. I had nothing to do with this act of evil, cruelty, or whatever has happened here. Because my love for these two girls and my wife... like I don't want anything to happen to them. I'd never want anything to happen to them. No matter if me and my wife separate or not. Or divorce or anything. I never wish harm on anybody. On a human being in general. Like just seeing that picture." He gestured to the picture of his daughters again. "I need them. I want them to run through that front door and just grab me. Or just bear - or just tackle me, knock me to the floor, bust my head, I don't care. The amount of love I have for my family is exponential, and it's never gonna die. I want them back. I have to have them back."

"Tell me about a normal day in your house," Coder said.

"Okay. So, I will get up about four o'clock, I'll go down, work out for maybe about an hour or so. There's a weight bench in the basement. So, get done with that, come back upstairs probably about five o'clock, I'll eat some breakfast, make some eggs...cottage cheese, something like that. I'll make the girls milk - I'll make CeCe's milk, I'll bring it upstairs, Bella's usually kinda iffy on milk in the morning, so I just... fill up the water bottles...from the refrigerator. Make sure that the backpacks have change of clothes, their hat, and if it's like a swim - like a water day or something, make sure they have water shoes in there, make sure they have sunscreen. Make sure that all that is in their backpacks and make sure they have their little blankie. They have all that with them. I have that all laid out, and then I go to work. So, Shanann will let the kids dictate when Shanann wakes up. And usually, it's Bella. She'll come in there, lay in the bed with her. And then Celeste. She'll wake up, and she'll come in and lay in bed with her, and they'll watch cartoons for a little while. And probably about 6:30, they'll get out. Shanann's getting ready, she'd probably take a shower, put her makeup on, all that kind of stuff. And then takes the kids over into their rooms, gets them dressed out of their pajamas, and Bella has a school uniform. CeCe didn't have one yet. Get them dressed, go downstairs, have breakfast. CeCe will probably have cereal, Bella, she likes cinnamon toast. She'll then put them in the car and go to school. And then they'll stay at school usually until about four o'clock, 4:30. I'll usually be home by then. I can go pick them up. I go in there, sign them out, get in the car, drive back. They'll be screaming the whole way because they want Mommy. And I get home, Shanann will have something for the girls, being whatever they want it to be. Might be pizza. Sometimes they want French fries, sometimes they want chicken nuggets, sometimes they're bossy, just like..." Chris stopped himself before saying "Shanann," realizing how that might sound to Coder. His secret disdain for his wife was slowly creeping in. That disdain was exactly what Coder was looking for.

"Mm-hm" Coder said, urging him to continue.

"Just whatever. Most time they have butter noodles. They love that. Wash their hands, sit 'em at the table. And they'll eat their dinner. And then usually go upstairs, take a shower, then get them all washed up, get them dried off, get some lotion, get their pajamas on, back downstairs, have a little nighttime snack. They'll have Cheez-Its, a wafer, or something like that. And they'll sit in their little couches, and they'll watch a cartoon until about seven o'clock and then between 6:30 and seven, we're giving them the medicine and any medicine they need at that point in time. If one of them has a fever... whatever else. And then brush their teeth, upstairs. CeCe gets an overnight diaper, Bella doesn't, and then read 'em a book. CeCe really wants the tiger book. I read that to her. We growl at the last part. Turn the rain machines on, give them both a kiss goodnight. CeCe wants me to put her to bed. Bella wants Shanann to put her to bed and close the door and night, night."

"Can we talk a little bit about the morning that they disappeared?" Coder asked.

"Mm-hm."

"We already talked about four o'clock alarm. Correct me if I'm wrong. 4:15 the challenging talk starts. You leave somewhere around 5:30ish, and then what? What was your day like?"

Coder had Chris walk him through the day again at Cervi 319. He circled back, attempting to get Chris to talk.

"Okay. So, let's have the hard conversation again. How old are they?" Coder said, looking for Chris to slip up someplace.

"Four and three. Bella will be five in December."

"Okay. You can imagine that every day that goes by..."

"It gets harder to find them," Chris said, filling in the sentence.

"Where we don't find your girls, and they get harder to find, we're gonna have less clues. Things that we need to get and need to use, and we need to do to find them, are gonna start getting blown away by weather, getting rerecorded over themselves that the surveillance part is gonna tell us. All of that is going to disappear. You can also imagine that every day that goes by, we're gonna be looking for the man who did this. Okay? And you can imagine that we're gonna include you as that man. So, let's talk about that," Coder said. "I think that you're trying to put on a brave face because you're a man and you're a father and you're a husband. I can tell that there's just something you're not telling me. And I'm not sure what it is, and I don't know why that is. I don't know why you're not telling me that there's something that's making you a little bit uncomfortable tonight. I just don't believe some of the things you're telling me. I just don't. Simply do not believe you."

"What makes you think?" Chris began. "What have I said that makes you not believe me at all?" Coder could see he was starting to get upset.

"This just doesn't make sense to me, doesn't add up," Coder said. "So, can we talk about two Chris's?"

"*Two* Chris's?" Chris asked.

"The tale of two Chris's. You need to help me know which Chris I'm looking at today," Coder told him. "And which Chris you really are. So, Chris number one is right here, right? And fell out of love with his wife, okay? Started wondering what it might be like if he didn't have a wife to take care of, any girls to take care of. Spent some time alone, liked that time alone. Came home, may or may not have had a conversation about how to get out of this marriage or how to fix it, but probably how to get out of it. Is looking at a bachelor pad in Brighton and did something terrible. To his wife and kids. And that may have been an accident, and I think it was an accident." He stared at Chris again, hoping he was getting closer to getting him to crack.

"That's not the Chris you're looking at right now," he insisted. "The Chris you're looking at is the man who loves these kids and loves his wife and would never, ever, ever do anything to harm them. That's the Chris you're looking at right now. The Chris you're looking at right now wants these kids and his wife back at his house. Right now. That's the Chris you're looking at."

"Why didn't you call 911?"

"I didn't think anything was wrong," Chris replied.

"I think you knew what was wrong."

"I did not know what was wrong, sir," Chris said. "I promise you that."

"What do you think it's gonna look like when someone finds out that it was not you that called 911?" Coder asked.

"Everybody's gonna have their own perception about what's going on here, but I know my wife. I know that sometimes she doesn't text me back. I know that happens. It's happened to me multiple times. Throughout many days. That she's busy with work. That's why it didn't register for me that day."

"We're back to this tale of two Chris's," Coder said. "There's a Chris who cares."

"I care. I promise," Chris interrupted him.

"Tell me about the call to your daycare." Coder abruptly shifted topics.

"To Primrose? I called them to see if the girls were there. They said they weren't there. I told them since they weren't there, to put them back on the waiting list."

"That's not what you told them," Coder said.

"I told them that we were gonna sell the house...put it on the market. We probably won't be in the area anymore."

"That's two different things," Coder said.

"Well, I want them to be back on. I put them on the waiting list as they weren't there."

"Why weren't they there?"

"I don't know," Chris said.

"Where were they gonna go?"

"They went to ... Shanann took 'em to a friend's house."

"Why wouldn't they go to daycare?" Coder asked.

"I am not sure. I, honestly, sir, I am not sure."

"It's hard for me as a father to talk to you like this," Coder said. "Not because it's a hard issue to talk about. It's because

I'm worried about your daughters under your care."

"You shouldn't have to worry about them under my care. I watched them all weekend. I went to a pool party at Jeremy Lindstrom's house. I love those kids. With all my heart. And nothing in this world would ever make me do anything to these kids. Or my wife."

"When you walk out of this room, there's nothing I can say to a room full of police officers that's going to convince them that you have nothing to do with this," Coder told him.

"I know."

"You know what they think. There's a guy who didn't call 911, who woke his wife up at a ridiculous hour because he was so guilty about something that he had to get it off his chest and say, 'I don't love you anymore, I'm leaving you.' That didn't go well. Okay, so what happened?"

"She told me she wanted me to wake her up before I left. That's why I didn't just wake her up, just to tell her this. I woke her up, that's what she wanted to do, and we talked," Chris said. "Usually at 4:00 a.m., I wake up, I go down and work out. This day, I wanted to talk to her about this. I love these girls. I love these girls so much. And this picture right here, Celeste and Bella. Those are my life. I helped make those kids. There's nothing in my life that means more to me than these kids. Nothing. Kids. That's your life, that's your lifeline. That's everything that - you make kids, they come first over anything. Kids, spouse, family. That's what it's always been."

• • •

Chris was trying hard to be persuasive, but he continued to fall flat with his disingenuous efforts to convince Coder of his innocence.

"Nothing you've told me tonight makes sense," Coder said. "Nothing you've told me tonight feels like the truth. Can we start over?"

"Sure," Chris said.

"I think that there's something that happened. That got maybe a little bit out of control," Chris said. "There was no fight. There was nothing physical. It was a conversation. We didn't raise a voice. Nothing. I promise you that, sir. There is nothing physical with this conversation."

"What was the last thing you saw about your daughters?" Coder asked.

"Last thing I saw, like when I left?"

"What did it look like?"

"Saw them on the monitor as it was switching back and forth," Chris said.

"What's the last thing you saw with your wife?"

"She was lying back in bed as I was walking out the door. Walking out the bedroom door."

"Okay. All right," Coder said, switching directions again. "What was your plan after you guys separated?"

"We'd just go our separate ways. I would probably get an apartment. She would try to sell the house first, of course... before we could do anything like that. And hopefully both get an apartment somewhat close. Maybe a 50-50 thing because I was going to go on the 8:00 to 6:00 schedule in September. And then I'd have six days off, and it would be perfect. I'd have kids for half, and she'd have half, and that would work."

"All right," Coder said quietly. "Tonight's been pretty intense I can imagine. How're you feeling?"

"I slept like two hours last night, so running on empty right now," Chris said.

"I know. I can see it. So why don't we do this? I'm sure you don't mind if we take a break for the night. I'm sure that you are feeling some of the pressure from me."

"You're doing your job," Chris said, resuming his affable demeanor.

"I wouldn't be doing my job if I didn't grill you a little bit, right?" Coder said.

"I've seen you turn into two different guys," Chris said, replying with a similar assessment to Coder's pointing out earlier that there were two Chris's. "Honestly, I've seen where you're smiling, and I've seen where it's different. You're doing your job though. I can't fault you for anything you've asked."

"So, can I make a commitment to you?" Coder said firmly. "I'm going to commit to you that we're not gonna stop working until we find them. And I want to commit to you that there is going to come a time when you're going to feel this pressure from other people. I'm not the only one who thinks that there's a possibility you have something to do with this."

"Like, another FBI agent?" Chris asked. "Pressure like this?"

"Everyone. Have you ever watched the news and saw two girls and a pregnant woman go missing? And if that's all you heard, what do you think the public thinks?"

"Husband," Chris replied.

"Husband. So, I'm going to make a commitment to you, okay? I'm going to commit to you that I'm going to be your guy, okay? I'm going to be your guy that handles the investigation. And I'm going to be your guy that you can come to. Because I hope that you realize I'm a nice guy. Tonight, we had to talk about some tough things, but I hope that you know that I did it respectfully. I think that you can see that. As we go on through tonight, the hours, the days - and I hope we don't get to hour or days - I hope its minutes, right, until this is over. But just in case it's not, I want you to know that I wanted to be in this room tonight. I wanted to talk to you. And I hope that you want to talk to me. When you have questions, when you have concerns, I want you to call the detective that you work with, and I want you to call me. I want you to know that if you have a question, if you think we're not doing something enough or well enough, I want you to say I gotta call Grahm. I gotta call Dave. When you need to have a night to yell at somebody, and maybe have a good cry, I want you to call me. I can't imagine what you're going through. I just can't."

Chris thanked Coder and left to stay the night with Nick and Amanda Thayer. He said he couldn't sleep in his house alone. Chris's dad Ronnie was flying into Colorado first thing in the morning for support. Coder wanted them to come directly to the police station so Chris could take the polygraph, and Ronnie could do an interview.

"I would love for you and me, as a team, to talk tomorrow, to do a polygraph tomorrow and move past all of it," Coder said. "Move past me wondering about Chris, about wondering which Chris I'm talking to. I want to move past it. I just want to get it behind us. And then our talks are gonna be a lot more comfortable than they were tonight. So, can we say that tomorrow at eleven o'clock?"

"Okay," Chris answered, knowing the walls were closing in on him.

CHAPTER 5

"Hold Me Tight"

At six o'clock on the morning of Wednesday, August 15, Colorado Bureau of Investigation agent, Matthew Sailor arrived at the Watts residence. Upon arrival, he met up with Detective Baumhover, Officer Steve Walje of the Frederick Police Department, and CBI crime scene analyst Dave Yocum. They had already received consent from Chris to search the house and gather evidence, but first Baumhover needed to call Chris to obtain the code to enter the residence. Once inside, they found Dieter in a kennel. They took him out and put him in the backyard while they conducted their search.

As they walked through the home, Sailor noted how neat and organized it was. The items in the kitchen were all labeled, and the clothes in the closets were organized by type and color. The beds had all been made, but Sailor knew that, in the initial search of the house, the children's beds were unmade, and the bed in the master bedroom had been stripped of its sheets.

As Sailor made his way through the house, he noticed that every single trash can in the bathrooms and bedrooms had been emptied. Lucky for investigation purposes, when he looked in the kitchen trash bin, he found the garbage bags from all the rooms. As he lifted a large trash bag up and out of the bin, he saw a bedsheet and three pillowcases underneath it. The bedsheet and one pillowcase had what appeared to be a dark substance smeared on it. The team took some photographs before collecting it as evidence.

When Sailor walked into the garage, he saw a cardboard box with a return address from Amazon in a trash receptacle. When he picked up the box, a book fell out. He reached down to pick up the book and examined the title: *Hold Me Tight: Seven Conversations for a Lifetime of Love*, a relationship self-help book by Sue Johnson. Sailor recalled hearing from colleagues that Shanann had sent Chris a book while in North Carolina in an attempt to save their marriage. This must have been the book, and it had clearly never been opened or read.

There may have been more than one reason Chris had no interest in reading a book intended to keep couples together when he wanted only distance between Shanann and him. As Coder had pointed out to Chris, he had improved his appearance since his marriage. And Coder had also pointed out that when something like that happened with a man, a woman was usually involved. He had even asked, "What's her name?"

Chris had denied the accusations, suggesting that if Shanann or he had wanted to stray they would have discussed it with each other. But Chris Watts was keeping a secret. There was another woman. Her name was Nikki Kessinger.

Even as Chris was speaking with the detectives, insisting on his innocence, Nikki, his coworker and lover, was obsessively searching for news stories on the whereabouts of Shanann Watts and her daughters. She was starting to get increasingly anxious about the fact that she was about to be in a situation that was way over her head. A contractor at Anadarko Petroleum, where Chris was a field coordinator, she had met him there, and since late June, had been having a very serious and intense affair with him.

At age thirty, Nikki had a few similarities to Shanann Watts. They were both curvy with long, dark brown hair and green eyes, but that was the extent of the similarities between the two women. Shanann was softer, more feminine and striking. Nikki was considered attractive by the men in her office. They would check her out as she walked in in the morning as they stood around together at their morning meetings. She was the athletic type: muscular and stocky in build.

Nikki wasn't aware that police already had work emails between Chris and her. Tony Huskey, Anadarko's regional security manager, had called the Colorado Bureau of Investigation and told them that something was going on between Nikki and Chris based on the emails he had retrieved. These emails, which began in early June, hinted that there was more than a friendship brewing between them.

Nikki likely knew that the longer Shanann and the girls were missing and the longer she withheld important information to the investigation, the more suspicious she would look to the police. The media attention was also going to bring out many secrets. As much as Nikki probably wanted to disappear, she had to know the affair would be discovered and didn't want to risk looking like an accomplice. For her to come out of this somewhat unscathed, she would have to help the police and give them any incriminating evidence she had on Chris, as soon as possible.

Nikki said Chris had acted as if everything were totally normal up until later in the day on Monday, the day Shanann and the girls vanished. He had nonchalantly texted Nikki that his family was "gone." She assumed they had some kind of spat, and Shanann would be back. Chris had told her Shanann had left her wedding rings behind, and perhaps it was over for good. He asked Nikki what he should do with the rings, and she suggested pawning them. Maybe Chris's marriage really was over, and they could be together now. But, no. Now, his wife and daughters were missing.

Nikki was probably aware how bad it would look if the affair came out in the media. It would give Chris a very real motive and expose him as a liar and a cheater. It would also make Nikki look like a super villain. After all, she had been sleeping with a married man with young children and a pregnant wife. Before she decided to contact law enforcement, she did a search on her phone to find out if cops could trace deleted text messages and how long phone companies kept messages. She deleted everything she could on her phone: text messages and internet searches. Nikki would later say she deleted her messages because she was embarrassed about the raunchy texts between her and Chris.

Then Nikki called her father, Dwayne. She was not about to deal with this alone, and she needed him to help her navigate the storm that she feared was about to ruin her life. As she called her father, Chris was also reaching out to his.

• • •

At 7:47 a.m., Chris texted his father, Ronnie Watts, and told him he would come pick him up at the airport. Ronnie had boarded a flight as soon as Chris told him he needed him to be in Colorado with him. Ronnie had come alone as Chris had specified; he wanted only his father there. A quiet, subdued man, who much like his son, never showed emotion, Ronnie had a slow, southern drawl and snow-white, neatly combed hair.

When Chris saw Ronnie at the airport, he had a strong feeling this would be the last time he would see his father outside a prison cell. Still, other than asking Chris if he had any clue about where Shanann, Bella, and CeCe were, Ronnie did not address the reason for his being there. Mostly the father and son made casual small talk. They talked about sports because that was all they knew how to do in the face of a crisis.

When they arrived at the police station around eleven o'clock that morning, Ronnie was taken to an investigation room to be interviewed separately, and Chris went to take the polygraph test.

In the questioning room, Ronnie explained some history about Shanann and Chris and how they met. He gushed about how Chris had always been a role model son as far as Ronnie was concerned. He was never in trouble, never did drugs, or had any mental health issues. He was a great student in school, focused on sports, and he prioritized those activities over dating and girls. In fact, for prom, a girl had asked him to go.

Ronnie gave background details about the recent trip Shanann had taken with the girls to North Carolina. The trip was designed so Shanann and the girls could spend quality time with both sides of their family. CeCe had never met her Uncle Frankie, Shanann's younger brother, or Jamie, Chris's older sister. Ideally, this trip would give CeCe and Bella the opportunity to get to know their uncles, aunts, and cousins better and spend more quality time with both sets of grandparents. The history between Shanann's and Chris's families were tense to say the least, and the visits with Chris's family were sometimes a disaster.

"So, I definitely want to hear about that and what's been going on," the interviewing agent said to Ronnie, referring to a blowout fight between Chris's mother, Cindy, and Shanann.

"We hadn't talked to her since that blowout, and she sent this text to us. When they got back (to Colorado) they did a sonogram for the baby. She sent this picture of the sonogram to me." Ronnie pulled out his phone and showed a picture of Shanann's unborn son to the agent. "No comment or nothing on it. No nothing. She was reaching out, and I think that's when Chris initially told her he wanted the separation and stuff. He told me he wanted the separation when he was down for the visit. He said, 'I don't love her anymore.'"

"And was that the first time... or were you aware of prior marital problems?" the agent asked.

"I didn't sense something was going on until now. They weren't all lovey-dovey like they used to be. And anytime we would come visit them a couple times a year and Face-Time with them and stuff, she's sitting on her ass, on her phone doing her Le-Vel (Thrive) stuff. Chris is running around, taking care of the kids, feeding the kids, doing this, doing that. He loves them kids. Believe me, he wouldn't do anything to hurt either one of the kids," Ronnie said, in an attempt to paint Chris as the "good" one.

"Did it seem like there were serious marital problems prior to this visit?" the agent asked.

"He said he should have done this a long time ago...and just like the baby now they're having. She was telling us it was Chris's idea to have it 80/20 because he wanted a boy. And I mentioned it to him, and he said, 'It wasn't me. It was all her. Everything is about her. She has this image, this persona that she wants. This image that she wants out there all the time. Everything is hunky dory. Everything is beautiful in the world and stuff. The things on Facebook is a mask she puts on.'"

Ronnie continued to speak unfavorably about Shanann. He called her "paranoid" and "extremely bipolar." In particular, he described Shanann as paranoid toward his wife, Cindy. With the recent trip to visit them, Ronnie said Shanann accused Cindy of trying to kill her children by exposing them to nuts. CeCe had life-threatening nut allergies, and Cindy did not take the allergies seriously, causing Shanann to feel a great deal of anxiety and distrust toward her mother-in-law. Ronnie also explained that the rest of the visit to North Carolina was extremely contentious. After the incident referred to as "nutgate," Shanann spent the rest of the trip with her family, refusing to let Bella and CeCe see him or Cindy.

CHAPTER 6

"I love those girls to death."

While Ronnie was being interviewed, Chris was taking the polygraph that would ultimately seal his fate. Special Agent Tammy Lee of the Colorado Bureau of Investigation administered it. Tammy, a skilled investigator with shoulder-length blond hair, a warm smile, and a jovial laugh, was astute and likable. People felt comfortable in her presence. On that day, she wore a navy-blue shirt with a black-and white-striped cardigan.

When Chris walked in the room and was introduced to Tammy, she got up from her chair to shake his hand and warmly said, "Hey Chris, how are you?"

In her mind, Tammy did a quick assessment of Chris as she watched him take a seat in the chair at the table where she sat. Chris, by all accounts, was kind, respectful, easy-going, calm, and cooperative. Every single person who had been interviewed for the investigation—coworkers, friends, family—not one had even the most miniscule criticism of

Chris. Everyone loved him and thought he was the greatest, most solid guy on the planet.

"How are you feeling?" she asked him.

"I feel sick to my stomach," he said lifelessly.

Tammy laid on the flattery, commending him for helping the investigation and being willing to do the polygraph. She assured him that this was just standard protocol, and they did it for all the missing persons cases. She made sure to tell Chris that he wasn't being singled out. Just as Coder had done, Tammy needed to make him feel comfortable so she could get him to talk.

Tammy carefully walked him through what to expect on the polygraph. She read him his Miranda rights and told him the polygraph was completely voluntary and that he would be recorded. He signed documents giving his consent, and the polygraph began.

Tammy eased into the test, asking basic questions first, about Chris's childhood, life, family, and occupation. She asked if he had any nicknames, and he told her people at work referred to him as "Rainman," after Dustin Hoffman's portrayal of an autistic savant in the 1988 film. This was because once Chris went to an oil site, he would always remember explicit details after. Chris recalled being a young boy and going to pick up his sister Jamie at middle school with his grandmother every day. While they waited for Jamie to come out of the building, his grandmother would quiz him on all the state capitals. He said he thought that maybe that's where his sharp memory and uncanny ability to recall tiny details came from.

Chris told Tammy that he had fallen out of love with Shanann and no longer felt compatible, and that they no longer had "that connection anymore." In North Carolina, when they were together, Shanann's parents and kids were around all the time, so most of their talks about their relationship were through text messages and not face to face. Chris said that he and Shanann both wanted to make it work and were at a point where they were wondering what they could do to make that happen. Shanann didn't know what to say, and she wanted to work on it, either by reading a book or going to counseling.

Chris mentioned that the last time they had sex was when their unborn son, Nico, was conceived sometime in May. He said he was usually the one to initiate sex, and most of the time, he was "shot down" but acknowledged that "that's married life," and on average, they had sex once or twice a week, and it was always enjoyable for him.

Tammy asked Chris if Shanann had directly asked him if he had been unfaithful to her. Chris said she did, but he denied it, saying, "You know that would never happen. You know what kind of guy I am."

Chris boasted that his friend Jeremy Lindstrom said, "You're the type of guy I could send you with my wife for a week and know nothing would happen."

Chris seemed to brag quite a bit about his stellar reputation with others.

"People know what kind of person I am," Chris said. "I'm

not the type of guy that's gonna say, 'All right, my wife is gone. Who's the girl I can find in five weeks?' That's not me. I respect my wife, and she respects me. If she's somewhere safe right now, I don't think it would be with a guy. If it is, I'm fine. I want her to be safe. I want the kids back home. If it was with a guy, great. Come back home. We'll talk about it later. I never had an inkling that she would do the same… that she would do anything to me." He quickly caught his slip up.

Shanann had also asked Chris over text if he was having an affair, and he shot that accusation down as well, telling her that should be the last thing on her mind. Chris told Tammy whenever Shanann would call him while they were apart over the summer, he would be on a run or working out, and she could tell he didn't want to talk to her.

Chris said he was open to Shanann's idea of marriage counseling, but he didn't want to do it. He didn't think they needed to do it. He said the disconnection was there, and he didn't think counseling was going to help. In other words, Chris's mind was made up about his wife, and he was unwilling to do anything that would help repair what he viewed as irreparably broken.

Tammy eventually got to the important part of the polygraph where she would ask Chris about what happened between the time Shanann got home from Arizona and the last time Chris saw her that morning. This was the make-or-break moment because if Chris had anything to do with this, he would have to constantly lie, and the polygraph would expose all his falsehoods. Chris was the only suspect they had, and if he failed the polygraph, investigators would hopefully be able to wrangle him into a confession. They needed to act quickly because if Shanann and the girls were dead, they needed to get to the bodies as quickly as possible to perform autopsies to have the significant evidence they would need to convict Chris in court.

Tammy asked Chris what he did Friday, the day Shanann left for her trip to Arizona. He said they knew what the sex of the baby was, but they weren't going to tell anyone until Shanann got back.

He told Tammy that, on Friday morning, he waited for the kids to wake up, and Shanann left early with Nicki to go to the airport. They hugged goodbye and exchanged pleasantries when she left. He hung out at the house with the kids, went to the grocery store, went to fix his glasses, went to Target. It was a teacher workday that day, so the girls didn't have school, and that's why Chris took the day off. They got home from running errands at 4:30, had dinner, and did the normal bedtime routine. Chris talked to Shanann that evening, but Shanann didn't Facetime with the girls because they would usually get too upset seeing their mother. Because they would get so worked up with reminders that she was not physically present with them, Chris and Shanann decided that while she traveled, it was probably best not to Facetime with the girls until they were older and could handle their mother's absence better. Whenever Shanann would travel, Bella would constantly ask about her, and this trip was no exception. Friday night after Chris put the girls to bed, he said he "chilled out."

Saturday morning, Bella came into bed with Chris, and they waited for CeCe to wake up. Chris and the girls hung out at the house and played outside until it got too hot. Jeremy Lindstrom's daughter, Mary,[3] came over to babysit that night so Chris could go to the Colorado Rockies baseball game with co-workers. He left the house at five o'clock and came home around eleven o'clock that night. He also had dinner at the Lazy Dog Restaurant with his co-workers. The girls were in bed asleep when he got home.

On Sunday morning, the girls watched the cartoon "Bubble Guppies" on television before starting the day. He put them down for a nap and had cold pizza from the previous evening before heading to Jeremy's house for his son's fourth birthday party, which was about 1:15-4:30 p.m. Jeremy and his wife had water balloons and inflatable pools set up for the kids, and the girls had a blast at the party. When they got back, Chris put the girls in the shower, dried them, and put their lotion on, dressed them in their pajamas, and gave them cold pizza again.

Chris described to Tammy the nightgowns he put the girls in. CeCe's was pink, and Bella's had a unicorn on it. They Facetimed with Shanann's parents and then had some snacks on their mini couches on the second-floor common area. Chris brushed their teeth, had them use the potty, and put them to bed.

---

3. Name has been changed to protect a minor

Bella came out twice because she knew Shanann was coming home that night, and Chris said he reassured her that she would see her mother in the morning when she woke up. Chris told Tammy that whenever Shanann would get home late from a trip, because the girls were light sleepers, she would never wake them up.

Around two o'clock that morning, Chris felt Shanann get into bed. She was in a T-shirt and underwear, her normal attire to bed. She always wore her wedding rings, even to bed, and would only take them off when coloring her hair. Shanann's wedding rings had been found on her nightstand, and Chris told Tammy that was very unusual.

Shanann had supposedly asked Chris to wake her up when he woke up for work so she could shower and "get the airport off" her. When Chris woke up, he showered and got dressed before he woke Shanann. He sat on the bed on top of the covers and gently nudged her awake. According to Chris, their dialogue went as follows:

"Are you going to shower?" he asked her.

"Yeah, I'll do it," she said groggily.

"Can we talk a little bit?" Chris asked her.

"Let's talk," Shanann said.

This was the supposed "emotional conversation" in which Chris, in his words, said they needed to sell the house and downsize. He told Shanann he didn't feel the connection anymore, it wasn't working, and he didn't feel the love they had in the beginning anymore. Shanann was crying and emotional hearing all of this. Chris said he was crying as well.

Shanann accused him of cheating.

"No. This isn't like someone came in my life and took me from you. There's no outside influence coming from this," Chris remembered saying to Shanann.

Chris hoped they could sell the house, separate, and live near each other because Shanann had told him recently that she wouldn't be able to afford to live in Colorado on her own with three kids. He said when she disappeared, initially he thought she was with somebody, but now he believed that something happened, and that she and the girls were not safe.

With a straight face, Tammy continued to the part of the polygraph where she would ask Chris directly if he had anything to do with Shanann's disappearance.

"So, if I asked you on the polygraph test if you physically caused Shanann's disappearance, can you pass that question?" Tammy said, staring at him.

"Yeah," Chris said nonchalantly.

"What do you think I mean by that? When I'm asking you if you physically caused Shanann's disappearance? What does that mean to you?" Tammy asked.

"If you asked me that, I feel like you're asking me, did I have anything to do with it myself, or did I help somebody do it, and I had no part in any of that," Chris stated emphatically.

"And I know it's totally awful to think about... but what are ways that you could make someone disappear?" Tammy asked Chris.

"I mean, if you're talking about what I've seen on the

movies or if you read about other people, you hire somebody," he answered.

"Like a hit man?" Tammy prompted.

"I'm just being honest," Chris said

"That's what I want," Tammy told him.

"You would hire somebody, or you would have somebody you know that would do it. It's a hard question to answer," Chris said, laughing. "Because I had nothing to do with the disappearance. If you're asking how I would do it."

"No. Anyone. How would anyone cause someone else's disappearance? By murdering them... what different physical ways you could cause someone's disappearance through murder?" Tammy asked.

"Stab someone. Shoot someone. Hit 'em with a blunt object. I mean, use a weapon a gun, or a knife. You could …." Chris paused.

"Smother someone," Tammy filled in.

"Smother someone," Chris echoed.

"Strangle someone," Tammy trailed off

"Strangle someone," Chris repeated.

Tammy pressed Chris to continue further by offering him more ideas of how one might murder someone else. Chris told Tammy that you could "lure someone into a trap."

Tammy asked him to explain further. Chris said you could have someone waiting around the corner, and an accident could happen, such as getting hit by a car. Tammy mentioned you could kidnap someone, and Chris added that you could take someone somewhere and torture them by leaving them without food or water. Chris continued by saying that you could beat someone to death or poison them.

"Chris, I just want to know if you're the one who caused Shanann's physical disappearance," Tammy said. "Sometimes people can feel guilty for causing someone to leave such as, telling your spouse you want a separation."

"That's why I feel like a jackass right now," Chris said with a sigh.

"Are you lying about the last time you saw Shanann?" Tammy asked.

"No."

"Describe to me the last time you saw Shanann."

"The last time I saw her was in bed after I talked to her. She said she was going to a friend's house and would be back later, and she was lying on her side with mascara running down her face from crying."

"Chris. If you are, in fact, lying and you did murder Shan-ann, then the image you just described would not be the last time you saw her. Do you know where Shanann is now?"

"I don't," Chris said.

CHAPTER 7

"I fell in love with her."

After the polygraph, Tammy excused herself from the room to speak with Special Agent Grahm Coder. She left Chris alone while he watched videos of his daughters on his cell phone. Coder and Tammy came back into the room, bringing with them a large printed photograph of Bella and CeCe.

"I brought Grahm back in to discuss the results," Tammy said in a serious tone.

Chris nodded.

"It was completely clear that you were not honest during the testing, and I think you already know that," Tammy said, cutting straight to the chase. "You did not pass the polygraph test. So now we need to talk about what actually happened, and I think you're ready to do that."

Coder leaned back in his seat as Tammy looked Chris directly in the eye.

"I didn't lie to you on that polygraph, I promise," Chris said, still refusing to give in to them.

"Chris. Take a deep breath," Coder said calmly. "I want you to take a deep breath right now."

"There's a reason you feel sick to your stomach and when you hold stuff inside," Tammy said. "It makes you physically ill. I can tell from your face that you want to come clean and be done with this, and I appreciate that. We're not here to play games. We just want to know what happened."

Chris continued to insist he wasn't lying, which made Tammy increasingly frustrated.

"I just want them to come home," Chris said.

"But you know they're not coming back home," Tammy insisted. "You know that."

"I hope they come back home," Chris said.

"But you know they're not."

"I hope they come back home," Chris repeated stubbornly. "I don't know that they're not coming back home."

Still leaning back in his chair, incredibly calm and poised, Coder told Chris that he and Tammy were confused. That they had been doing a lot of work overnight and had found some leads. They knew a lot more than Chris realized.

"You're a great guy," Coder told him. "And I know this because everyone tells us that, okay? We can't find *anyone* to say anything bad about you. Chris is a *great* guy. He's a good father. He's a good man. We're confused as to why you're not taking care of your beautiful children."

"I'm not taking care of them right now?" Chris gasped.

"Where are they?" Coder demanded.

"I don't know. I do not know where they are at," he insisted.

"If I could have my babies back home now, I would. I want them back. I want everybody back. That's the God honest truth."

Tammy and Coder stared at him in silence. The only sound that could be heard was the steady tick of the clock in the interrogation room.

Coder told Chris he couldn't reconcile the two Chris's that they were witnessing. He said it warmed his heart that he was the type of dad who could pack a bag in the morning for his daughters. He went on to say he knew Chris loved his daughters, and that he wasn't faking it. Then he pleaded with Chris to tell him about the other parts he was lying about.

Chris, now knowing he was backed into a corner, admitted there was something he was lying about.

"I'm not proud of it, and I feel horrible about it," he said. "I've been cheating on her while she was pregnant. But I hurt her emotionally, not physically." Then he continued, trying to distract Coder and Tammy. "I didn't go to the Rockies game. I went to dinner with *her*. The five weeks I was alone, I was with *her* most of the time."

"This is the Chris who I knew would come out today," Coder said. "This is Chris the truth teller." Coder spoke almost as if he were encouraging a small child.

"I fell in love with her," Chris said.

"Absolutely," Coder said.

"Who is *her*?" Tammy asked.

"I don't want to get her involved in this. I don't want to ruin her life," Chris said. "I don't want her involved in this.

She's a wonderful person. She knew I was married, yes. At the end, I told her I was going to get separated. When I saw her, she took my breath away, and never in a million years, did I think that was gonna happen. I never felt this way about anyone in my lifetime."

It was very strange that Chris was gushing about his mistress and showing more concern about protecting her than the whereabouts of his own family.

"I know you want to take care of her, because you're the type of guy that takes care of women," Coder said, continuing to stroke Chris's ego. "You took care of your wife. You took care of your daughters. You were very good at taking care."

As Coder moved the conversation back to the missing family members, Chris continued to deny having any knowledge about what happened to them. Coder, again, trying to appeal to the "good" and "helpful" Chris everyone loved, reminded him that his father was waiting in the lobby, and that Chris was lying to everyone. They needed him to tell everyone what happened to his family. Coder told Chris they already knew about his girlfriend, Nikki, and that they had the Watts family's "Alexa" device that was trained to record distress. If Chris did kill them in the house, Coder wanted to scare Chris into thinking they had audio evidence, which could potentially force him into a confession.

In another attempt to try to get him to talk, Coder said he thought Shanann may have been a controlling person who did whatever she wanted. This wasn't necessarily what

Coder thought, but perhaps he could get Chris to admit to something if he painted Shanann in a negative light. Coder pleaded with Chris again and again to find his babies.

"I promise you. I have nothing on my hands that's…I did nothing to those kids or her to make them vanish," Chris said again, unwilling to take the bait.

Coder tried a different tactic, trying to get Chris to confess to a lesser crime. He asked Chris if there had been an accident. Maybe something that happened that wasn't supposed to happen. Perhaps a fight that went horribly wrong by mistake.

Chris denied he had done anything to Shanann and the girls on purpose or by mistake. He also continued to emphasize that Shanann, although suspicious about his affair, did not know for a fact that it had happened, and that he had always denied it.

Coder told Chris that he found it odd that he described an "emotional" conversation with his wife in which they were both crying, but he hadn't shed one tear since his family vanished without a trace. He didn't appear to be upset at all.

Chris stated that he loved his girls and his lack of tears didn't mean he wasn't upset. He then forced a sniffle, trying to muster up some type of human emotion that he knew the investigators were looking for from him.

"I love those girls *to death*," Chris said.

Seeing that they were still getting nowhere, Coder tried another tactic, offering Chris another possible scenario that might seem more "socially acceptable" while still shifting blame away from him. The risk with this technique was that it could elicit a false confession, but it would at least get Chris to admit partial guilt. The hope was that the bodies would be recovered as soon as possible, and that the forensic evidence would be enough to paint the picture of what really happened, regardless of a false confession from Chris.

"Did Shanann do something to the girls?" Coder asked.

"No. I don't know. I have no clue."

"Did Shanann do something to them, and then did you feel that you had to do something to her?" Coder said, knowing he was getting closer to squeezing something out of Chris.

"No. No," he said, sighing. "They were at the house when I left. They were there."

Bringing up the video footage from neighbor Nate Trinastich, Coder reminded Chris that the only way his family could have left the house was in his truck. Shanann was seen entering the home by the doorbell camera and then never leaving the house again. Coder reminded him that the truck had a GPS that would ping every ten minutes. They would know every single movement Chris made that morning. There was nowhere left to hide.

Coder continued to further push the idea that Shanann may have done something that would give Chris a "reason" to hurt her. He told Chris he knew that sometimes mistakes happen and offered stories of cases he had personally worked on—specifically stories of parents who had murdered their own children. One story was about a mother who had smothered her children because she didn't want her husband to take them away from her. This mother believed she was doing right by her children, because in her mind, she was saving them from pain.

"Why?" Chris asked, completely dumbfounded and not connecting with the story. "How's she saving them pain?"

"She didn't want them to have to live a life without her," Coder said.

Chris still looked puzzled.

Finally, Coder cut to the chase. He gave Chris two options to choose from. Either Chris did something to all three of them, or Shanann had done something.

"I didn't do anything to the girls," Chris said.

"What did Shanann do to the girls?" Coder demanded.

"Can I speak to my dad?" Chris finally said, defeated.

At this point, the entire interrogation was creeping over five hours.

"Will you promise to tell everything to your dad?" Coder asked, exchanging a look with Tammy.

Chris nodded.

Coder and Tammy left the interrogation room and went out to the lobby, where Ronnie waited. He stood up when he saw them, and they could see that he was wearing a light blue polo shirt with the words "Papa Ronnie" stitched on its breast pocket.

"Chris wants to talk to you alone and tell you what happened," Tammy said. "Just so you know, everything in that room is being recorded." Ronnie nodded that he understood and followed Tammy and Coder back into the interrogation room.

"Take as much time as you need," Tammy said softly, and then closed the door behind her, leaving Ronnie and Chris alone.

Ronnie sat close to Chris and looked at him.

"That polygraph…I failed it…" Chris said in a hushed voice. "They're not gonna let me go. They know I had an affair. I came clean about that."

"Anything else you wanna tell them about what's going on?" Ronnie asked, not fully prepared for the information he was about to hear.

Chris told Ronnie that the morning they had the emotional conversation, he told Shanann he wanted a separation.

"I don't want to protect her…I don't want to protect her, but I don't know what else to say," Chris said in a whisper.

"What happened?" Ronnie said softly, as if making sure he understood what he believed his son was implying. "Did she hurt them?"

"She hurt them," Chris said. "And then I freaked out and hurt her."

• • •

"Talk to me, Chris," Ronnie said in disbelief. "Tell me what happened."

"She…she smothered them…they were smothered," Chris whispered.

"They what?" Ronnie gasped.

"She strangled them," Chris said, changing his story.

"She smothered them, or chokin' em?" Ronnie mumbled.

"I didn't hear anything when I was downstairs, I came back up, and they were gone. I don't know, like me talking to her about the separation and everything. I don't know what else to say. Because I freaked out, and I did the same thing to fuckin' her," he said, trying to muster more emotion. "Those were my kids."

Ronnie's face looked as white as his hair.

"After our conversation, I went downstairs and heard some kind of commotion upstairs, but I didn't think much about it. When I went back upstairs, I saw Shanann on top of CeCe, choking her. Both were blue."

"Shanann choked the girls to death?" Ronnie said, still in shock.

"I freaked out and did the same thing to fucking her." Chris's voice was a loud whisper.

"Oh my God," Ronnie whispered, putting his head in his hands briefly and taking a moment. "So, then what'd you do? Haul the bodies off or something?"

"I didn't know what else to do. I freaked out. It's just rage. I'm sorry," Chris said sheepishly.

"I know you're sorry, son." Ronnie gently rubbed Chris on the back as he continued to sit with his head buried in his hands.

"I'll never see the light of day again," Chris said.

"Why did Shanann have to hurt them babies?" Ronnie said, still in complete shock. He continued to rub Chris's back and console him. "I love you, no matter what. We're going to find a good lawyer and see what the hell they can do"

• • •

While Chris was being questioned, a search team had been on foot and using a drone at the Cervi 319 site where they believed Chris had disposed of the bodies. The drone had picked up an area where there appeared to be white fabric, so the team went to go check it out, assuming it was related to the investigation. As they approached the large white piece of fabric, they could see it was the bedsheet from the Watts home that matched the fitted sheet that had been found in the trash in the kitchen.

Not far from the sheet, an area of dirt appeared to have been recently disturbed. While the team waited for further instructions, they received a call from CBI that Chris had confessed and was going to tell them where the bodies were hidden. Photos of the Cervi 319 site—including photos of the disturbed ground, the sheet, and two oil tanks—were sent to Chris.

Tammy and Coder asked him to mark exactly where all three bodies were. Pointing to the photos of the two oil tanks at the Cervi 319 site, Chris marked where he had disposed of Bella's and Celeste's bodies, one girl in each tank. The openings of the hatches of the tank were only about 8-inches wide, and he explained he had to use some force to get Bella's lifeless body through the opening. He heard her body make a splash when it hit the oil and based on the sound of the different splashes his daughters' bodies made, he felt that one tank must have contained more oil than the other. When Tammy asked Chris to confirm if he was positive his daughters were dead when he put them in the oil tanks, he said he was. He also confirmed that Shanann was buried in a shallow grave beneath the disturbed ground.

Officers easily recovered Shanann's body first. She was found face down in her grave, wearing only a purple T-shirt, black bra, and blue underwear. Her body had already started the decomposition process. She had a coffin birth, and baby Nico had been expelled from her body.

On Thursday August 16, the extensive and traumatic recovery process for the bodies of CeCe and Bella would begin. This was an incredibly disturbing event for the first responders and those who were involved in the process. First, the oil tanks had to be drained.

CeCe, who had been so vibrant in her short life, was recovered first. Her body was removed, completely covered in crude oil. She was wearing a pink nightgown and a pull-up diaper and was taken out of the tank in a decontamination box with handles. The first responders patted her stomach with oil absorbent pads, which caused some of her skin to slip off. They gently wrapped her tiny body in a white sheet and put her in a body bag. They recovered Bella, who wore a pink nightgown covered in butterflies, last.

On the same day the girls' bodies were recovered, Chris's girlfriend Nikki was picked up at her home by CBI Agent's

Kevin Koback and Timothy Martinez and taken to the Thornton Colorado Police Department. She had asked the agents to pick her up and escort her to the station. Her father Dwayne met them there.

Nikki was wearing her thin dark hair in a messy ponytail pulled high on her head. It looked as if she had not washed it in days, and the rest of her appearance seemed in equal disarray. Her sunglasses were pushed on top of her head, and she had bags under her eyelids. She wore a gray zip-up pullover, jeans with ripped holes in them, and sneakers. Agent Koback told her she was not being investigated as a criminal suspect and that she was free to leave at any time on her own accord.

Speaking to the agents, she told Koback that when she had met Chris at the end of May or early June, he wasn't wearing a wedding ring. She said she wasn't aware he had kids until right around Father's Day, somewhere around the second week of June.

She thought it was cool that he had kids, she told Koback. "That sounds sarcastic," he said.

"No… it was kind of cute. It was like, *oh he's a daaaad*…it was around Father's Day too," she said.

She said Chris was always excited to talk about his girls. When Chris mentioned his "significant other," he explained they were in the process of getting a separation. This was not the same story Chris had told the officers, which was that she knew he was married when they met and when they began dating.

Nikki also told Koback that she didn't know Shanann's

name when they met, but the records from her phone suggest that she was internet searching the name "Shanann Watts" as early as September 17, 2017, almost a full year before she and Chris started the affair. Shanann's online profile was easy to find and completely public. Anyone doing a search on her up until the time of her death would have found a treasure trove of information about her personal life, including her third pregnancy.

Nikki told Koback that Chris would usually come to the Anadarko office in the mornings and meet with his team. That's where she usually saw him. They would pass each other in the hallway of the office and say hi, which soon led to casual small talk. They hit it off right away because they felt they had a lot in common.

The first time they saw each other outside of work for an official date was at a park when Chris got back from a Le-Vel/Thrive San Diego trip with Shanann at the end of June.

Every time Chris spoke about his children, or even Shanann, Nikki said he was never hostile and always civil and kind. There were no red flags that would indicate he was angry with his family or wanted them gone. Chris was always calm, peaceful, and relaxed, she said, and she never once saw him lose his temper.

Although he was an introvert, he told Nikki he enjoyed talking to her because he could get out of his shell when he was with her. He felt like he could really be himself. She thought it was because they had things in common such as fitness, eating healthy, and cars. She said she would classify him as a 4 or 5 out of 10 on an introvert scale but not necessarily the extreme introvert everyone was making him out to be.

On two occasions, Nikki said she was at the Watts family home. Chris told her he was living in the basement, and they were getting ready to sell the house. Koback asked Nikki if she knew Chris's street number or name. She said she didn't, but her internet searches showed that she recently searched for "2825 Saratoga Trail," the address of the Watts family home.

Nikki said Chris was very open and communicative, and in her opinion, he was different from other men because he seemed so open with his feelings. She found that refreshing because she hadn't had the best of luck dating men in the past. He was kind and thoughtful with her and would often text her pictures of flowers because she loved them. In fact, he had texted her a picture of a sunflower, her favorite flower, from Cervi 319, the morning Shanann and the girls went missing.

She said her second and final time at the Watts house was the weekend of July 14. Nikki recalled this time because she felt incredibly uncomfortable. She remembered seeing a photograph of Shanann and the girls and thinking to herself, *Why would Chris want to leave this seemingly amazing life? He has a beautiful wife and children, a gorgeous home, and an awesome job. Why would someone just walk away from that?*

Nikki claimed she wanted to make sure Chris really

wanted to leave this amazing life behind before he moved further in their relationship. She said she urged him to try to fix things with Shanann. Chris, apparently lying, said they had been trying to fix things for a long time, and it wasn't working.

Nikki said it almost made her feel bad that she was engaging in a relationship with a man who described his marriage as contractual and not emotional. She wished that the contractual part of the relationship was over before she got involved with him.

She eventually backed away from the relationship, Nikki said, claiming she wanted to know that he really tried to make it work with his wife before he left his family for her. She felt some "cold feet" about her relationship with Chris after visiting his house the weekend of July 14. She said she was holding back with Chris and trying to take things slower. She also said she would sometimes allude to the future with Chris, telling him if she ever met his daughters, she would like to do things like paint pottery with them and help them grow plants.

Before Chris went to North Carolina in early August, he told Nikki that he was going to try to save his marriage with Shanann. Yet once in North Carolina, he was still in constant contact with Nikki. She said he told her that he tried to convince Shanann to work things out with him, but she refused, and that they agreed to proceed with selling the house upon their return to Colorado.

Chris had referred to Shanann as "bossy" and said he

couldn't have an opinion around her. He said he didn't feel heard, and that Shanann was always scrolling through social media when he tried to talk to her. Chris made it sound as if he and Shanann had drifted apart over six years and were in mutual agreement that splitting everything 50/50 was a good idea. They rarely fought, he said, and were always calm.

Chris confided in Nikki about their financial troubles and bankruptcy, saying they were always "house broke," and that Shanann had a hard time controlling her spending. He said Shanann wanted it to appear as if they lived a certain lifestyle, even though they couldn't afford it. Chris never called her a bad mother but said the marriage lasted as long as it did only because of the children.

Nikki knew about the blow-out fight between Shanann and Chris's family when they were in North Carolina. Nikki vaguely knew the fight had to do with Chris's mom, Cindy, exposing CeCe to nuts despite her life-threatening allergy. Chris told Nikki when he got to North Carolina, his family didn't pick up the phone for days. When he finally showed up at their house, he found a note that said, "Son, if you stop by, we're at the beach." In Nikki's words, the Watts family "ignored Chris most of the time he was out there."

"His own family?" Koback asked, finding it odd that Chris's family would shun him in such a way.

"Yesss," Nikki said, as if agreeing with Koback's reaction. "His mom, his dad and his sister…" Nikki continued.

"What's the significance?" he asked. "Do you know why?"

"Yeah, he said… and again, I don't know what's true with

this man anymore and what's not. But I asked, 'Why are your folks ignoring you?' because I was really concerned about it. I talked to him every day when he was out there, and I would ask him, 'Did you talk to your family? Did you talk to your dad?' I wanted him to see his people because it's important. Family is an important thing. And he was like, 'Well, they're ignoring me.'"

Nikki was also aware that Cindy Watts (as well as Ronnie and sister, Jamie) did not show up to Shanann's and Chris's wedding. Chris told her it was because Cindy really didn't care for Shanann.

Nikki admitted that in the six to eight weeks she and Chris had been involved in a relationship, they exchanged "I love you's" several times. Nikki said Chris said it a lot more to her than she did to him. When Chris was in North Carolina, supposedly trying to patch things up with Shanann, he told Nikki he loved her. Nikki claimed her reaction to him was hesitant because she wanted him to try to work things out with Shanann. "Don't say those words to me, try to make peace with your wife, and then lay in bed with another woman," Nikki said she told him.

These statements were somewhat confusing because Nikki was acting like she was trying to push Chris away but at the same time willingly engaging with him and communicating with him daily.

"It's gonna affect me long term," Nikki said, her voice cracking for the first time. "I'm going to wake up every day knowing this mom and her unborn child, and two little girls are not around anymore, and it breaks my heart. My God…and then I have to think about the consequences of his actions and how they affect everybody else. All her family is impacted. My name is about to be slandered, for probably a while. I don't know how long it's going to take to heal, but I wouldn't be surprised if it's going to be hard to go out in public sometimes for a couple of years, and that really hurts me." She started to cry. "This is a horrible, horrible thing. How dare you? And people aren't going to understand that. They are going to say, *oh you're the woman who had this affair with a man who took out his whole family*… and I take a step back and it's like…*I didn't know!* Ughhh. He's so disgusting and I'm so ashamed of him and everything and I just…*ohhh those little girls. They're sooo little. They're sooo little."* She then began to sob uncontrollably. "It's so sad and she's pregn-naaanntt. God, they're so cute and they're so little. Why? Why? How? How? How can you bring yourself to do that to someone who is like, that big?"

Nikki collected herself and then tried to recall her interactions with Chris the weekend Shanann went to Arizona until the present. The Saturday before Shanann disappeared, Nikki admitted she was with Chris at the Lazy Dog restaurant and her apartment when Chris lied to everyone, saying he was at the Colorado Rockies game with co-workers. Nikki said although she was pulling back from the relationship because his kids were back home, Chris wanted to see her more.

Nikki said they first went to a different Lazy Dog (there

are two in the Denver area), but when they got there, she looked at the menu and realized she didn't want to eat there. She told Chris she wanted to go to the other one instead. Interestingly, Chris felt he could be more himself around Nikki and called Shanann bossy, yet Nikki seemed to be calling the shots in her relationship with him. Chris would often go to her for advice, and Nikki would advise him on clean eating, counting calories, apartment hunting, and helping young children through divorce. Nikki's parents were divorced when she was a little girl, so she was familiar with that experience through the child's perspective.

Sunday night, the evening Shanann was supposed to return from Arizona, Nikki remembered hearing a television in the background when they were talking on the phone. This was odd to her because when she would talk to Chris on the phone at night, he would be downstairs sleeping in the basement, and there was no television down there. That night the thought had crossed her mind that maybe he was waiting for Shanann to come home because he wasn't in the basement as he usually was.

Chris told her he would be going to the Cervi 319 site in the morning and not the office. That wasn't particularly strange to Nikki because although typically, the guys would usually go to the office first, there were times when they would go out to the field beforehand.

Nikki talked to Chris Monday morning, the day he murdered and disposed of the bodies of his family. At some point on Monday, he texted her saying it had been a busy day.

Later, when Nikki got home from work, she had another text from Chris saying his wife and kids weren't home and asking her to call him when she was able to. When she finally reached him on the phone, the conversation was brief because the police were at his house, which meant most of their communication over the rest of the day was over text message.

Over text, Nikki said she asked Chris where he thought Shanann was. He played it nonchalantly, saying he and Shanann got into a disagreement, and she most likely went to a friend's house and would be back the next morning. He said Shanann's friend Nicki Atkinson was insisting they involve the cops, but he didn't seem too concerned about it.

According to Nikki, when she talked to Chris on the phone later that evening, he told her he was going to go to work in the morning and the conversation went like this:

"I think you should probably stay home and help the police," Nikki told him.

"I'm worried that Shanann will see my truck and won't come home because she thinks I'm there and doesn't want to see me," Chris told her.

"So, move your truck so she won't see it," Nikki advised him. "Make sure you have a friend with you when she comes home, in case there is a conflict you'll have a witness with you and if someone isn't there, record whatever happens with your phone."

By Monday evening, Nikki said she realized that Shanann still wasn't back, and no one had any clue where she was or how to find her. When Nikki said she confronted him again about what happened the morning Shanann supposedly left, Chris told her that they had gotten into an argument and Shanann was being mean. He said Shanann told him she was pregnant, and the child wasn't his. Chris denied knowing that she was pregnant, even though Shanann had posted the information on social media.

Nikki said she still believed this was just a dispute between a couple, and that Chris's story was believable. But by Tuesday morning, Shanann still wasn't home. Nikki asked Chris multiple times where his family was, and he kept telling her he didn't know. During her lunch break, she went through all the news stories about Shanann, Bella, and CeCe and read that Shanann was fifteen weeks pregnant. Nikki said this was the time she started to get suspicious and knew Chris had been lying to her. If Shanann was that pregnant, she would be showing, and there was no way Chris would not know about it.

Nikki allegedly texted Chris and confronted him about his lies:

"I read your wife is 15 weeks pregnant. You lied to me. You knew she was pregnant. I know the baby is yours and not from an affair your wife had."

"Does this ruin everything with us?" Chris asked her.

"You should be focused on your family. Stop lying and go find your family. I don't want to talk to you until your family has been found."

Nikki thought it was bizarre that he seemed more

concerned about the demise of their relationship than his missing family. That was the last contact she said she ever had with him.

On August 19, after her initial interview, Nikki conducted multiple internet searches related to Amber Frey, the former girlfriend of Scott Peterson, convicted killer of his wife, Laci Peterson, who was nine months pregnant at the time. She had vanished on Christmas Eve, and her body washed up on the shore months later. Shortly before Scott murdered Laci, he was living a double life and having an affair with Amber Frey, whom he told he was widowed. Amber had always been a sympathetic character in the media and in the public eye because it was obvious that she was completely unaware that she was involved with a married man. Equally important, without her testimony, Scott Peterson might have gotten away with murder.

Nikki might have been looking to elicit sympathy for herself. Given that the Watts family murders had similarities to Laci's murder, Nikki may have thought she could find a way to show the public she was a victim the way Amber had been. As you will see, those closely following the case did not view Nikki as a victim once the police discovery documents were made public.

CHAPTER 8

"This is the heartless one…"

The days and weeks following the explosive news regarding the Watts family murders were filled with the most soul-crushing and devastating heartbreak for Shanann's loved ones, especially her parents and younger brother, Frankie. The cycling emotions of grief, consisting of a never-ending rollercoaster of anger, confusion, and overwhelming sadness hit everyone hard. The ripple effects of the murders were wide and extended everywhere, from the small suburbs of Denver, Colorado, to locations across the world, where many people had been following the case through the media.

It was especially difficult because Shanann's loved ones knew that she would *never* do anything to hurt her children. To have to endure any speculation that she was responsible for their deaths was another stab through the heart. Never in their wildest nightmares did anyone who knew Shanann and Chris fathom that something this sickeningly awful could happen. It was too surreal, too shocking, too hard to process.

Because Shanann's life so was so public on social media, many people following the story began to judge and criticize her, picking apart every little move she made. Some would blame Shanann for everything and call her controlling. Some would speculate she had some form of Munchausen's and faked her illnesses and the girls' medical conditions. Some people expressed sympathy for Chris, and some women even wrote him love letters in prison.

The Rzucek family received death threats and attention they never wanted nor asked for. All they wanted to do was mourn their loss in private and in peace. Although there was a massive outpouring of love for the Rzucek family, unspeakable cruelty was constantly torturing them with the added layer of negativity and threats.

The prosecution on the case was led by Michael Rourke, an experienced and savvy attorney. A deeply compassionate man, Rourke was handsome and tall, with kind brown eyes and short, slicked-back silver hair. Rourke felt an overwhelming loyalty to the Rzucek family from the moment he met them. This case hit him hard, as it did many of the other people involved in it. He and the prosecution vowed to do everything in their power to clear Shanann's name and expose all the lies Chris had told. This case was one of the most shocking and horrific cases Rourke had dealt with in more than twenty years as a prosecutor. As a father of a daughter around Bella's and CeCe's ages, he was especially horrified and sickened by the crime. It was too close to home.

While the media continued to speculate, the evidence the prosecution had against Chris was kept secret, with the expectation that this case would go to trial, and a jury would decide if Chris committed the crimes they were seeking to charge him with. These counts included five counts of first-degree murder, three counts of tampering with a deceased human body, and the unlawful termination of a pregnancy.

In late October, an interesting development in the case suddenly surfaced. Chris's defense team proposed a resolution, offering a plea deal that said he would plead guilty to all charges, in exchange for not seeking the death penalty. If the case were to go to trial, it would involve years and years of drawn-out proceedings with all the sordid details exposed to the public. Chris could avoid all this and a lengthy trial by pleading guilty. He was also made aware that in the worst-case scenario, if he was sentenced to death, there would be years of appeals. He knew the evidence against him was overwhelming, and he cared deeply of what others thought of him, so pleading guilty seemed the easiest way to escape everything as much as possible.

Michael Rourke flew to North Carolina to meet with the Rzucek family in person and discussed all possible scenarios with them. The family wanted Shanann's name cleared, and Chris's pleading guilty to all charges would be one way to do it. Second, the family, specifically Sandi, held strong beliefs that they should not get to decide the fate of someone else's life, not even Chris's life.

The *Denver Post* did an exclusive interview with Nikki.[4] It is unclear who initiated the interview. In the accompanying photographs, her face was illuminated against a black background with her long brown hair styled past her shoulders. The expression on her face was serious.

Nikki told the Post that when she met Chris, he told her he was at the end of divorce proceedings, and she had no clue he was still very married. She said it was a brief affair, and that she had been totally duped by him.

Ahead of the sentencing, Chris's family members were struggling to comprehend what happened in their own way. Understandably, raising a son with zero warning signs of violent behavior, (in fact, one who displayed the opposite characteristics), created a surge of denial and confusion. How does a parent who believed their offspring was a role model son, husband, and father deal with the fact that he is capable of such a thing? For Cindy, Ronnie, and his older sister Jamie, the idea of Chris killing his children wasn't a real possibility because it just couldn't be true. Not the Chris they knew.

Chris's mother couldn't accept the fact that he was going to plead guilty, and she didn't want him to. She went to the media and gave an interview, saying she wanted him to fight.[5] This interview was controversial because Cindy did

---

4. Schmelzer, Elise. "'It's Horrific': Christopher Watts' Girlfriend Speaks out for the First Time as Sentencing in Frederick Murders Draws Near." The Denver Post. The Denver Post, November 16, 2018. https://www.denverpost.com/2018/11/15/christopher-watts-murder-mistress-nichol-kessinger/.

5. Watts, Cindy. Interview with *9Wants to Know*. 9 News.Com, Denver Colorado, November 15, 2018.

not speak well of Shanann. Cindy shared that she did not attend Chris's and Shanann's wedding because she couldn't get along with Shanann and didn't like the way she treated Chris. Cindy thought the marriage was toxic. Admittedly, she said she knew very little about their marriage, but Chris always seemed anxious to her. When Shanann needed something, "he wouldn't walk, he would run" Cindy said.

Cindy said Chris wasn't excited about the third baby, and he was "finally seeing the light" when it came to Shanann. When Cindy first heard they were missing, she believed Shanann took the children and ran off to punish Chris, because that's the kind of person Cindy believed Shanann was.

Cindy was very angry that she wasn't allowed to speak to Chris before his sentencing. She wanted to know why he would plead guilty to the crimes if he was innocent, and at the time, Cindy firmly believed that he did not kill his daughters. She said it scared her to death to think Chris could have done all of it, and she couldn't mentally go there. She couldn't see why he was pleading guilty, because if she were in his shoes, she would fight to the end. Cindy believed if the attorneys had let Ronnie and her talk to Chris, that would have made a difference, and maybe he wouldn't have pleaded guilty. The guilty plea was Chris's choice, but it seemed that Cindy was still hoping her influence could change the direction she envisioned the trial going.

Ronnie stated somewhat cryptically in the media interview in what appeared to be a jab at Shanann, "You have to get to know her to be around her. We'll put it that way."

Shanann's family responded to Ronnie's and Cindy's statements with their own retort: "Their false statements, however hurtful or inaccurate, will never alter the truth about Shanann. And will never alter the truth about the crimes committed by their son. Her memory and reputation deserve to be protected. And her family is fully prepared to do so."

The day before the sentencing, the prosecution briefed Ronnie and Cindy on the evidence against their son and why he decided to plead guilty. Frank, Sandi, and Frankie Rzucek would be making victim impact statements at the sentencing. Ronnie and Cindy wanted to make victim impact statements as well. Being that they were the grandparents of the victims, they were granted permission to speak at the sentencing.

On November 6, 2018, Christopher Lee Watts was formally sentenced to life in prison. Many of Shanann's loved ones were present at the sentencing, and all were visibly distraught. Tammy Lee, Grahm Coder, and Detective David Baumhover were also present. Wearing an orange jumpsuit, Chris sat with his attorneys. He appeared disheveled. His buzzcut and facial hair had grown out a bit and looked greasy and unwashed. His eyes appeared nervous behind his dark-rimmed glasses, and his body trembled slightly as if he had a little twitch of electricity pulsing through him.

Judge Marcelo Kopcow welcomed the observers in the courtroom and laid out the rules of proper conduct for the sentencing before letting DA Michael Rourke begin. Shanann's family would make their victim impact statements first.

Frank Rzucek Sr. went first, his voice breaking with emotion and tears as he fondly remembered his daughter and grandchildren. Frank, voice shaking, unable to look at the man he once considered a son said:

They were taken by a heartless one. This is the heartless one, the evil monster. How dare you take the lives of my daughter Shanann, Bella, Celeste and Nico? I trusted you to take care of them, not kill them. And they also trusted you. The heartless monster... then you take them out like trash. You disgust me. They were loving and caring people. You may have taken their bodies from me, but you will never take the love they had for me. They loved us more than you will ever know because you don't know what love is. Because if you did, you would not have killed them. You, monster, thought you would get away with this.

Frankie Jr., Shanann's younger brother, was next but opted to have DA Rourke read his statement for him. He detailed the torture he had been through for almost three months from losing his beloved and only sibling. Frankie adored and looked up to Shanann, and they had a beautiful brother and sister relationship. Being an uncle was one of the most special parts of his life, and the hole that was left by the loss of his beautiful, sweet nieces and unborn nephew felt too much for his broken heart to bear. Frankie stood next to DA Rourke, wearing a suit, hands stuffed in his pockets, eyes downward, chewing on gum with a hollow look on his stunned face. His words articulated how he would forever struggle to understand how Chris went from being someone worshipped by the whole family to someone who could take away their entire world:

You took away my privilege as an uncle to the most precious little girls I have ever known. I will never hear the words Uncle Frankie again, but you will never be called Dad again. I just can't comprehend how they weren't enough for you. Shanann, Bella, and CeCe loved you more than anyone. I pray you never have a moments peace or a good night's rest in the cage you'll spend every day of your life in. I just wish that you would tell the truth, but that's asking more than you are capable of. I stayed up all night writing this statement. I don't sleep because of you. My life will never be the same because of you.

Sandi spoke next as the matriarch of the Rzucek family, composed and strong in a navy striped suit with a purple pin on the breast to represent lupus. She thanked everyone who had prayed for them, for everyone involved in the investigation, Nate Trinastich, and Nicki Atkinson. She called them her heroes. And then she spoke to Chris:

We loved you like a son. We trusted you. Your faithful wife trusted you. Your children adored you, and they also trusted you. I know the angels were there in the moment their lives were taken to bring them to paradise. I want the world to know how loved my daughter and grandchildren were. I didn't want death for you because that's not my right. Your life is between you and God now, and I pray that he has mercy for you.

After the Rzucek family spoke, Cindy and Ronnie Watts had a turn to make their victim impact statements as the grandparents of the youngest victims. They addressed the courtroom, first through a victim's advocate. After their shocking media interview that was aggressive in nature, they had the opportunity to speak with the prosecution before the sentencing to hear the evidence against their son. They also used this as an opportunity to correct and clarify any erroneous statements they had made to the media. The victim's advocate said:

We are not here to ask for leniency. We are not in any way condoning or tolerating the crime that has occurred and the pain that has been caused. We join in our daughter-in-law's family in saying this never should have happened. This is not condonable. This is something that we will never get over. We appreciate the consideration that everyone has paid, most especially the families that have lost everyone. We appreciate that they begged for Christopher's life. We agree and echo what they have said that it is not his place to take anyone's life nor would it be our place as a community to take his life. So, we thank you for the opportunity and for every consideration and effort that has been put out. The prosecution in this case has in fact respected the victims bill of rights. They took the time to explain that the information that my clients had at the time that they were interviewed was not correct. They were misinformed, they were searching for answers, they were not intending to cause any pain to anyone, and they appreciated that the prosecution answered their questions and gave them the time, the respect, and the consideration so that they could tell this court and everyone in this community that the interview content was not their message. That they accept that their son has done this. That they accept that he chose to plead guilty, he sought and requested their agreement for a life sentence and appreciate that he's given an opportunity to serve a life sentence. It is his responsibility; it is his sentence and it is not enough to make up for what he has done. We understand and we join the family in that we have questions. We don't know how such a thing could possibly happen, or that a man who was responsible for raising his children and protecting his wife would take the steps that he did and disregard their bodies and the love that he had for them and they had for him and everyone else and take the gestures and put this community through the investigation and discovery and the responsibility of bringing justice. We do not understand that. We do not think that was appropriate. We do not think that an explanation will ever justify it. My clients indicate that they understand that a full opportunity for a confession and all the responsibility and accountability has not occurred and they support the family in the request that that happen. Not today. In an appropriate time. In an appropriate manner. So that everyone can have peace. To understand to the best of their ability, the details that they need and to have their questions answered. And by giving this opportunity of a life sentence, we hope he embraces that moment.

Cindy Watts spoke next. She spoke about how the families were irreparably broken and how she would never understand what happened. She did not say much beyond that. She instead, decided to address Chris, who sat behind her, head down and still quivering, his leg and foot shaking uncontrollably. Cindy spoke through tears and a trembling voice:

To my son Christopher: I have known you since the day you

were born into this world. I have watched you grow from a quiet, sweet, and curious child, who Bella reminded me so much of, to a man who worked hard in sports and later mechanics to achieve your goals. You were a good friend, brother, father, and son. We have loved you from the beginning, and we still love you now. This might be hard for some to understand. How I can sit here under these circumstances and tell you all that we are heartbroken, although we can't imagine what could have led us to this day. But we love you. Maybe you can't believe it either. As the lord said in Jeremiah 331: I have loved you with an everlasting love. Therefore, I have continued my faithfulness to you. As your mother, Chris, I have always loved you, and I still do. I hate what has happened. Your father, sister, and I are struggling to understand why, but we will remain faithful as your family just as God remains faithful because of his unconditional love for all. We love you, and we forgive you, son."

Cindy turned around and looked directly at Chris, who could not bring himself to meet his mother's gaze.

"We forgive you, son" she said sobbing as she stepped aside to make room for her husband to speak.

Ronnie could not personally read his statement, but a victim advocate read on his behalf. This was the only point in the trial where Chris looked up and directly ahead. Ronnie spoke of being involved in his son's life, enjoying coaching Little League and going to the races with him. Ronnie knew in his heart that Chris loved his girls in the same way Ronnie loved his own children. He urged Chris for answers and said:

Chris, I want to talk to you as a father. You are here today accepting responsibility, but I want to tell you this now: I love you. Nothing will ever change that. And I want you to find peace, and today is your first step. The Bible says if we confess our sins, God is faithful and just and will forgive us. Chris, I forgive you and your sister forgives you and we will never abandon you and we love you. Dad.

After Ronnie spoke, the television cameras panned to Chris, catching one lone tear trickle down the side of his face.

Finally, DA Rourke approached the podium, ready to present the evidence they had against Chris. Up until this point, other than the immediate family members and the investigators, no one knew what was coming. There had been speculation and rumors in the media, but it was unclear as to what evidence law enforcement had that compelled Chris to plead guilty to all charges.

DA Rourke, with deep sadness in his eyes, looked at the judge. He knew what he was about to say would be traumatic for so many in the courtroom:

Your Honor, there are no words to adequately describe the unimaginable tragedy that brings us before this court today. By my comments, I'm not even going to try to express the horror, the pain, or the suffering that the defendant has caused these families, this community, and to all who were a part of this investigation. However, I do want to spend a few minutes sharing with the court the details of the crime, and so far, you've only had an opportunity to review the affidavit and a few facts here and there that have been offered to the court in the motions and the pleadings that have been filed.

The questions that have screamed out to anyone who will listen since August 13th of 2018 are why and how? Why did this have to happen? How could a seemingly normal husband and father annihilate his entire family? For what? These are the questions that only one individual in this courtroom or on this planet knows the answers to. I fully expect we will not receive the answers to these questions today, nor will we at any point in the future. I don't expect he will tell the truth about what really happened, or why. Even if he did, there is no rational way that any human being could find those answers acceptable responses to such horrific questions. The best we can do is try to piece together some kind of understanding from the evidence that is available to us. And the evidence tells us this: the defendant coldly and deliberately ended four lives. Not in a fit of rage, not by way of accident, but in a calculated and sickening manner.

Shanann was 34 years old. She had married the defendant in November of 2012. Over the weekend leading up to August 13th she had been at a work conference in Phoenix, Arizona, and returned home in the early morning hours of August 13th. We know she got home at about 1:45 in the morning. The doorbell camera on her home shows her arriving back home from the airport. Shortly thereafter, at least according to the defendant, they had, what he referred to as an "emotional conversation" about the state of their marriage and what their lives would look like going forward. What was said during that emotional conversation, only he knows. What we do know is that shortly after that, the defendant strangled her to death with his own hands.

We know that he slowly took her life the morning of August 13ᵗʰ. We know that this was not done in an uncontrolled vengeful manner that he tried to describe to agents from CBI and the FBI. If that were the case, you would expect to see vicious, horrible bruising about her neck, shoulders, and face. You would expect to see the highway bone in her neck broken. You would expect to see defensive wounds on his body as she struggled and fought for her own life. None of those were present. The only injuries that were on Shanann's body were what appeared to be fingernail or finger mark bruising to the right side of her neck. We know that our experts will tell you that it takes 2–4 minutes to strangle someone to death manually with their own hands. The horror that she felt as the man that she loved wrapped his hands around her throat and choked the life out of her must have been unimaginable.

Even worse, what Bella, age 4, and Celeste, age 3 must have experienced or thought as their father, the one man on this planet who was supposed to nurture and protect them, was snuffing out their lives. They both died from smothering. Let me say that again. The man seated to my right smothered his daughters. Why? Imagine the horror in Bella's mind as her father took her last breaths away. Your Honor understand between her upper lip and her gum had a centimeter and a half laceration. She bit her tongue multiple times before she died. She fought back for her life, as her father smothered her. Celeste had no such injuries. In fact, she had no external injuries at all but according to the medical examiner, she was smothered, nonetheless.

The defendant then calmly and methodically loaded their bodies into his work truck. Not in a hasty or disorganized way. He was seen from his neighbor's doorbell camera backing his truck into the driveway, going back and forth into the house and back out to the truck three different times. One time for each of their bodies. He then drove them away from their family home, one final time, intent on hiding any evidence of the crimes he just committed.

In one final sign of his callousness for his wife, his daughters, and his unborn son and their remains, he drove them to a location where he thought no one would ever find them, to one of the oil tank batteries with which he was so familiar. He knew this was safe. He had texted a coworker the night before saying *I'll head out to that site. I'll take care of it.* He had carefully ensured that he would be alone in the middle of the plains to secrete away the remains of his family, in a place that he hoped they would never be found.

In one final measure of disrespect for the family he once had, he ensured they would not be together, even in death, or so he thought. He disposed of them in different locations. He buried Shanann and Nico in a shallow grave away from the oil tanks. Bella and Celeste were thrown away in the oil tanks at this facility. Different tanks so these little girls wouldn't be together in death. Imagine this, Your Honor: this defendant took those little girls and put them through a hatch at the top of an oil tank 8 inches in diameter. Bella had scratches on her left buttocks from being shoved through this hole. A tuft of blond hair was found on the edge of one of these hatches. The defendant told investigators that Bella's tank seemed emptier than CeCe's because of the sound the splashes made. These were his daughters.

Significantly, when his coworkers arrived later that morning, they all described him as acting completely normal. It was a normal workday. Even while his daughters sank in the oil and water not far away from him. And then his efforts at deception truly began. We've all seen the emotionless interviews the defendant gives to the media, asking for help in locating his family. We watched as he claimed the house was empty without them and he hoped they were somewhere safe and that he just wanted them to come home. He told investigators that they were at home sleeping when he left for work that morning and that she had told him she was taking the girls to a friend's house for the day. What is striking about this case, your Honor, beyond the horrors I have already described to you, is the number of collateral victims he created by his actions. While he stood in front of TV cameras asking for the safe return of his family, scores of law enforcement officers, neighbors, friends, and family scoured the area, fretted for her safe return. They texted him begging for any information and sending him their best wishes, all the while, he hid what he had done.

The list of indirect victims does not end there. Think of all the firefighters and the border state patrol and hazmat experts who had to don protective suits and who were called upon to pull Bella and Celeste out of those oil tanks. Or the coroner employees who had to conduct these autopsies, or the victim's assistants who frantically attempted to ease the suffering of those affected. All this, Your Honor, for what? Why? Why did this have to happen? His motive was simple, Your Honor. He had a desire for a fresh start. To begin a relationship with a new love that overpowered all decency and feelings for his wife, his daughters, and his unborn *son.*

While Shanann texted the defendant over and over in the days and weeks leading up to her death, attempting to save her marriage, the defendant secreted pictures of his girlfriend into his phone and texted her at all hours of the night. While Shanann sent the defendant self-help relationship and counseling books, one of which was ironically enough thrown in the garbage, he was searching for secluded vacation spots to take his new love and researching jewelry. And while Shanann took the girls to visit family in North Carolina, the defendant went to car museums and the sand dunes with his new girlfriend. The stark difference between the content of their text messages and internet searches is absolutely stunning. Even the morning after he killed them and disposed of their bodies, he made several phone calls. One was to the school where the girls were supposed to start, telling the school that the girls would not be coming back to school anymore. That they were being unenrolled. Presumably to give him more time before law enforcement notification about them going missing. He contacted a Realtor to start discussing the selling of his house, and he texted with his girlfriend about their future. None of this answers the questions of why, however. If he was this happy and wanted a new start, get a divorce. You don't annihilate your family and throw them away like garbage. Why did Nico, Celeste, Bella, and Shanann have to lose their lives in order for him to get what he wanted?

After Rourke spoke to the courtroom, Judge Kopcow said that this was the most inhumane and vicious crime he had handled out of the thousands of cases he had seen.

He formally sentenced Chris to five life sentences in prison without the possibility of parole, including forty-eight years for the unlawful termination of Shanann's pregnancy and thirty-six years for the disposal of the bodies. Chris would serve his sentence at Waupun Correctional Institute in Wisconsin, the same prison where infamous serial killer Ed Gein served his.

Three months after arriving in Waupun, in February of 2019, Chris received a visit from Colorado Bureau of Investigation Agents Grahm Coder, Tammy Lee, and Detective David Baumhover. They had been haunted and puzzled by this case and were seeking answers from him. They showed up unannounced, and Chris, somewhat surprisingly was willing to speak candidly with them about his life, the evening of the murders, and the days following. Chris spoke to them for more than five hours in a more detailed confession. Before we explore that, we need to investigate the past and examine the lives of Chris and Shanann.

CHAPTER 9

"He's a keeper."

Shanann Cathryn Rzucek was born on January 10, 1984 in New Jersey to Frank and Sandi Onorati Rzucek. Frank Rzucek, Shanann's father was always a gentle, emotional and loving man, fondly known for wearing his heart on his sleeve. Physically fit, tan, and handsome, Frank had a dazzling smile and personality to match, much like his daughter.

Sandi was outgoing, dominant, and strong willed but also fiercely loving and loyal. With her strong and fiery personality, Sandi was the dominant one in her partnership with Frank.

A few years after Shanann's birth, Franklin Rzucek Jr. was born. As an adult, Frankie was a tall, lean, attractive man who had inherited his father's bright smile and chiseled cheekbones. Shanann seemed to be a perfect mix of her mother and father. When she smiled, she resembled Sandi.

The family of four soon moved to North Carolina, and Shanann and Frankie Jr. would attend high school there. In high school, Shanann was extremely well-liked and described by others as someone who everyone wanted to be around. She was always her own person. Incredibly independent and ambitious, she left home at eighteen and never looked back.

As an adult woman, Shanann was strikingly gorgeous. She had the signature Rzucek smile that lit up her whole face. Her eyes sparkled and danced, and her face would glow when she smiled. Her energy was contagious. More important, Shanann was one of the most loving and loyal people one could ever wish to have in their life. If you were her friend, she would do anything for you. If you were having a bad day, you could call her, and she would drop everything for you.

Not only was she determined, driven, loyal, and kind, but she was also raw, honest, and real about herself. Shanann once said:

I'm far from perfect. I didn't complete college, I'm not the best writer or speaker, I'm insecure and scared!!! I have so many fears and doubts! What I am great at is not giving up! I get knocked down over and over again, but I get up and FIGHT! I fight harder and harder every time I fall! I want to set the best example I can for my children, my husband, and myself!

Christopher Lee Watts was born on May 16, 1985 in Spring Lake North Carolina to parents Ronnie and Cindy Watts. His sister Jamie was seven years older than he. Ronnie worked as a parts manager at a Ford Dealership, and Cindy was a notary and secretary for a used car dealership. The family was religious and regularly attended First Baptist Church.

Chris described having a relatively normal, happy and uneventful childhood. Ronnie was quiet and never really spoke about feelings or showed them. Cindy was more emotional and made many of the decisions in the relationship. Chris's older sister, Jamie, was very outgoing, pretty, popular, and well-liked. From a young age, Chris was in her shadow. He has ardently stated that he never wanted to be like Jamie. He wanted to be his own person. Jamie doted on Chris in childhood. She was very motherly with him and always wanted to know how he felt.

Chris's weight fluctuated throughout life. He loved to eat, and his family joked that he was like a garbage disposal. He was overweight and socially awkward throughout some of his relationship with Shanann. When he started using the Thrive products Shanann was selling and began to work out and eat healthier, he became tan and fit. His co-workers nicknamed him the "silver fox," a tribute to his silver hair and all-American good looks. Chris had light brown eyes. They didn't sparkle like Shanann's, but when he smiled, his teeth were bright white, and he appeared to be a friendly, nice guy who was easy to talk to and be around.

Chris attended Pine Crest High School in North Carolina. He played sports and did very well in school. While he wasn't popular by teenage social standards, he was very well-liked by peers and teachers. Chris always played by the rules and did everything right. He was the type of kid who never got in any trouble and would de-escalate rather than instigate conflict. He was incredibly introverted and withdrawn, although always respectful and deferential. Even though he wasn't a lady's man, some girls had crushes on Chris, despite his being shy and awkward.

Chris kept in touch with his childhood best friend, Mark. They became friends when they were eight or nine. Mark joined the military, and in adulthood, Chris and Mark didn't speak or see each other much, but they had that special childhood bond and would always pick up where they left off whenever they reconnected.

Chris mostly kept to himself in high school. He didn't have a group of friends, and when it was time for prom, he went with a girl who asked him. He didn't really date in high school or show much of an interest in doing so. Instead, he chose to focus on school and sports. He was described as incredibly intelligent with a photographic memory. In 2003, he won a $1,000 scholarship to attend NASCAR Technical Institute in Mooresville. Chris loved cars and was an aspiring mechanic. After graduating from NASCAR, he worked for a Ford dealership in Morrisville.

Chris always gravitated toward his father, Ronnie, who was his hero, best friend, and the one person he looked up to. Ronnie was equally attached to Chris. In fact, when Chris moved out of the family home to go to college, Ronnie became so depressed about his son leaving that he started using what Chris had referred to in his prison confession as "white powder." Chris had tried to talk to him about it, but much like everything else, sensitive topics were off limits in the Watts household and not to be brought up for discussion.

This was perhaps why Shanann and Chris' family struggled to find common ground with each other. Shanann was an open book and the Watts family were very private people.

After Shanann left home, she faced numerous and diverse challenges. In 2002, she married an attorney, Leonard King. They had met when Shanann was in high school, and Leonard described her, not surprisingly, as having a "compelling" personality. When they were married, she worked as a manager for Dirty South, a tire company in Charlotte.

In her Facebook videos, Shanann alluded to the fact that the marriage to Leonard was dysfunctional. Chris had mentioned that Shanann couldn't be herself with her ex-husband, and she could finally be herself when she met Chris. In any case, the marriage with Leonard was short-lived, and there were no children, so a clean break and a fresh start for Shanann were easy.

From Leonard's point of view, according to police interviews, he had tried to make things work with Shanann. He said when the marriage was on the rocks, she threw herself into work and wouldn't come home at night. He had attempted marriage counseling with her, and they had gone to a few sessions, but she just wasn't interested in working things out. Once the marriage was over, Shanann and Leonard never spoke again.

Post-divorce brought some of the darkest moments in Shanann's life. Around that time, she became very ill. She went from doctor to doctor, running tests, trying to figure out what was wrong. Eventually, she was diagnosed with lupus, an autoimmune disorder that causes the immune system to become hyperactive and start attacking the tissues, causing pain and inflammation in joints and organs. Shanann was also diagnosed with fibromyalgia, a disease characterized by widespread musculoskeletal pain. Shanann also thought she might not be able to have children because of an endometriosis diagnosis.

Chris and Shanann met in 2010 when Shanann was in the thick of her health struggles and not at all interested in dating. Chris's cousin's ex-wife had suggested that Chris and Shanann become friends on Facebook, guessing they would hit it off. Shanann, although not interested, accepted the Facebook request from Chris, thinking it was just Facebook and wouldn't amount to anything.

Their first date was at the Epicentre in Charlotte, an entertainment complex. They had planned to see a movie, and the theatre had full-service bar and dining options. It was more of an upscale establishment, not a typical movie theatre, and Chris had shown up in shorts and sneakers. Shanann was not impressed. She had even told him that he wasn't her type and tried to push him away.

On the first date, Chris was so nervous he couldn't eat. He knew right away that he liked Shanann, so he pursued her, despite her lack of interest. Chris knew how to win her over and to prove himself indispensable to her. Perhaps he liked the challenge.

• • •

In the early months of their relationship, he would sort her medications for her into a pill box and even went to a colonoscopy with her. Shanann said she knew Chris was "a keeper" after he did that for her. He had proved his loyalty to her, and Shanann knew this type of kindness was exactly what she needed in a partner.

Chris fit the mold of every fairytale. He swooped in when Shanann was sick and at her worst. Despite her best efforts to push him away, he stuck around. He did the things that people usually don't do unless they've been together for years. He showed her loyalty, devotion, and he adored her. He let her be who she was without any apologies.

As a therapist, I tell my clients to look for people who show their kindness through actions. Chris was kind and helpful to everyone he knew. He was a man of few words but certainly a man of action.

This was a stark contrast from her marriage to Leonard, and she began to realize that the way Chris treated her was the way someone should treat the person they love. He had all the traits of a man who would make a great husband and father, and Shanann desperately wanted to be a mother despite her concerns about possible infertility.

Both described the relationship as a happy one. They were young and appeared to be in love. However, much like Shanann's health, the relationship did not come without its challenges, and those reared their ugly heads early on. In the first year they were together, Chris said his mother was hesitant about Shanann.

In his opinion, Cindy didn't know how to handle the fact he had a serious girlfriend because he was the "baby" of the family and never dated in high school.

According to Shanann's mother, Sandi, Shanann wanted to be accepted by Cindy, Ronnie, and Jamie, and in hopes of connecting with them, she decided to have a cookout at her home to introduce her family to the Watts family. Sandi mentioned in one of her letters to law enforcement that the cookout didn't go well. Sandi said Cindy made comments to undercut Shanann the entire time. Furthermore, Sandi felt that Cindy seemed outwardly suspicious of Shanann and didn't like that she lived in such a nice house and had expensive things at such a young age.

At one point during the cookout, Sandi said that when Shanann was out of earshot, Cindy leaned over to her and said, "Was your daughter married before?"

"Yes...just like your daughter Jamie was," Sandi said, uncomfortable with where the conversation was going.

"I just don't see it," Cindy said, shaking her head.

"See what?" Sandi inquired.

"I just don't see or feel that your daughter loves my son," Cindy replied.

Sandi was taken aback and immediately felt nervous for her daughter. She knew that Cindy would cause trouble for Chris and Shanann. She knew because she had a similar experience with her own mother-in-law. According to Sandi, Cindy and Jamie continued to be distant and aloof with Shanann and her family and never really warmed up to them.

Despite the tepid relationship with Chris's family, the relationship between Chris and Shanann progressed quickly. They got along well, except for one fight early in the relationship, when according to Chris, Shanann was upset that he had been texting with a female friend.

In 2011, Chris proposed to Shanann at Ocean Isle Beach in North Carolina. Everyone was happy that day, including both families, and it appeared the future was bright after all. Shanann knew exactly what she wanted, and Chris was happy to go along with her agenda. They made plans to marry in November 2012 at the Double Tree Hilton in North Carolina.

Sandi told investigators in a letter that Shanann was having an engagement party, and Jamie offered to help her by sending the invitations out to everyone. Only immediate family whom Shanann had directly invited showed up to the party. It has been said that when Shanann checked with friends to see why they didn't come, they said they never received invitations.

Shanann was absolutely devastated, as several friends have reported. To my understanding, Jamie and Cindy have said that the invitations had been sent. Although there is no way to know exactly happened with the invitations and why, it seems that Sandi and Shanann believed that Jamie and Cindy were responsible.

These stories from Sandi in the police discovery do not include the perspective of the Watts family who may very well have their own version of these stories. There may have been several misunderstandings, miscommunications and different perceptions of what happened with these events. Nevertheless, Sandi's testimony and perspective are important to share as they illustrate the animosity and breakdown of trust between Shanann and the Watts family.

Chris told investigators in his prison confession that right before the wedding, he had a blow-out fight with his family and told them he didn't need them anymore. He even went as far as cussing out his mom. This was extremely out of character for him because he had always been obedient, and this probably fueled Cindy's negative feelings toward Shanann. Because this was so unlike Chris, Shanann was an easy target to blame. In retrospect, in his prison confession, Chris said he didn't remember if Shanann had "coached" him to confront his family or if it was just his own built-up rage that had been accumulating over the years. It seems like Chris always had a dark side. Although he hid it well, occasionally it would rear its ugly head when he had seldom outbursts of a rage that had been quietly building inside of him.

Chris's immediate family did not attend the wedding, seemingly as a result of this blow-out fight. Despite the absence of the Watts family, the wedding was memorable and wonderful for both Shanann and Chris. Shanann looked beautiful in a strapless princess-style gown with a sweetheart neckline and beaded embroidery. Her dark hair was pulled back, highlighting her cheekbones. The wedding colors were purple, to represent lupus awareness, and the men wore purple vests and ties.

Only Chris's grandmother and best friend, Mark, showed up from his close-knit circle. When it came time for the mother-son dance, as is traditionally done in weddings, Chris danced with his grandmother and Mark's mother. Anytime in the future when he looked at pictures of his wedding, he said he would always be reminded that his family wasn't there. It was a very happy day for Chris, but the nagging thought of his absent family always haunted him.

CHAPTER 10

"I couldn't have asked for a better man!"

After the wedding, Shanann and Chris decided to move to Frederick, a suburb just miles outside Denver, Colorado. Frederick is a beautifully picturesque Colorado suburb, boasting views of white-capped mountains, serene lakes, and clear blue skies. Shanann and Chris had visited friends there and decided it would be a nice place to move—for a change of scenery, to get away from family drama, and to start a family of their own. Chris and Shanann decided to build their dream house, a spacious five-bedroom, 4½-bathroom home on Saratoga Trail, a quiet street with beautiful views. They lived with a friend for a year while the house was being built.

Chris and Shanann both got jobs at the Longmont Ford Dealership in Longmont, Colorado, Chris as a mechanic and Shanann in sales. They met several of their good friends, including Jeremy Lindstrom, at the dealership. Chris would stay in touch with Jeremy, even after Chris left the dealership for several reasons, including carpal tunnel syndrome.

Chris and Shanann said they used fertility treatments to try to conceive their daughters. With Shanann's illnesses, getting pregnant was a challenge, and any pregnancy would put significant stress on her body and would be considered high risk.

Chris and Shanann were excited to become parents, documenting the pregnancy on social media and a blog that Shanann created called, "The Watts Journey." Shanann documented her pregnancy milestones on the blog for loved ones and, most important, for Bella to look back on when she got older.

Shanann posted sentimental things: photos of her growing bump, thoughtful baby gifts, and Bella's 3D/4D ultrasound. She posted pictures of Chris and her, including one that she captioned this way. "Today is 3 years your daddy and I have been together! I couldn't have asked for a better man!" Shanann also blogged, sharing a photo of the positive pregnancy test.

In the comments on the post, Chris wrote: "OMG, I was so happy when your mother told me she was pregnant! I felt extremely lucky! I can't wait to meet you in December!" When the first ultrasound was posted on the blog, Chris commented, "Was a very exciting moment for your mother and I. To be able to see you for the first time was an amazing feeling!"

The blog also seemed to depict happier times between the both sides of the family. There were photos of Shanann with

Jamie, Chris's sister, at the baby shower in North Carolina and of all the gifts with which both sets of grandparents were showering Bella. After a lot of heartache and pain in Shanann's life, things seemed to be finally working out for her.

Bella Marie Watts was born on December 17, 2013. From the beginning, everyone thought Bella took after her father in personality. She was always calm, thoughtful, sweet, nurturing, affectionate, and quiet. At the time of her death, she had a short, light brown, pixie-cut hair. Her angelic, deep brown eyes had a unique sense of sweetness and innocence to them.

Celeste Cathryn was conceived with fertility treatments not too long after Bella. Chris acted thrilled at the idea of another child. Shanann loved surprises and grand gestures, so she put an "eviction notice" on Bella's crib and secretly filmed Chris's reaction when he came home from work and saw the exciting news. Chris seemed elated in the video footage.

Both pregnancies were rough on Shanann, but carrying Celeste was more challenging. Not only would the pregnancy exacerbate her lupus, but having a little toddler at home while having a stressful pregnancy was no easy feat.

Celeste was born on July 17, 2015, and she was the opposite of Bella in personality. "CeCe," as they fondly nicknamed her, also had the nickname "rampage" because she was so over the top with energy. CeCe had an ear-to-ear grin that took over her entire face. She would often wear her white blond hair in two pigtails on top of her head, sticking up like little cascading fountains. Even though Bella and CeCe were so different in personality, they quickly became the best of friends. They adored each other and did everything together.

At the time, Shanann was working evenings at a call center in a children's hospital and sold different products on the side for extra income. Because Shanann had difficulties while pregnant, her parents moved in with them temporarily to help. Shanann and Chris were still working to pay bills and keep their house in North Carolina and were in Frederick for a total of fifteen months.

Chris found living in the very full house with Sandi and Frank's dogs, Dieter the dog, two babies, and four adults stressful, but he got along well with his in-laws and appreciated the help. According to Chris's prison confession, although Frank and Sandi lived in the basement, Sandi and Shanann clashed from time to time because of their dominant personalities. Chris said he felt he was walking on eggshells because he had to keep the girls upstairs in the morning so he wouldn't wake Sandi in the basement. When Sandi and Frank started working, they weren't in the house all the time, and that made life easier because everyone wasn't on top of each other. Sandi and Frank were devoted and loyal grandparents and a tremendous help to Shanann and Chris.

Shanann started working for Le-Vel in January of 2016 and decided to focus on that full time because it gave her more flexibility to be a stay-at-home parent and bring in income. Shanann sold Thrive, a weight-loss and lifestyle regimen consisting of capsules, shakes, and patches of vitamins, probiotics, and other natural substances for boosting health and energy. When she recruited more promoters to sell products, they worked underneath her in typical pyramid fashion.

Shanann was fully committed to Thrive and was doing well with it. She had earned a car allowance that went toward monthly payments for a Lexus, Lifestyle Getaway, trips to locations such as San Diego and Puerto Vallarta, and she didn't feel the need to work for anyone but herself. She felt she could focus on being a good mother to her girls and simultaneously bring in income. Chris had left his job as a mechanic and started working as a field operator at Anadarko Petroleum. Anadarko offered good health benefits, a decent salary, and the work didn't aggravate Chris's carpal tunnel issues.

Life was good for the Watts family but not without its stress. Beyond Shanann's health struggles, she had surgery on a compressed disc in her neck in 2017, and the girls struggled with their own health issues. CeCe was diagnosed with allergies, including a life-threatening nut allergy, asthma, and acid reflux. Both girls had tubes in their ears, their adenoids removed, and both took medications.

The cost of Shanann's surgery, the girls' medical procedures, medications, and private school tuition at the Primrose School put the couple in financial trouble. They filed for bankruptcy in 2015, reporting $448,000 in debt. Their credit cards were maxed out. At the time of Shanann's death, they would be three months behind in mortgage payments, and Shanann had taken $10,000 out of Chris's 401k plan to catch up on those payments.

The couple was stressed about money, but outsiders looking in wouldn't have been able to tell. Shanann was a big dreamer and loved nice things. She painted some of the walls in her home bright colors.

The level of meticulous organization was because of Shanann's self-professed OCD. She did everything well. Her house was immaculate, she was an excellent cook and baker, and she loved fashion. She would often coordinate her outfits with her daughters' and Chris's clothes. Pictures of an idyllic family life adorned her social media pages.

Chris and Shanann seemed, by all accounts, totally in love and devoted to one another. They were doting, affectionate, caring, and loving, in public and in private. Chris was close to perfect in terms of how attentive he was to his family, and Shanann would often say she couldn't have handpicked a better husband and father. On many occasions, she referred to Chris as the best thing to ever happen to her.

Chris was known in their social circles as an outstanding father. People observed him as being incredibly hands-on with Bella and CeCe. He did everything for his family and gushed about his daughters to everyone who knew him. Most people who knew Chris would easily say his girls were his life. In the mornings, Chris usually woke up first because he had to be at work very early. Often, he would leave Shanann's, Bella's, and CeCe's daily vitamins out on the counter with notes on them. One of the notes to Shanann said: "You are the best leader!! Love you beautiful!!" That day, Bella and CeCe had notes written on their vitamin packets as well: "Bella, Love You" and "Celeste, Love You."

Shanann was constantly praising Chris and sharing the story of how they met and fell in love. On his birthday, three months before he killed her, Shanann shared a birthday post for Chris on her Facebook page:

Today I celebrate you Chris. You are absolutely the BEST thing that ever happened to me in 2010! That year you were placed in my life when I was at my worst! I was just diagnosed with Lupus and Fibro, and I felt like my world was crumbling around me! Then I met you! We have so many incredible memories these past 8 years, two beautiful girls, moved halfway around the world, sold house, built our home for our family and all you constantly do for us! You work your ass off, you're an amazing husband and even better dad! You are the blessing I've been looking for my whole life! You are chasing big goals and dreams and never stop. You support me in so many ways! I hope you have an amazing birthday! I love you baby!

Many people roll their eyes at proclamations like these on social media. It is true that people who are overly saccharine are often embellishing or portraying an image they want others to believe rather than the reality. However, in Shanann's case, she seemed like she really believed she had won the lottery with her husband. There didn't seem to be any secret abuse behind closed doors. Shanann felt she genuinely had a happy, loving, and affectionate marriage. According to her text messages with friends, if there were any problems, Shanann would have considered them minor issues every couples goes through after being together for a long time.

Shanann, always looking to a big, bright future, created vision boards and had them for her daughters as well. She was envisioning 2018 as her best year yet. On New Year's Day of 2018, she posted a photo of her with Chris and the girls with the caption: "*To the future. Bigger. Better. Greater. 2018.*" Shanann had claimed 2018 was her year. She was on the right track to achieving all the goals she was setting for herself, and she was extremely excited about her future.

Chris had always wanted a son, and because he was always so hands-on and helpful, Shanann agreed to try for a third child. Chris probably imagined a relationship with his son that was like the relationship he had with his father. Shanann had even gushed on Facebook on Father's Day of 2018 to Chris, saying the following:

Chris, we are so incredibly blessed to have you! You do so much every day for us and take such good care of us. You are the reason I was brave enough to agree to number 3! From laundry to kids to showers! You are incredible and we are so lucky to have you in our life! Happy Father's Day!

Shanann was excited that everything she had ever dreamed of was finally falling into place. She had no way of knowing that her world would fall apart only a month after this post and that her husband would murder her in cold blood two months after this Father's Day post.

• • •

In early June, Shanann discovered she was pregnant with their third child. She wanted to surprise Chris with a creative pregnancy announcement and knew that the news would be a huge shock to him. Because they needed fertility drugs to conceive Bella and CeCe, the thought of getting pregnant naturally and right away was not something either of them had banked on.

Shanann set up her iPhone camera so it was directly filming Chris as he walked through the door as he came home from work that afternoon. She wore a shirt she had made just for the occasion that read, "Ooops We Did it Again."

Before Chris walked in the room, Shanann stepped in front of the camera with a teasing grin on her face and flashed the message on the shirt before going back to hide behind the camera. Dieter was barking excitedly when Chris got home. Chris, dressed casually, wearing a long-sleeved gray shirt, jeans, and tinted sunglasses, stopped dead in his tracks with his arms frozen out at his sides as he spotted Shanann, read the words on her shirt, and chuckled.

"Oops, we did it again," he said in his soft-spoken Southern drawl, a grin breaking out on his face. He laughed as he walked toward her. "I like that shirt," he said, still smiling. Then, after a moment of silence, "Really?"

"Really," Shanann answered.

"That's awesome," Chris said. "So pink means…?" he trailed off in a teasing tone.

"That's just the test," Shanann said from behind the camera.

"I know…just the pink is gonna be girls?" Chris said with

a goofy smile.

"I don't know. That's just the test," Shanann said.

"That's awesome," Chris said again as he leaned in to kiss her. Then he looked directly in the camera and flashed a smile. "I guess when you want to, it happens."

He pulled the pregnancy test away from him and examined it, shaking his head in disbelief.

"Wow," he whispered loudly.

This pregnancy video was just one of many examples of Chris's phony acting. Unbeknownst to Shanann, more than another child on the way was brewing for Chris that June. Around the first of the month, he started chatting with Nikki Kessinger.

She had been talking to Chris at work and had found him very attractive. The attraction was mutual. Chris hadn't been wearing a wedding ring because of his rapid weight loss. His ring kept falling off, so he was getting it resized.

According to Chris, during one of their first conversations, he said something along the lines of, "We moved to Colorado from North Carolina."

Nikki responded with, "What's all this 'we' stuff?"

Chris told her about his wife and daughters. He also had pictures of them as the wallpaper of his phone that Nikki saw.

On June 12, one day after Shanann's pregnancy announcement on Facebook, Chris received an email from Nikki. In the email, she thanked Chris for being so honest with her and told him that truthfulness was underrated.

Chris responded with a brazenly forward email. He told Nikki he was just a straightforward guy who didn't like lying. He also mentioned that he thought she was stunning and amazing. He said he wanted to get to know her better.

Nikki responded again, saying she enjoyed talking to him and felt she could relate to him. She told Chris she was looking to build a beautiful life with someone, similar to what he had done with Shanann and the girls. Mentioning her belief in karma, Nikki said she wanted to keep their friendship at work.

Chris responded with the final email in the chain. He said he thought that people always have an agenda for everything, and that a beautiful life was hard to find because of it. He said he also believed in karma but gave Nikki his work number in case she ever needed to get in touch with him in the field. He signed off with hopes that she would have an amazing day.

CHAPTER 11

"My daddy is a hero."

After the email exchange between Chris and Nikki, Shanann was oblivious and ignorantly blissful, starting to think about life with a third child. On June 14, only a few days before Father's Day, she happily captured a video of Bella singing in her car seat. "My daddy is a hero. He helps me grow up strong. He reads me books; he ties my shoes. You're a hero through and through. My daddy, daddy, I love you."

Shanann's voice in the background squealed with emotion. "Awww, I love it!"

Chris and Shanann were very busy the rest of the month of June. They planned to leave for a Lifestyle Getaway in San Diego with Le-Vel at the end of the month, and her father Frank traveled from North Carolina to stay with the girls, so Chris and Shanann could enjoy some relaxed time together. However, Chris wasn't looking forward to the trip because he already had made up his mind about starting a relationship with Nikki. Upon their return to Colorado, Shanann was set to fly with the girls to North Carolina for six weeks to spend the summer with their families. Because Chris had to work, he would join them only for the last week of the trip in early August.

Shanann was preoccupied with Le-Vel and her Thrive business and getting ready for her trips. She was packing and meal prepping for Chris, jokingly calling him a "bachelor" who would be on his own for five weeks, not realizing how literally he would take that role.

Shanann went to an ultrasound to check on the baby without Chris on June 19. He was out working in the field that day. There was a tornado in the area, he had to take cover, and couldn't make the appointment on time. Shanann took Bella, who had joked that there were five babies in her mama's belly.

When Shanann texted a photo of the ultrasound to Chris, he replied, *"No 5 babies?"* and then added, *"Little peanut!! Love her/him already!!"*

Still blissfully unaware of her husband's intentions to stray, Shanann proudly boasted the text exchange on Facebook with a screenshot of the exchange, saying, *"I love Chris! He's the best dad us girls could ask for."*

A few days later, on June 22, Shanann and Chris flew to San Diego for the Thrive Lifestyle Getaway. Shanann's best friends, Nicki Atkinson, Cassie, Addy, and Cristina were all there, including Cassie's and Addy's husbands. Cassie's husband, Josh, got along well with Chris, and the two men texted and kept in touch every now and then. The Thrive getaways were something the group looked forward to because the women didn't live in the same state. Addy was in Maryland, Cristina in Hawaii, and Cassie and Josh would soon be moving to Colorado near Nicki and Shanann.

Everyone had a great time in San Diego and spent most of the time lounging by the pool, walking on the beach, taking a cruise on a boat, and attending social gatherings where they connected with Le-Vel people from all over the country. Josh took beautiful, candid photos of Shanann and Chris strolling on the beach. Although the sky was overcast, Chris and Shanann looked happy and in love, embracing each other, holding hands, and smiling.

Chris had someone else on his mind, though. During this trip, he and Nikki texted back and forth the entire time. Aware that Chris was in San Diego, Nikki suggested they meet up for the first time outside work when he returned to Colorado (according to Chris). Shanann and Chris flew back to Colorado on June 26. Twelve hours later, Shanann flew to North Carolina with Bella and CeCe.

To Shanann, everything seemed great between Chris and her. She had told several friends that they had been "all over each other" in the weeks leading up to her departure to North Carolina. She had even shared that Chris couldn't keep his hands off her, and they would have sex in the kitchen pantry when the girls were watching television in the next room.

As early as June 27, however, Chris and Nikki exchanged flirtatious text messages. The first one recovered was from

Chris to Nikki.

"*Promise! I'm about loyalty, truthfulness, and being dedicated. I don't like playing games...unless its role playing (wink face emoji). If you want me there, I will be there! Ice cream, cookies, and lollipops. Sounds like a cheat meal night lol.*"

Immediately after Shanann and the girls left for North Carolina, Nikki and Chris met at a park in Thornton, Colorado. The affair ramped up very quickly from that point on. Some deleted text messages have not been recovered, so many of the text messages may seem out of context or confusing. What is clear is the haste with which Chris accelerated his relationship with Nikki once his pregnant wife left town.

On the evening of June 29, Chris texted Nikki, "*I'm still going to see you! It won't be as often as we like but I will make it happen! You think you're the only one addicted right now? I'm so hooked on you.*" Shortly after that, he texted again. "*Sleeping without your warm body next to me isn't going to be fun tonight.*"

On June 30, Nikki texted Chris. "*I have an idea btw. I have a free hotel stay at a Holiday Inn. Not sure if you can swing it this month but we can road trip to the mountains or southern Colorado for a day or two if you want. Won't cost a dime lol.*" She also texted, "*She supports me...but her parents were in a situation like that when she was a kid, and it came up. It won't bother me. I'm not going to stop seeing you. I made up my mind. Are we bad people?*"

On July 1, Chris sent Nikki a text, saying, "*I'd love to be a part of it. Being in your life is something that I crave. Conserve it while you can. I enjoyed our conversation tonight. I hope you have a great night. Sweet dreams. Nikki (kiss face emoji)."*

Soon after, Chris and Nikki started spending four to five nights a week together. Chris was barely at home, and it is unclear how much attention Dieter the dog was getting.

July 3 was Nikki's birthday. Chris got her a birthday card, one that made it seem as if they had been dating in an exclusive relationship for years.

The card read, "A year of stuff you love to do and brand-new dreams to make come true. One that brings you smiles and laughter and fills your heart with love long after. A million moments day by day, that simply take your breath away. Have a birthday as wonderful as you are." Chris wrote his own message after, saying, *"This sums up you! Big things will happen this year, dreams will come true. That smile (that stare), that laugh (that giggle) gets me every time!! You are a truly amazing, inspirational and electric woman that takes my breath away every time I see you! You are wonderful!! Don't EVER stop being you!!!!! HAPPY BIRTHDAY!!! Chris."*

He also added a quote from the song "Take You There" by Through the Roots: *"Your energy is so insane. You heat me up, you make me melt and then you cool me down like rain."*

• • •

The next day, on the Fourth of July, Chris was off work and had spent the night at Nikki's. He woke up that morning to a livid Shanann, who was just starting to pick up on Chris's emotional distance and lack of receptivity toward the girls and her. The first week Shanann was in North Carolina, she and Chris were chatting on the phone and having frequent phone sex, but now something was starting to feel off to her. That morning, she had been trying to reach Chris on the phone and didn't know where he was, which was unusual because he was an early riser and would have been awake early. She called multiple times in a row, getting angrier with each call that he didn't pick up. When Chris saw the missed calls, he went outside to call her back, and she started yelling at him, asking him where he was and telling him the kids wanted to talk to him.

Chris went back inside to the house and told Nikki he had to go.

"Are you coming back?" she demanded. In his prison confession, Chris said she was angry and realized she would always be "second fiddle" to Shanann. Nikki told investigators she recalled telling Chris she needed to take a step back.

"Just because I have to leave doesn't mean you have to take a step back," Chris supposedly said to calm her down. He was already feeling stressed after Shanann's call, and now he had someone else angry with him.

"I don't think we should see each other the rest of the day," Nikki said.

While in prison, Chris was writing to a woman named Cheryln Cadle, who has since published *Letters from*

Christopher,[6] which details her correspondence with Chris in letters and in person. In his account to Cadle, he says later that day, Nikki came over and went over a "protein eating plan" for him.

In North Carolina, Shanann was struggling with the pregnancy, the humidity of Southern summers, and trying to parent active toddlers. It had poured rain that evening, and Shanann and her family were unable to see the fireworks.

In the evening in Colorado, Chris had plans to meet up with good friends Nick and Amanda Thayer and their daughter. They all went to a firework show at the Thornton Recreation Center.

As they sat together on a blanket, Nick recalled making small talk with Chris.

"What's it like to be a bachelor?" Nick jokingly asked.

"It's weird being in an empty house. I'm working out all the time," he replied. "Shanann got upset with me today because I missed her calls. If I don't answer the phone because I'm in the shower or working out, she gets upset. If I'm having any fun without her, I have to hide it."

Amanda, Shanann's friend, overheard the comments and picked up that Chris was feeling a little annoyed. While out with the Thayers, Chris was texting Nikki.

"I'm getting drenched right now lol. Like to see you all wet in the rain."

The text messages mostly involved what Chris was eating.

---

6. Cadle, Cheryln. *Letters from Christopher: The Tragic Confessions of the Watts Family Murders.* Pittsburgh, PA: Dorrance Publishing, 2019.

He told Nikki he "crushed tacos," avoided eating funnel cake and tater twists, and had a protein shake before he left the house.

After he said goodbye to the Thayers, he headed back to Nikki's apartment, resuming his new double life. At eleven o'clock that evening, he texted her, "*Just pulled up to your place.*"

CHAPTER 12

"How does it feel when someone says, I love you?"

The next few days would leave Shanann frustrated and confused by Chris's continued aloof behavior.

On July 8, at 5:15 am, Chris texted Shanann to cover his tracks for being so distant. "I'm sorry Boo. I fell asleep as soon as I got home. The heat killed me yesterday. I love you so much!!!" Sadly, he was duping his wife here, using scripted and disingenuous sentences to keep Shanann off his back.

On July 9, Shanann took the girls to visit with Chris's parents, Ronnie and Cindy, his sister Jamie, her husband, and their two children. Shanann was hoping the trip to North Carolina would be a bonding experience for the girls and both sides of the family. Despite all the tension that had transpired, Shanann had said to friends that she was always willing to try to put the past behind her and have a good relationship with her in-laws, especially for the sake of Chris and the kids.

After lunch at Cindy's and Ronnie's house, the incident

known as "nutgate" happened.

CeCe was so allergic to tree nuts and cashews that during her allergy testing, she vomited multiple times and broke out into hives after the smallest amounts were given to her. The little girl had apparently been diagnosed with an anaphylaxis reaction to the nuts, which is life threatening. Children who experience anaphylaxis reactions must always have Epipens because they could potentially die from ingesting whatever they are highly allergic to.

In Chris' account in his prison confession, Cindy did not take the allergies seriously. She always thought Shanann was overreacting, controlling, and overbearing.

According to the police discovery, Cindy's other grand-children were eating ice cream that either contained nuts or were processed in a factory with nuts, and CeCe wasn't allowed to have any. Shanann had told people that Cindy had said the girls "have to learn that they can't always have what they want." Shanann disagreed, saying that they were two and four and shouldn't be taunted with ice cream when they couldn't have any. Shanann's friend also relayed in the police discovery that Shanann said Jamie had put a bowl of pistachios within arms-length of CeCe. However, this is hearsay, and it is unclear as to what happened or what was said in those moments.

Shanann had enough and flipped out. She called Frank, her father, and asked him to come pick them up immediately. She said she didn't want her children unsupervised around Cindy and Ronnie, and she felt she could never trust them again. As much as she felt that she had tried to make amends over the years, this was putting her children's lives at risk, and she couldn't excuse it anymore.

After they left Cindy's and Ronnie's house, Shanann was still furious. She vented to people in an allergy Facebook support group in hopes that people who could truly understand what her experience was like could validate her. She felt that Cindy didn't take her seriously and would call her crazy and say she was overreacting.

Shanann called Chris several times to explain to him what happened and to convey how angry she was.

She also texted him late in the afternoon: *"You should call your dad and tell him you did not appreciate your mom putting your daughter at risk today, nor do you like that she teased our girls. You should also say you don't appreciate her saying they have to learn they can't always get what they want! They are 2 and 4!"*

Chris responded as she had hoped. *"I will call him and tell him what I think about this. It's not fucking cool at all because it is the kids. I will set this right."*

Chris called his parents as he said he would, but he also told them not to worry because he was done with Shanann and would be leaving her. He told them he had finally "seen the light."

The next morning, Shanann texted Chris again.

"You ok? It's like you don't want to talk I kept trying to talk and I had to dig it out of you?"

"I'm fine baby. The last few days at work have put a lot of responsibility on me with new people. I didn't mean to seem short

Boo. I love you to the moon and back!" Chris replied disingenuously, yet again.

Even though his words were loving, Shanann still didn't feel reassured. She knew something was wrong.

"*I miss you and I feel like you just want to work out and run,*" Shanann said, looking for attention she felt he was withholding.

"*Running helps clear my head. It's a way to free it all.*"

"*I wish my husband wanted to talk to me,*" Shanann texted back.

Shanann wasn't aware that Chris had been texting Nikki that day, also calling her "Boo," the nickname he always used with Shanann.

On July 14, Nikki and Chris went to the Shelby American Collection, a museum showcasing Mustang cars in Boulder, Colorado. While they were there, Shanann made four unanswered calls to Chris. After the fifth missed call, he called her back briefly.

Nikki visited Chris's house that day, supposedly the second and last time she would ever be there. She recalled in her police interview that she felt uncomfortable there as she looked at pictures of Shanann and the girls framed all over the house. Chris had asked her to come over to help him set up an app for managing his calories, and she had agreed, happy to share her knowledge with him. She was a fitness junkie and enjoyed helping as his interest grew in a lifestyle she was passionate about.

In his letters to Cadle, Chris said that Nikki had been

playing with Dieter and went upstairs, where she saw pictures of his family. She came downstairs with a shocked look on her face and asked him why he would want to leave everything he had built with his wife. Chris confessed that before he and Nikki started their relationship, he and Shanann were actively trying for another baby. Nikki lost her cool and told him that his relationship with Shanann must not have been that bad if they were trying to conceive again. She stormed out of the house and sat in her truck, texting Chris for thirty minutes. Chris said he somehow managed to calm her down. Even though Chris seemed to think his relationship with Nikki was great, it's clear that there was some drama present from the very beginning.

During the rest of the afternoon, even when Nikki was not with him, Chris ignored all Shanann's calls. He spent forty-five minutes on the phone with Nikki, and during that phone call, Shanann called him four more times. After he got off the phone with Nikki, he called Shanann back briefly and then spent the next two hours researching gems and minerals on his phone for Nikki.

Later that evening, Chris said Nikki acted as if nothing had happened. In Cadle's book, Chris said Nikki told him, "I got mad because I thought I could give you a son, and when you told me you and your wife were trying, that made me upset." Apparently, Nikki was also upset because she didn't have any "firsts" with Chris, clearly feeling threatened by his relationship with his wife. She was actively competing for him now and didn't seem like she was planning on backing off. Chris mentioned in his correspondence with Cadle that this was when the idea to murder his family started.

On July 17, CeCe celebrated her third birthday in North Carolina. Her birthday party was scheduled a few days afterward. Ronnie and Cindy Watts did not show up to the birthday party or call to say they wouldn't be attending. Shanann was upset that they would not show up for the birthday of their grandchild, regardless of what had happened. They also unfriended Shanann on Facebook, which she seemed to feel was another way of communicating their disapproval.

Around this time, Chris had started using the Secret Calculator, an app designed to look like a calculator that would discreetly store photos and videos. The photos would not be easily found by someone potentially snooping through his phone. This app is where he would store nude and semi-nude photos of Nikki.

On July 21, he and Nikki headed to the Bandimere Speedway, a racetrack in Colorado. Nikki was showing interest in all the activities Chris loved, and he was enticed by that. Before, he played a role where he went along with whatever he believed Shanann wanted. Now, he thought he had someone who was actively showing an interest in the things he cared about. Before he left, he texted Shanann, *"Headed out to the track Boo. I will text you when I get there."*

Shanann was noticing that Chris was putting up more walls with her, despite his texts making it seem as if everything was fine. In addition to internet searching for minerals and gems, Chris was also researching places to take Nikki on dates. He searched items like, "Spanish dancing near me," "red wine made in Argentina," "The Cheesecake Factory" and "clean eating restaurants near me." Nikki was into a healthy lifestyle and clean eating. Presumably, she had told Chris some of her interests or new things she would like to try, and he was thinking of ways to make this happen.

Toward the end of the month, around July 24, Chris started telling Nikki he was going to leave Shanann. Nikki, hopeful about this prospect, searched *"man I'm having an affair with says he will leave his wife."*

That same day, a frustrated Shanann, unable to get hold of her husband yet again, texted Chris, *"Are you alive??"*

"Tire light came on when I was leaving King Soopers last night. Got the tires aired back up. Spent a lot of time looking for anything in it. Nothing at all," Chris replied.

Immediately after his reply to Shanann, he searched the internet for "Victoria (sic) Secret" at the Orchard Town Center, clearly for Nikki and not his wife.

Twenty minutes later, Shanann decided to call Chris out on his distant behavior via text: *"I realized during this trip what's missing in our relationship! It's only one-way emotions and feelings. I can't come back like this. I need you to meet me halfway. You don't consider others at all, nor think about other's feelings."* Shanann was starting to pick up on the lack of empathy Chris was displaying. She was spot on. Chris cared only about his needs.

"I'm sorry. I love you," Chris replied, continuing to tell

Shanann what he believed she wanted to hear, but this tactic wouldn't work this time. Shanann was too perceptive and understood his actions did not match his words.

"I try to give you space, but while you are working and living the bachelor life, I'm carrying our 3rd and fighting with our two kids daily and trying to work and make money. It's not hard texting love you and miss you. If you don't mean it then I get it, but we need to talk. I kept looking at my phone all night and no response from you. Like seriously! We didn't just start dating yesterday! We've been together 8 years and have 2.5 kids together."

Shanann was horrified that Chris had no sympathy for her and showed little interest in trying to connect with her. What she was picking up on was correct because Chris really could not care less about Shanann, the girls, or anything about his life before Nikki at this point.

The next day, Chris conducted more internet searches, inquiring about things such as: *"When to say I love you," "When to say I love you for the first time in a new relationship," "What do you feel when someone tells you they love you?" "How does it feel when someone says I love you?"*

These are odd questions to ask at thirty-three years-old when you supposedly married the love of your life and constantly leave her notes about how much you love her. One would assume that Chris already knew what love felt like. These internet searches would give an alarming amount of insight into how emotionally void Chris Watts really was and is. Furthermore, it was a chilling look at what a fantastic actor he could be.

Later that afternoon, while Chris was speaking to Shanann on the phone, Nikki left him a voicemail.

"1 miss your face. I was just calling to say hi. Call me back, bye," she said, with a giggle that a police transcriber described as "eerily disconcerting."

On July 28, shortly before Chris was to leave for North Carolina to join his family, he and Nikki had their first overnight getaway at the Great Sand Dunes National Park in Colorado. They set up a tent in the Zapata National Falls campground and went hiking and surfing the sand dunes together. Chris took many photos and videos of the two of them on the trip, including a video of their tent with the song, "Forever Girl" playing in the background: *You're everything in my whole world, that's my forever girl, oh yeah, that's my forever girl."* In another video, Nikki is in the shot speaking directly to the camera:

"Thank you so much for coming out here with me Christopher, I am having a wonderful time. You mean a lot to me, and I'm glad you're having a blast." She then blew a kiss to the camera.

The next day, they left the Dunes. Chris texted Shanann around 11 o'clock in the morning. *"Finished the hike! Packing up and heading home!"*

Shortly before 6 o'clock that night, Shanann sent a text to Chris. *"I'm assuming you're safe considering it's been 3.5 hours."*

"There was a car fire and the Renaissance Festival traffic in Colorado Springs. Just got our car. Headed home," Chris replied.

At 7:30 pm, Shanann called Chris, and he talked to her for

fifteen minutes. Right after they got off the phone, an agitated Shannan texted him: ""*Sorry you're so tired, but I haven't talked to you in 48 hours and I had a hard weekend. Glad I have you to talk to! If you care...*"

"*I'm sorry you had a hard weekend Boo. I will make it up to you I promise. I'm sorry I'm out of it tonight,*" Chris replied, being duplicitous as ever.

"*It would have been nice for my husband to show interest in how the girls and I are, and the baby. I'm done with begging for you to talk. See you Tuesday,*" she responded testily.

Over the next twenty-four hours, Chris searched the lyrics to love songs, such as, "Down to Earth" by Through the Roots: "*When I'm around you, I can feel peace in the atmosphere.....but when I'm lost yea, you capture me and bring me right back down. If I'm ever cold, I can count on you to heat me up with your presence, and when you send your love to conquer me, I don't fight it, I just let it.*"

He also searched the lyrics to the song "Love You Like That" by Canaan Smith: "*I wanna love, wanna love, wanna love you like that.*"

Throughout the day, he exchanged logistical text messages with Shanann about their alarm company, Vivint. Bella potentially dislocated her ankle, and they traded a few texts about that. In the evening he texted Shanann: "*Letting Dieter out and going to bed Boo. Love you.*"

Chris also made good use of the song lyrics he searched for. Before he left to meet his family in North Carolina, he wrote Nikki another handwritten card: *Nikki, Wow, where do I even start? The first day I saw you, you took my breath away. The first day I had the guts to talk to you, I got lost in those stunning green eyes. The first day we hung out in the park together, I knew I was addicted. The first time we kissed, I knew I had met the most amazing, unique and electric woman EVER!!! We have a lot of firsts together, Nikki. And I want to keep having them with you!! "All night til the sun comes back, I wanna love, I wanna love, wanna love you like that." Love, Chris.*

CHAPTER 13

"I don't want to lose anyone."

On July 31, Chris flew to North Carolina to be with Shanann, the girls, and both his and Shanann's families. Before he boarded the flight, he made sure to hide any evidence of his affair with Nikki, transferring all the photos and videos from their Sand Dunes excursion to his secret calculator. One of the videos was of Nikki surfing down a sand dune with short shorts and a scarf covering her face. Chris commented out loud in the video, "So damn sexy."

He boarded the flight and sent a quick text to Shanann: *"On the plane. Love you Boo."*

Shanann placed a quick call to Chris. She was angry because he had driven the car to the airport and parked in an expensive lot.

"You never ever listen to me. How much a day?" Shanann texted him, exasperated.

Chris texted her pictures of the parking signs and told her the number of the lot.

"$130 we can't spend at the beach. Text me when you land in Atlanta."

When Chris landed in Raleigh, North Carolina, he texted Shanann that he landed.

"Let me know when you're coming down escalator so I can record girls," she replied.

"Ok Boo," Chris responded.

As promised, Chris alerted Shanann, so she could film a happy reunion between him and his girls. The girls, cute as ever, started running toward Chris, squealing, "Daddy!" An alarm started to sound obnoxiously in the background. When Chris and the girls made their way over to Shanann, who was still filming, Chris kneeled beside his daughters.

"Now, I can hug you. Come here. Come here, little girls!" he said in a gentle voice as he embraced both simultaneously.

Later that evening, before she went to bed, Shanann sent Chris a message from another room, presumably because Chris was keeping his distance and didn't want to stay with his wife:

"Can you set alarm for 5 am and wake me please?" she requested.

"Yup. I got it. Love you," Chris said, continuing to use his automatic, rehearsed statements that meant nothing to him.

"Love you too," Shanann sent back.

Chris' ruse would not last long after this.

In an interview with law enforcement, Shanann's brother, Frankie Jr., mentioned he thought it was very odd that Shanann got very sick the evening Chris arrived in North

Carolina. She spent the entire evening vomiting and complaining of a bad headache. Frankie spent all night checking on his sister and thought it was bizarre that Chris couldn't care less that Shanann was sick. He told investigators, "She slept on the couch, which I thought was odd… and that he never came out to see her, because he used to be so nurturing, and I was almost like, dude you're a little much. I mean he went from being the best guy I could have pictured for my sister to could care less what happened to them. I hugged him a week ago… he helped me with my brakes with my truck. He's a very smart mechanic, he used to give me advice with things. It's just so mind-blowing."

In Chris's deleted internet search history, he had typed, "80mg of oxycodon (sic) will…" After speculation online about whether Chris gave Shanann oxycodone to try to make her miscarry, he confessed that accusation was true. In his letters to Cadle, he has given conflicting stories about the oxycodone. At first, he told Cadle he gave the oxycodone twice—once in North Carolina, to try to cause a miscarriage because he thought it would be easier for him to leave her for Nikki if she were not pregnant, and immediately before her death. He later changed the story and said he gave it to her only once in North Carolina to try to get Shanann to miscarry.

In any case, Shanann became sick with unusual symptoms at fifteen weeks pregnant and immediately after Chris arrived in North Carolina. In texts with a friend, she shared, "The last week I have not been able to pee normal. (Hard to pee). Feeling great otherwise. 10pm-Last night Chris rubbed my back for the first time in over a month. When he was done I sat up and I was lightheaded, body felt kinda numb/tingly, itching all over and just weird. – (11pm ish) about 1 hour later I stood to pee and vomited (mildly) about 30 minutes later massive instant migraine came out of nowhere. Took Imitrex around 2:30am. Usually gets rid of migraine within 20 mins. It's still just as bad right now. Maybe 1.5 sleep last night and I just vomited again 5:30am. Still lightheaded, shaky, blurry vision and exhausted. Went out to eat last night for dinner. Could this be vaginal infection, migraine, virus, food poisoning, or morning sickness starting at 15 weeks?"

It's very likely Chris is telling the truth here, at least the part where he secretly slipped her oxycodone in North Carolina. It may have been after this failed attempt of getting rid of the baby that he started to seriously plot the murders.

• • •

Chris and Shanann took Bella and CeCe to Pavilion Park in Myrtle Beach, and the girls had fun on carnival rides and bouncing on the trampolines. Chris was easily agitated, snapping at them and losing his patience, which was extremely out of character for him. He was annoyed with his daughters in a way that he had never been before.

While he was in North Carolina, Shanann told him that he was welcome to see his family, but she and the girls would not see them after "nutgate" and the snubbing of CeCe's birthday party. Chris continued to hide nude photos of Nikki in the secret calculator.

On August 4, while Nikki spent two hours searching for wedding dresses on the internet, Shanann finally confronted Chris over text in a lengthy message:

"Truth came out last night. I didn't create no dagger between you and your dad. That was done by your mom and your dad and I won't change a thing. My daughter's life is way more important and you better believe I wanted to say a whole lot more than I did, but I was being the bigger person. I didn't tell your dad not to come to party. I didn't tell him not to text, or call your grand-daughter, on her birthday. I didn't tell him to start acting like he only has 2 grandkids instead of 4. I didn't block your family on Facebook, he did. Myself and your kids have nothing to say to them. They do. They owe your kids their life. Your parent's home isn't a safe zone. Your mom isn't safe! You can let them tell you what you want, but I didn't tell anyone to stop loving your kids or stop acting like it. He did that, not me. You can believe I cre-ated this dagger, but I didn't do that. I stood up for our kids, I advocated and protected our children. I don't ever want to hear I'm sorry I killed your kid because I was stupid.' That would kill me... These kids are my world and I have to protect them from the evil of the world. I shouldn't have to protect them from evil family. Our kids deserve the same love and attention the other kids get, nothing less. I'm not accepting I'm sorry from your mom, because she doesn't mean it and she knew what she was doing. I made it very clear not to eat it around Celeste, because she doesn't

MY DADDY IS A HERO

understand, way before that happened. She's evil and willing to risk your daughter's life just to get under my skin. You and your dad are no different if you are ok with her behavior. There's nothing wrong with me and I'm not crazy. I just love my kids way too much. From the day I left you never said I missed you before I said it. Something changed when I left. You may be happier alone and that's fine. You can be alone! This pregnancy, you have failed to acknowledge it, or to acknowledge how I'm feeling. The first trimester is the scariest and most dangerous, yet we can lose this baby at any point till delivery. I'm not going to be treated this way for having the balls to protect our family and kids. I should get a gold fucking medal for handling it the way I did, because I had a lot of choice words I wanted to say to her and your dad for his stupidity. No one stands up to your mom and your dad for that. He's just as guilty by not doing anything. I have nothing to do with him stopping sharing memories of his grandkids. What does that have to do with me? They are fucking with our kids' feelings and that I'm not ok with."

In a small twist of foreshadowing, Shanann continued: *"I am their mother and I will protect them. I have enough to worry about with the world out there, I'm not going to worry about family. I will just remove it. I also don't control what you do. If you want to go hang out with your parents today, by all means do so, but without us. Don't put it on me why you can't go. You are your own person."*

In his most lengthy response to Shanann in a long time, Chris finally responded: *"These kids mean the world to me and always will. Yes, my mom truly screwed up in a huge way, more* than a huge way. I don't know what I would've done if something happened to CeCe. These kiddos are the light of my life and seeing their sweet, incredible smiles and playfulness makes me smile every day. I'm sorry for the way I've been acting, I've just been in my head and I haven't been right at all."

There are several psychopathic traits highlighted in this text. He is clearly lying about everything. He would not have cared if something happened to CeCe. In fact, thoughts of killing his entire family had entered his mind at this point. Even his words sound completely phony and syrupy sweet, as if he were reciting from a Hallmark card.

"Yes, that I created this dagger between you and your dad and that wasn't me. That was them. I protected our daughter from their stupidity. They created that and you belong with them thinking otherwise. I didn't tell your dad to remove himself from the kid's life... I did and do not deserve to be treated the way you have. I defended our daughter," Shanann fired back.

"Yes, you protected our daughter and I thank you for that a million times a million. I don't think they are innocent in any of this. They do want to be in the kids' life and I'm not sure they even know how to right now. They should've swallowed whatever they needed to and came to CeCe's birthday party and called her and shouldn't have blocked all social media contact with them. I don't care what they do with us, just as long as they love and respect the kids. I'm not used to not having a relationship with my dad. I should've just called him before it got to this point where it got in my head- I didn't and that's my fault" Chris responded in his typical conflict averse fashion. He was used to talking people down from the ledge and he was good at it. He automatically reverted to his default way of operating.

"Why should you beg them to be in their life? They pick up the phone and apologize for starters. They show up to her birthday, especially since we were an hour away. They did this. They make the effort. You blame me for this so-called dagger between you and him. Fuck that. You are just like them. Believe what he tells you and move back home where you weren't appreciated when I met you. No one ever protected you from your mom and someone should have before me. I'm done being the bad guy in all this. Especially when I had more balls to stand up for you a long time ago with them. My bad for thinking you deserved better. Now my kids are in the pic and I'm done."

Shanann continued: *"While it's on my mind: if I'm in the wrong that's one thing, but I'm not here, and you not standing up for us and the girls is not cool. You just make it, so they feel they did no wrong and brush it under the rug. I will never trust your parents alone with our kids. EVER! This is the week we started dating 8 years ago. They ruin everything special. I won't forgive you, or them, for that. I'm tired of it. I'm the one that takes care of you, not them. You are making me feel like complete shit these last several weeks, especially this week and I'm not ok with it and I won't change my ways when it comes to our kids. And I always defended you. Always."*

Three minutes later, Shanann added to her text messages: *"I'm not asking you to choose who to be with I shouldn't have to ask you to choose right from wrong. You are not happy, then you know where to go... Worst summer ever."*

Meanwhile, back in Colorado, Nikki was searching Facebook for Chris's and Shanann's profiles.

• • •

On August 5, Shanann and Chris communicated via text messaging about Chris visiting his family for the remainder of his time in North Carolina. Chris wanted the girls to see his grandmother (Maw Maw).

"*Are you wanting to go to see just Maw Maw tomorrow? or family too?*" Shanann asked.

"*I was hoping both. If not, that's ok too. I wanted to see Maw Maw in the morning, if possible. You wanted the girls to see her too, right?*" Chris replied.

"*If both then that's fine, but alone. If just Maw Maw we will go... They saw her twice and they can go again but I'm standing strong with your family. You can use the truck and see both. But I just need to know... I'm not going to be the reason you don't see them. So, if you do, you just go,*" Shanann responded.

"*I know they would love to see Maw Maw one more time,*" Chris wrote. "*I bet Maw Maw would love to see them too since she remembers them. I don't want to leave anyone without a car here though either. Should I have someone pick me up at nursing home so the girls can still see Maw Maw?*"

"*I'm not going to be where there's a chance we will run into your family. I'm not kidding, Christopher. I'm having a bad experience these last few days with my pregnancy and I'm spotting. I'm not dealing with it well... Have your parents pick you up when kids go down tonight then and do what you need to..."*

"I want kids to see Maw Maw. I will make sure there is zero chance anyone will see them," Chris reassured Shanann.

Later, that evening, Shanann sent a screenshot quote to his phone.

"Husbands: stand up for your wife and protect her from the attacks that come from the people close to you. Let your family and friends know that when it comes to your wife and marriage, there is a line they cannot cross. If you have to take sides, then always take your wife's side. From the day you said 'I do' your wife displaces your parents, friends and siblings. Apart from God, your wife now occupies and assumes the privileged first place of honor in your life. Oftentimes it requires that you lovingly stand up for your wife in front of your parents, especially your mother. Therefore, what God has joined together, let no (mother, father, brother, sister, friend or boss) separate." - Isaac Kubvoruno

Shortly after sending this quote, Shanann confronted Chris over a series of vulnerable text messages about his odd behavior. She seemed desperate to figure out what was wrong. She wanted to fix it. She wanted the old Chris back and the marriage she treasured so much.

"I don't know how you fell out of love with me in 5.5 weeks, or if this has been going on for a long time, but you don't plan another baby if you're not in love. Kids don't deserve a broken family... I left you, you couldn't take your hands off me. You show up and I have to practically ask for a kiss in airport....

"Being away from you, it's not the help I missed because I handle that. It was exhausting, but with school that's not hard. I

missed the smell of you, you touching me when I'm cooking, you touching me in bed, you touching me period! I missed holding you and snuggling with you. I missed eating with you, watching TV with you. I missed staring at you, I missed making love with you. I missed everything about you. I couldn't wait to touch you, hold you, kiss you, make love to you, smell you, laugh with you. I couldn't wait to celebrate 8 years with you... If you are done, don't love me, don't want to work this out, not happy anymore and only staying because of kids, I NEED you to tell me.

Would you stay with me if we didn't have kids?

I just don't get it. You don't fall out of love in 5 weeks. How can you sleep? Our marriage is crumbling in front of us and you can sleep."

• • •

The morning of August 6, while Chris was staying with his family, he searched the internet for the distance from the moon to the earth. (He seemed fond of the phrase, "Love you to the moon and back"). The phrase is a cliché, and because Chris had become very good at mimicking phrases and words that sounded good, he had probably used that phrase as a robotic response to his wife and daughters. He knew that's what he was *supposed* to say, but it held no weight for him. Perhaps he confused the lustful feelings he had for Nikki with love. For the first time in his life, something was stirring in Chris, but completely unaware of his own emotions, he needed an online website to figure them out.

I wonder if these new emotions for Nikki were piquing his curiosity to find out how much love existed between the moon and earth.

Shanann continued to text Chris after a brief conversation they had.

"Your only response last night was 'I don't want to lose the kids!' You used me to just have a boy!' Only reason you wanted another kid?! I can't handle this and you are ok with it. Why didn't you just tell me you were done?!? Why get me pregnant?!?"

"I'm not just staying because of the kids," Chris replied. *"They are my light and that will not change. I didn't fall out of love in 5 weeks, that's impossible. I don't want to erase 8 years just like that. I'm not sure what's in my head. I don't know if it's my parents, the third pregnancy, if I'm just scared or what. I didn't use you."*

"That's what you said last night... you can't even say why you're married to me. That's a stab in the heart... You didn't say you didn't want to lose us, you said you didn't want to lose the kids."

"I don't want to lose anyone," Chris replied.

Shanann responded in another ironic and sad hint of fore-shadowing of what was to come.

"This has been the worst week of my life! We were supposed to celebrate love and family. But instead, hate and whatever you call it. I'm not willing to watch something dangerous happen to one of our kids with your family for you to wake up. They will give you sorry excuses today!! I don't know what to say.

You don't see you, or how you're treating me... 8 years of 'love' and you are treating me horribly. I fell deeper in love with you this summer, you fell out. That's not love. Love falls deeper in love when apart, not out. *You don't love me. or you have a horrible way of showing it. You haven't fought for me this week. It's only the kids."*

As usual, Chris continued to casually transfer photos of Nikki into his Secret Calculator throughout the day while his marriage was imploding. Later, he told Shanann that his parents didn't want to drive him to the location where she was. Shanann asked him if he wanted her to come pick him up. He told her it was up to her, and his dad was cool bringing him back to where she was first thing the next morning.

Shanann, agitated again, snapped, *"We fucking leave tomorrow. I need help."*

She told Chris she was on her way to pick him up, but ultimately Ronnie agreed to drive him back to Shanann. Before he left his childhood home, Chris took pictures of photos in the house, including a childhood family portrait.

Later that evening, after he was back with Shanann, she texted him again from another room:

"I was trying to get you to fucking hug me. Make me feel safe. This is much deeper than 'lack of conversation!' Make me feel like everything is going to be ok."

"It will be ok. This will all get fixed," Chris replied, reverting back to his aversion to conflict.

"No. I don't need words damnit. You just told me you don't want this baby," Shanann said, sounding anxious and angry.

"I am scared, ok," Chris retorted. *"You wanted the truth and I told you how I felt."*

"You hold me after that conversation, you hold me. If you want

this to fucking last you make me feel safe after that bomb... Don't you get it? "How many times do I have to ask you to hold me? You hate me that much?" Shanann said, seemingly feeling overwhelming anxiety.

"*I don't hate you. I will fix this. It will be better,*" Chris was lying again, clearly not knowing what else to say to calm down his wife.

"*You didn't answer me. I'm begging you to hold me and you still can't.*"

"*I don't know where my head is at. I will fix it though,*" Chris repeated.

Shanann knew in her gut something else was wrong. She knew she wasn't crazy. She needed Chris to tell her what was really going on.

She texted back to him: "*This isn't the only thing. This doesn't get your head all screwed up. Something changed in the last 5 weeks... Something you won't say.*"

Chris didn't respond.

• • •

Shanann was devastated, and the physical strain of the pregnancy didn't help. She didn't feel comfortable fully confiding in her parents about her marriage troubles. They could tell Chris was acting weird, distant, and not his usual self, but they didn't realize how bad things were.

Shanann decided to confide in one of her closest friends and Thrive team members, Addy. In heartbreaking text messages to her, Shanann detailed how emotionally tortured she had been from everything that was happening since she arrived in North Carolina.

"*Addy, he's changed. I don't know who he is anymore.*"

"*What do you mean?*" Addy asked.

"*He hasn't touched me all week, kissed me, talked to me except for when I'm trying to figure out what is wrong. He's been distant since I left.*"

"*What's the deal with his parents? Maybe he's distant because of that. Was he on board with you leaving for that long? Could he be resentful?*" Addy asked.

"*He said they apologized, and they didn't come to Celeste's party because they were scared of me. That's bullshit. If you are sincerely sorry and love your son and grandkids you reach out and say that. He was totally on board. We decided it together. Quality time with everyone. I'm supposed to go tomorrow for 4D ultrasound and gender reveal next Saturday. I just want to cry. We've never had a problem in our relationship like this. No joke. NEVER. THIS IS TOTAL LEFT FIELD. He was submissive to his parents last night, as usual. He hasn't asked me once about how I'm feeling or the baby. I was vomiting the other day so bad and he just existed. I don't know where my head is at. I'll fix it though (he texted me).*"

"*Aww honey, it will be ok...just give him time,*" Addy said. "*He's adjusting to the idea of the baby. He's scared. He shouldn't be doing this to you, but he's a good guy, he will fix it.*"

"*What if he really doesn't love me anymore?!*" Shanann texted. What Shanann didn't realize was that Chris never truly loved her to begin with. He was incapable of real love.

"Not possible honey. He LOVES YOU!" Addy replied.

But Shanann wasn't so sure anymore, and with good reason.

On the morning of August 8, Chris went back to work, and Shanann started texting with another friend, Sara.

Sara asked her if things were any better with Chris. Shanann filled her in on the conversations over the past few days and told Sara she tried to initiate sex with him the previous night, but he had rejected her. She was feeling sick to her stomach and told her friend she had never cried this hard in her entire life.

"He said he feels there's lack of communication and it's not from me. I sent him 12 texts over the month begging him to talk to me. He fell asleep at 7/8 pm. I tried talking to him after rejection last night and me crying for an hour alone on couch - he slept. I kicked his sorry ass out of bed, and I refuse to sleep on couch anymore this week. Told him this morning to not come home today if he can't tell me the damn truth on what the hell is wrong! We are supposed to go to ultrasound tonight and he doesn't want the baby. He'd abort if I said it was ok."

In Sara's mind, it seemed the only logical explanation was an affair. She asked Shanann if it was a possibility.

"He said he's not having an affair," Shanann said.

"Are you sure?" Sara asked.

"Honestly no, but what else would make him do a complete 360... We couldn't get enough of each other before I left," Shanann replied.

Throughout the day, Shanann texted her other good friends, Nicki and Cassie, and updated them on all the trouble with Chris. They tried their best to support her and give advice, but they were just as perplexed as Shanann was.

Shanann told her friends that Chris didn't want a divorce right away, but she would fight for full custody. Feeling defeated, she told them she couldn't afford three kids by herself in Colorado.

Cassie's husband, Josh, texted Chris to check in about the ultrasound. They would soon find out the sex of the baby, and Josh knew Chris really wanted a boy.

"Are you excited for the ultrasound? Today's the day, right?!" Josh asked.

"Just got back to work. Yep, today's the day. I'm excited. It's at 7:00," Chris replied.

While Shanann searched the internet for *"couples' therapy"* and *"emotion focused therapy,"* Nikki Kessinger was searching topics about *"marrying your mistress."*

Later, in the evening, Josh checked in with Chris, eager to find out the sex of the baby. Chris told him the envelope was sealed, and they would find out at the gender reveal party that was scheduled a week from the coming Saturday. Except that gender reveal party would never happen.

CHAPTER 14

"My sexy empanada"

On the morning of August 9, Addy woke up to another distraught message from Shanann. *"He said we are not compatible anymore! He refused to hug me after he said he will try to 'work' it out! Said he thought another baby would fix his feelings. Said, he refused couples counseling!"*

"What!?! That doesn't sound like Chris. Did he go to the appointment?" Addy asked in disbelief.

"Yes, but cold. Addy, I have no idea what happened."

"Go through his phone, make sure there isn't some other bitch I have to kill," Addy said, maybe thinking that Chris was having an affair after all.

"This is total left field," Shanann said, still in shock.

"Why no to counseling?" Addy asked.

"He said he's not sitting on no damn couch saying what he just said to me to a stranger."

"Oh Jesus," Addy replied.

"I found some in our area, and if anything, this baby and kids

deserve him to go," Shanann said.

"*Is this his parents' influence?*" Addy asked.

"*He refused to hold me. Said he's not there. He can't. I haven't slept most of the week. My eyes burn from crying so much. I canceled gender reveal. Nicki is going to tell me today. I need happy news right now. I said to him, how is this a few months? We were so intimate and what I thought 'in love' when I left! He said he had a lot of time to think. The baby in my belly deserves his full love. Either way.*"

"*I'm so sorry, honey,*" Addy said, at a loss for the right words.

"*I said, you sat here in this living room and said you think it would be a great thing to have another baby. We talked it out a lot beforehand and we agreed to do this. You were so excited and happy,*" Shanann said, still in shock.

"*I think he will come to his senses and feel like an ass in a few months,*" Addy said, trying again to be reassuring.

"*I grabbed his hand during the ultrasound, and he didn't grab back. I cringed. He rejected sex night we arrived here. Only thing I can think of, even though I don't think he has it in him, is another girl,*" Shanann said. This is a very frightening example of how little Shanann really knew about Chris, and how convincing Chris was with his "nice guy" image.

"*Did you look through his phone? Did you ask if there was someone?*" Addy asked again.

"*He said last night...opposites attract but this isn't working anymore. I did. He denied. No, I didn't look. He's deleting messages from his dad. I'm sure he's not that stupid.*"

"*Why is he deleting messages from his dad? This makes no sense.*

Any of this. It's not Chris. He loves and adores you."

"*I don't know if I suck it up again and call his mom today (tape a call) so she can't lie and twist my words and talk to her and tell her I want to have a relationship but I need her to love and respect my kids,*" Shanann said, trying to brainstorm ideas as to what might make things better.

"*I think maybe you tell him that if you want to work it out with them. I thought he was on your side about what happened with CeCe?*" Addy said.

"*I did last night because I thought maybe that is the only thing that happened while I was away. I told him I have been sucking up my feelings when they throw their jabs at me for him. But when it came to putting our daughter's life in danger, I said I want to continue to have a relationship with them, but they need to love, respect and care for him and the kids better. He is (on her side with CeCe) but then he said at the beach that I put a dagger between him and his dad. His dad is the one that didn't come to her party. He's the one that didn't make contact with his son and he's the one what blocked us on Facebook, not me. It's taking everything I have to not flip on him and them. Like every ounce of my body.*"

Shanann and Addy exchanged *I love you*'s and said their goodbyes. Both would be meeting up in Arizona the next morning for the Le-Vel weekend getaway.

Shanann asked Chris if he wanted to find out the sex of the baby with her that evening, and he agreed. Shortly before noon, in perhaps the most eerie foreshadowing of all, Chris texted her a photo of the girls' life-size doll covered in a white sheet with only the feet sticking out. Shanann assumed the girls had been playing and positioned the doll like that. It was very morbid, especially in hindsight. The doll looked like a dead body at the morgue, lying lifelessly and stiff on the black leather couch. Shanann, finding it amusing, posted it on Facebook with the caption, "*I don't know what to think about this*," followed by hysterical laughter emojis. Shanann added, "*at least they covered the body together. At least we know they have each other's back.*"

We now know at this point, Chris's fantasies of killing his family were forming into an actual plan. In a letter to Cadle, he forthrightly admits the killings had been brewing in his dark mind for weeks. "All the weeks of me thinking about killing her."

That day, Chris deleted his Facebook page. Shanann texted him, asking him why he did, and he didn't respond to her. When his father Ronnie asked him the same question, Chris answered, "*Yes Sir! Finally liberated myself!*"

Nikki apparently just told Chris she had told her friends about him. Now that she was starting to tell people about their relationship, he wanted to make sure anyone deciding to snoop on Facebook and look for him wouldn't find out he was presumably happily married with a baby on the way.

Even with all the turmoil, Shanann was starting to feel a glimmer of hope from Chris. He had suddenly agreed to go away for a weekend in Aspen with her when she got back from her trip to Arizona. She had placed an order on Amazon for the well-known self-help relationship book,

Hold Me Tight: Seven Conversations for a Lifetime of Love" and was eager for him to read it. He seemed to be talking to her a little more, although he was still aloof. He had also agreed to go with her to take Bella to her first day of kindergarten on Monday morning. Shanann thought maybe he was finally seeing the light and starting to come around. However, his change of heart was most likely because he knew he would soon be rid of her and playing along was easy knowing he wouldn't have to do it much longer. Once Shanann was out of the way, he would be free to be with Nikki.

That evening, Chris and Shanann opened the envelope revealing the sex of the baby and Shanann at least, was very excited to find out it was a boy. Shanann wanted to name their son Nico Lee. Nico would be honoring her Italian heritage, and Lee was Chris' middle name. Chris told her to hold off on sharing the news with others and on Facebook until Monday. Chris, plotting to kill Shanann on the coming Sunday evening, knew she wouldn't be around on Monday to share the news.

Finally showing a change of heart, he agreed to go to counseling and said he would read the book Shanann had ordered for him. They also discussed selling the house and moving somewhere cheaper together. Then, when Shanann told Chris she loved him, he reciprocated the sentiment. However, he still didn't want to sleep in the same bed. He gave her a quick kiss before leaving their bedroom to sleep in the basement, and that gave her some hope as well.

The flicker of hope Shanann felt was for nothing though,

because after Chris left the bedroom and went to the basement, he transferred more semi-nude selfies of Nikki into his secret calculator app.

The morning of August 10, Shanann left for Arizona very early before the kids woke up. She sent a text message to Chris that was filled with her usual optimism and exuberance.

"Good morning honey! Sorry to make you wake up twice today. I didn't want alarm going off. We are checked in and everything, it's already a mad house here today! Enjoy the girls! Don't forget King Soopers 10-11. I told Bella I was leaving for work with Nicki and I assured her I was always coming home. They usually don't eat right away, lately. Give them lots of kisses for me. Thank you for everything last night. I miss and love you so much! I am still in shock we are having a little boy! I'm so excited and happy! I really thought it was another girl. Thank you for letting me hold you this morning, it felt good! Your letter is on the counter. Have a great time with kiddos. They truly missed you. Love you baby. Send me pics."

On the counter, was the letter she mentioned. What is reprinted here was taken from a screenshot sent to Sara, Shanann's friend.

My Dearest Chris,

I don't know where to begin. I am so lost for words. I can't even explain how hard the pain is. The last five weeks have been the hardest. I missed everything about you. I missed your morning breath, your touch.

Your lips. I missed holding you. I missed smelling you in the sheets. I missed talking to you in person. I missed watching you laugh and play with the kids, that I love so much about you. I missed seeing you naked and on top of me, making love to me. I missed having you around when I first felt alone and upset. I just flat out missed the hell out of you.

I really don't know how we fell out of compatibility or if that is someone else's words. The only thing that changed this month was everything going down with your family. I can't change what happened, but I can try to work things out with you, with them. But there must be a mutual respect with everyone…

The rest of the letter was cut off.

Later that day, Shanann texted Chris, saying she landed in Arizona, but Chris was preoccupied with making other plans. Now that Shanann was out of town for the weekend, he was eager to be with Nikki. Because of the state of their marriage, Shanann wanted to stay home in Colorado, but Chris encouraged her to go. Then, he reached out to his friend Jeremy Lindstrom in hopes that Jeremy's teenage daughter Mary would be able to babysit for a few hours Saturday night.

"Do you think Mary is available to watch the girls for a few hours tomorrow night? I won a raffle at work for a Rockies game. It's with people I don't know from work, but I haven't been to a game in a while where the kids aren't involved and only last an

inning lol."

"*Of course,*" Jeremy replied. "*Which house?*"

"*I would say my house because the girls would fall asleep easier and all it would be is watching the monitor,*" Chris responded.

Jeremy agreed to Mary arriving the next evening at 6:15 and staying until 10 pm.

That afternoon, Chris took Bella and CeCe on a car ride to meet up with his co-worker, Troy McCoy. Chris buckled the girls into their car seats in Shanann's white Lexus SUV and made the drive to a Safeway parking lot so he could give Troy an Amazon Firestick.

Troy gave Chris a smile and a wave when he pulled into the parking lot. Just as Chris was handing Troy the Firestick, their co-worker, Kodi Roberts, called Troy.

"Hold on one sec," Troy said to Chris, taking the call.

"There's a leak in the bypass line at 319," Kodi said over the phone.

Chris strained a bit to try to make out what Kodi was saying to Troy. Then Troy hung up and exchanged goodbyes with Chris. As Troy peered in the backseat of the Lexus, he saw Bella and CeCe laughing and smiling. He waved to the girls, and they waved back to him. Troy watched the Lexus drive off into the distance.

When Chris and the girls were back home, Ronnie asked Chris if he could Facetime with the girls since Shanann was away. Chris told him he was afraid Bella would tell Shanann and Ronnie agreed it was a good idea not to talk to them and avoid drama.

After a day of catching up with her Le-Vel friends in Arizona, Shanann got into bed and started searching for resorts and Groupon deals in Aspen. She thought it would be a good place for a romantic weekend getaway and was looking forward to quality time with Chris.

He had been with his daughters that night and wasn't able to see Nikki. She had been out that evening and Chris texted her. *"Hope you had a great night beautiful. Miss you! Get home safe! Sweet dreams my sexy empanada."*

• • •

When Shanann woke up the morning of August 11, she texted Chris first thing.

"Good morning baby! Are the girls up?"

"Good morning. They are watching cartoons in bed," Chris responded. Chris and Shanann sent some casual messages back and forth. She told Chris about the crazy thunderstorms the night before and asked him if he wanted the cable NFL package for the fall, trying to put her focus on planning for a happy future together as a family.

Chris spent the day with the girls, and Shanann spent the day with friends in Arizona. Chris told Shanann that Mary, Jeremy Lindstrom's daughter, would be coming over to babysit for a few hours so he could go to the Colorado Rockies game. Always a careful and attentive mother, Shanann asked him to make sure Mary knew not to feed CeCe anything she was allergic to.

That evening, Chris dressed in black jeans and a white T-shirt ordered pizza for his daughters and Mary. He gave the girls their medication and told Mary she could put them to bed at seven o'clock. He also gave her the baby monitor and said he would be back by ten o'clock. Mary had never babysat the girls before, but she found them very sweet and easy to take care of. While she was watching them, she received a text from Shanann in Arizona. "*Hey love, this is Shanann. How are the girls?*" Mary told her they were doing great and that CeCe had three slices of pizza. Shanann graciously thanked her for watching them and told her if she needed anything to just ask.

Chris drove to Nikki's apartment first. When he got there, they drove to the Lazy Dog Restaurant and Bar for dinner. Nikki looked at the menu and realized it wasn't the same menu as the Lazy Dog she usually went to. She told Chris she wanted to leave and go to the other one, and he obliged. After all, Chris was always the easy-going one.

Over dinner, they talked about Chris and his fitness plan. Since he had lost so much weight, he had become focused on a healthy lifestyle, working out, running, and clean eating. Chris paid for the meal on his joint credit card with Shanann. Up until then, he had been using gift cards he received from his company, but again, he knew he would no longer have Shanann to deal with, and he could be careless if he wanted to.

After dinner, they went back to Nikki's place and had sex. Chris noticed it was close to ten o'clock and told Nikki he had to leave because his babysitter had to be home soon. He rushed out, but he had to stop at the ATM first to get cash to pay Mary.

While he was driving home, Shanann called him because she had received an alert on her phone about a $62 charge on their credit card at the Lazy Dog Restaurant. Shanann asked him what he ordered there. He told her he just had a salmon and a beer. As stated earlier in this book, after they got off the phone, Shanann searched on her phone for the Lazy Dog Restaurant to see how much a salmon and beer cost. She was easily able to deduce that the meal did not amount to $62.

When Chris pulled up to the house, Mary's mother, Jennifer, was waiting in a parked car in the driveway. Chris paid Mary, thanked her, and said he would see her tomorrow at her little brother's birthday party.

Nikki, by herself in her apartment, started her internet searching again, this time for "Chris Watts," "Shanann Watts," "Ronnie Watts," and "2825 Saratoga Trail," where Chris and Shanann lived. It is unclear what motivated her to search for those things and what she was looking for.

Before he went to bed, Chris called Shanann, knowing she would soon be gone for good. Shanann went to bed that night, unaware that the next day would be the last day of her life.

CHAPTER 15

"Ready to be home with Chris and the girls"

August 12, the last day of Shanann's, Bella's, and CeCe's lives, seemed like a typical day. Shanann woke up, and before anything else, sent Chris a text saying, "*Good morning baby. Love you.*"

Although she was with Addy in Arizona, Shanann texted her afterward, telling her she had a lot of work to do for the week because she wanted to go completely offline when she and Chris went to Aspen. Shanann was often glued to her phone, but she knew her relationship with Chris needed 110 percent of her attention.

Before starting her day with her Le-Vel crew in Arizona, she checked in with Chris again, asking how the girls were. He told her they were drinking shakes. Shanann told him she missed them and asked Chris to give the girls kisses from her.

Cassie's husband, Josh, also texted Chris that afternoon. Most likely, he was aware of the issues Chris and Shanann were having and all the talk of selling the house and downsizing. Josh, Cassie, and their young children had plans to move to Colorado, and they had arranged to stay with Chris and Shanann until they got settled. This was normal for Chris and Shanann to have house guests long term. As stated earlier, Shanann's parents lived with them for a while, and Shanann's good friend, Cristina, and her daughter moved in with them to help after Shanann had neck surgery.

Josh asked Chris if it was still cool for their family to stay with them when they arrived in Colorado. Chris, always the people pleaser, said of course it was. When Josh asked him how the Rockies game was, Chris lied once again and told him it was "epic."

Shanann had been doing some introspection and trying to think of things she could change about herself to make the relationship better. She was invested in making her husband happy, and she was trying to dig deep to figure out what she could do to improve the situation.

She texted Addy again. "*I need to do better with my calendar! I don't block out family time, I fill in family time. He said to me last night it has nothing to do with business though.*"

Addy told Shanann she agreed and that Shanann needed to make more time for the family.

"*No, I agree. I think its itty-bitty things. I sometimes can be bitchy, and he gets that side of me. I know I tend to make him feel like he isn't able to do things because I have control issues. He said the other night he wishes I'd just let him hang up a picture, he also never calls me out. He never fights me, just goes with flow. He knows I like things done a certain way, but I never thought about how that may make him feel as a man. I don't even know if this is what's bothering him. He still hasn't said! I'm praying he wrote me a letter like I asked since he can express himself better in a letter than talking. I'm the pusher and he's the withdrawer. He has strengths that are my weaknesses and vice versa. The lack of communication isn't on my part. I can be better at how I communicate, but he doesn't communicate! I say things sometimes just to get him to react in any way since he doesn't react and that's not good. It's not even all the time. 99% of the time we are perfectly fine. And we have never ever fought. Literally over anything serious. I have fought with him over stupid shit like not doing something I asked in a timely manner. I did belittle him without realizing it with his parents. Told him he needed to find his balls and protect his family. He is submissive when his parents are involved."*

There is a little clue in this statement from Shanann about Chris's personality. She mentions that in order to get her husband to react, she has to say things to try to rile him up. She needed more emotion from him, but she didn't realize that she was dealing with someone who was probably void of real emotions and attachment.

Addy told Shanann that being submissive was just who Chris was. She added, *"He would kill for you."*

Shanann told Addy, *"Told him in a letter I would for him and there has to be mutual respect. I did respect his parents enough to deal with them. His mom just didn't and when alone with me jabs at me... it's not fair... I mean fuck, I agreed to spend*

5 weeks with both parents. That's hell for me. But I did it for him and kids."

Shanann continued, *"He was NEVER close to anyone but his dad. I, being the family person tried bringing them closer and it backfired... I need to feel like he will stand up for us faced with difficult situations... that's his flaw... or weakness. My weakness is I have an Italian temper that can't hold back when pissed... I'm a fixer and I want to talk this out and he just wants to work it out in his head. I've just been acting kind of normal. Morning baby, love you, etc., but not over doing it... Over doing it is what we do. We are so affectionate, can't stop touching each other, etc. not just the sex but the touch."*

This is one reason it was impossible for Shanann to know what her husband was capable of. He was consistently affectionate with her. She felt loved, appreciated, and cherished for most of their marriage.

Before Shanann met up with friends for the day, she texted Chris asking him if he would get the girls' backpacks ready for their first day of school the next day. He said he would, knowing full well that he wouldn't need to. Shanann also asked for photos of the girls. Chris obliged and sent her one photo of Bella and one photo of CeCe. Later Shanann checked in at the girls' naptime and told Chris that if he was available, she would love to talk to him. He never called or returned her message.

When the girls woke up from the nap, Chris took them to Jeremy Lindstrom's house for his son's birthday party. The girls had fun playing in the inflatable pools with the other kids. Chris was acting normal to everyone at the party, and, as usual, he was attentive to the girls. But his mind was on more than his daughters. He knew this was his last day with them.

While at the party, he texted back and forth with Nikki. She had spent the day with her family, and he texted to her, *"Nice!! That sounds like a good time! I haven't seen IMAX in a while. Sounds like you're having a fun day with the folks! I'm still at the bday party. Kids are soaked from water balloons."*

An hour later, he went back to texting about his favorite topic, what he had been eating. *"Been pounding fruit and had a whole jar of asparagus. He didn't smoke any bbq this time. He did hot dogs, so I did the fruit and veggies."* The messages were banal and surprisingly normal, considering Chris would murder his family less than twenty-four hours after texting these messages from a child's birthday party.

CeCe fell and hurt herself during the party. She was crying, and Chris ran over to console her. Nobody would have sensed anything was amiss. He seemed totally normal to everyone who interacted with him, chatting about Shanann's pregnancy and the gender reveal party (that Shanann had canceled). He mentioned it would be cool to have a boy and said he was excited to find out the sex—even though he already knew it was a boy at this point. Shanann checked in again, asking if the girls were having fun at the party. Chris said they were. When Shanann responded with *"love you,"* Chris didn't respond. He was finished pretending.

At 5 pm that evening, Chris' co-worker Kodi Roberts, was

surprised to get a text from Chris, which was unusual on weekends.

"*I have the whip checks for the Cervi 6-29. I'm gonna go straight out there from my house in the morning. I will look at that 3-19 as well and run the 11-29 if you want?*" Chris said.

"*l was going to head out there first thing tomorrow to check out the 3-19. Did Troy talk to you about what I had found out there Friday afternoon??*" Kodi asked.

"*Yup. I was standing right next to him LOL... l was giving him a Firestick to look at... I can go out there though. No sense in both of us going out there LOL.*"

"*Alright sounds good man,*" Kodi replied. "*I appreciate it. I think I still have a couple Konys left out there. I can let you know in the morning. And let me know if you find anything at the 3-19. If not, we may pressure test that BP line and see if it's leaking underground.*"

On a normal day, Chris would almost always head to the office before doing a site visit. In this exchange, he was orchestrating a scenario where he would be out in the oil fields alone so he could dispose of the bodies of his family.

Still in Arizona, Shanann, Addy, Nicki, and another friend, Cindy, headed to dinner at 5:30 pm. Right before they left, Shanann made a quick Facebook post, sharing her excitement. "*Felt the baby move twice this weekend!*" Even though Shanann's Facebook posts sounded upbeat, she wasn't acting like herself at dinner. She wasn't feeling well, but she was also still distraught and worried about the state of her marriage. She confided in the small group about her worries as she sipped on ice water with lemon and picked at her chicken Caesar salad. She told them about the strange credit card charge at The Lazy Dog restaurant for $62 that Chris said was for a beer and salmon. She also mentioned her concerns about his possible infidelity but didn't think that could be the case because Chris had "no game."

She told her friends she was going to have another talk with him upon her return, although it would have to wait until the next day because her flight would land too late, and he would be asleep. She said she planned on putting her arm around him in bed when she got home. She wanted to make a simple gesture of affection toward him since they had almost no physical touch recently. The sudden shift of always being physically affectionate to nothing was jarring and unsettling.

In general, Shanann's friends had been concerned about her in Arizona because she wasn't acting like herself. She wasn't eating or drinking enough water, and they tried making sure she was getting proper fluids, so she didn't dehydrate.

It was a great dinner, and the women were so happy to be together celebrating such close-knit bonds. If there was ever a time in Shanann's life where she had found her "tribe," it was in this season of her life, and she didn't take any of it for granted.

Shanann and Nicki left for the airport, only to find out that their flight was delayed due to storms. Shanann was anxious to get back home and to see if Chris had read her letter and responded. She was ready to go to Aspen and begin repairing the relationship. The utter confusion and helplessness she had felt the entire summer was something she was ready to leave behind in the dust. She wanted to move forward, and she wanted to do it quickly. She knew something was wrong, but she didn't know what or how to fix it. That was torture for Shanann. She was a fixer.

She texted Chris to ask if the kids were in bed and asked for more photos. Chris had fed the girls cold pizza and candy. He and the girls Facetimed with Shannan's father Frank. It was 7:45, and Bella had just gone to bed. Bedtime was normally at 7 pm, but she missed her mom and knew she was coming home that evening. Chris told her she would see her mom in the morning, even though he knew she wouldn't see her mother alive ever again. He also sent Shanann one last picture of Bella, taken earlier in the day at the birthday party. Chris told Cadle in a letter that he was fully aware it would be the last time he would put his children to bed, saying: "August 12th when I finished putting the girls to bed, I walked away and said 'That's the last time I'm going to be tucking my babies in.' I knew what was going to happen the day before and I did nothing to stop it!'

"*The power went out in the restaurant when we were there,*" Shanann texted, sending Chris a photo of a dark restaurant. "*Great job on Bella's hair!*" she added, referencing the picture he had sent of Bella in her party dress, her hair up in little pigtails.

"*That sucks! Yea, she cooperated,*" he answered back.

"Really bad dust storm, rain, thunder, and lightning. Praying it doesn't cancel flight. Addy's flight was cancelled this morning," she said, trying to make normal conversation with her husband. Things hadn't been normal for a while now, and she was probably craving normalcy again.

She decided instead of texting, she would pick up and call him, just to chat. She would not have thought twice about doing that before, but now she felt as if she were walking on eggshells. The call didn't go as she had hoped. She turned to her friend Nicki.

"He was short with me," she said glumly. "I think he was working out."

Wanting to smooth things over and feeling hyper aware of her every move, she texted him. *"Sorry I bothered you. I just wanted to talk to you."*

Shanann then texted Addy and told her she could call Chris because he was still awake. Chris gave Addy mechanical advice for her car, and Shanann texted him, trying to show her appreciation. *"Thank you for taking good care of the girls this weekend so I can learn and work,"* she wrote. *"I appreciate it!"*

Chris got off the phone with Addy and responded to Shanann, *"You're welcome! I just talked to Addy."*

Shanann, always organized, was already thinking of meal planning for the week.

"What kind of vegetables do you want with dinner tomorrow?" she asked Chris, assuming the week would be a completely normal one.

"*Green beans*," he replied.

"*I'm ready to be home. I'm ready for bed*," she texted, exhausted.

While waiting for updates on the status of her flight, she texted Addy again. Her mind was obsessing over the talk she planned on having with Chris.

"*This is what I'm planning on sharing with Chris tomorrow night when we talk: Can you please tell me something, because just like you, I'm in my head? I try to fix things and make them better and this is making me crazy. I know that you need time. I want to give you what you're asking for and respect your space. I need some time. This place that I'm in, in my head, is not a good place. It is not healthy for me, or Nico. I need you to help me help you. I need you to give just a little bit of what I did, or didn't do, so I'm not going crazy in my head to figure it out. I know I can't fix this by myself; that, we are going to have to work together.*"

At 9:28 pm, Shanann called Chris to try to give him an update on her delayed flight. He didn't pick up, but he did call Nikki a minute later and spoke to her on the phone for almost two hours. While they were talking, Shanann texted him again at 9:44 pm: "*Tried calling you to give you update. Was starting to board and they announced that our crew isn't here yet and it's going to be a minimum of an hour before they are here.*"

Shortly after 11 pm, Shanann made the last Facebook post of her life, sharing her flight info with the message, "*Ready to be home with Chris and the girls.*"

After Chris got off the phone with Nikki, close to 11:30

pm, he texted Shanann back, lying to her. "*Holy crap. Sorry, I passed out on the couch. That's gonna be late.*" This was the last text exchange between the couple while Shanann was alive.

CHAPTER 16

"Mommy doesn't feel good."

***Before reading any farther, the reader should be warned that the content in this chapter is disturbing and depicts the murder of Shanann and her daughters. It may be wise for some readers to skip this chapter. It should also be stated that the events portrayed in this chapter are Chris's version of what happened. This chapter is based on his interview from prison with law enforcement, his letters with Cheryln Cadle, and the evidence in the police discovery. Chris has changed his story and contradicted himself numerous times, but this is the only account we have to go on. Readers can decide for themselves what they believe. Regardless of what truly happened, what Chris has testified to and, in all versions of the story, is beyond evil.*

Around 1:50 am, Nicki watched Shanann walk inside her

house and close the door behind her. Shanann, wearing jeans, a black cardigan and gray T-shirt that had the word "love" on it in pink letters entered her home that was mostly dark except for the lights on the porch. She kicked off her favorite black flips flops and left them by the door with her suitcase.

Exhausted, she made her way upstairs to the master bedroom, shed her clothes, pulled on a purple T-shirt and crawled into bed next to Chris. Chris had been sleeping in the basement since the family had returned from North Carolina, but he was in the master bedroom this evening.

According to statements by Chris, this is what happened next. Soon after she snuggled under the bed covers, she put her arm around Chris. She started caressing his hand and chest. Although it had been months since they had been intimate, and Chris had been rejecting sex, he was receptive to Shanann's advances this time. This was the first time Chris had been sexually intimate with his wife since he started sleeping with Nikki.

Chris knew what he had to do to take care of the mess. He'd found it easy to shower Nikki with attention when Shanann and the girls were away, but now he wouldn't be able to see her at all if he was still living under the same roof as his family. He felt Shanann would keep him from being with Nikki, and the only way he felt he could be with her was if he killed his family.

Chris knew he would go through with his plan. Even though he had enjoyed the previous day alone with his daughters, laughing, playing, and singing with them, he still had no desire to stop his evil plan from happening. In his letter to Cadle, he claims he went to Bella's room, then CeCe's, took the pillows from their beds and smothered them. Then believing they were dead, he was ready to talk to Shanann. The affair with Nikki, the anger and disappointment of the drama with his family and Shanann over the years, and his inability to deal with emotional problems all boiled to the surface.

He crawled back into the large mahogany four-poster bed and decided to have the talk with Shanann. He planned on telling her he was leaving her and no longer loved her. It is strange and incredibly cruel to think that, knowing he was going to kill her, he still wanted to make her suffer emotionally before he took her life.

Shanann had married Chris partially because he was a safe choice. He was always loyal, devoted, and submissive. They never fought. Chris rarely raised his voice. He was so easy going. Shanann thought they would be together forever. Shanann had given everything to Chris as a wife. They had always been so happy. Her own anger, despair, and sadness came to the surface all at once.

Shanann started to cry, and mascara streaked down her face as she told Chris she loved him. Chris told her he didn't love her and wasn't compatible with her. He said he became angry again when Shanann told him if he left her, she would not let him see the kids. In his words to Cadle, "She was used to getting her way and when she saw she wasn't, she would revert as always to threats and anger to get what she wanted. This time, though, I was not giving into her demands. That's when my anger for her began. Years of her telling me what to do and what not to do. Keeping me from my own family for sometimes months at a time were over, keeping me in the background was over."

Chris was not necessarily upset about losing the kids. According to one of his versions of the story, he had already smothered his daughters at this point. His anger was about his feelings of being out of control, and he resented Shanann for it. Now he felt empowered to have ultimate control over his wife.

Chris spent his entire life being the helpful guy everyone loved and wanted to be around. There was no way he could face being the bad guy. He knew if word got out that he had cheated on his pregnant wife, everyone would look down on him, and that was not something Chris could handle. Shanann was suspicious about possible infidelity. In a version of Chris's story, she had even said, "I knew there was someone else!"

In his mind, he blamed Shanann for all his problems. In his mind, it was Shanann's fault he had grown distant from his family and her fault his children didn't have a close relationship with them. In his mind, it was Shanann's fault he had cheated on her and put him in this mess. Everything was her fault. Chris' narcissism and entitlement had reached their peak.

Chris watched her as she got drowsy, and then he put his hands around her neck, squeezing her jugular vein and cutting off the oxygen to her brain. Shanann did not fight back as she helplessly watched her husband, the man she had always referred to as the best thing that had ever happened to her, slowly squeeze the life out of her. As she died, Chris noticed she evacuated her bowels, and her eyes filled with blood.

Chris' adrenaline began coursing through his veins. He claimed he was shaking uncontrollably. It was over. His wife was lying dead in front of him, and he had killed her with his own hands.

• • •

Sandi was having a spiritual connection to her daughter around this time. As she shared with Dr. Phil,[7] at 4:30 am, she shot out of bed in a cold sweat. Trembling, she got up and sat at the foot of the bed. She felt as if a spear had gone through her forehead.

She heard a whisper in her ear. "Shanann."

"Did something happen to my daughter?" she asked out loud.

An overwhelming feeling of pure horror and dread overcame Sandi. In that moment, she knew deep within her soul, that her daughter was gone.

Frantic, she woke up her husband Frank.

"Something is wrong with Shanann," she said, panicked.

"She's fine, don't worry," Frank said to her, patting her gently.

---

7. Rzucek, Sandi Onorati. Interview with Dr. Phil. *Life-After-Death: Did Spirits of Shan'ann Watts And Her Daughters Visit Mom After Murders? The Dr. Phil Show.* CBS. March 11, 2019.

Sandi got up and rushed to her son Frankie's room and pushed open the door.

"Frankie, something is wrong with Shanann."

"Mom, you're worrying again," Frankie said.

"I'm telling you. Something is wrong," Sandi insisted.

"Mom. You're being paranoid. She's probably sleeping or something."

Sandi closed the door to Frankie's room, but she was still shaking uncontrollably.

• • •

At the Watts house, Chris stood hovering over the bed and Shanann's body. He glanced at Shanann's hand and noticed her wedding and engagement rings were still on. Chris pried her rings off her finger. He would deal with them later. Chris decided he would stage the home to appear that Shanann left him. He could make it look as if she took off and left. No one would ever believe Chris would hurt her, but maybe they would believe that Shanann could get angry enough to leave him and never return. As far as the outside world could see, she was the fiery one with the Italian temper, and Chris was the rational, logical one,

Chris had just started wrapping Shanann's body in the top bedsheet when he heard rustling at the door. As told to Cadle, and this was Chris changing his story yet again, much to his shock and surprise, it was Bella and CeCe. They stared at the lifeless body of their mother, lying face down, wrapped in a sheet.

"What's wrong with Mommy?" Bella asked quietly with trepidation in her soft-spoken voice.

"Mommy doesn't feel good. We have to take her to the hospital," Chris responded. Chris said he noticed Bella's eyes were bruised, and both girls looked confused and traumatized after his initial attempts to smother them. Chris felt no empathy for them at all. In fact, he told Cadle he was overwhelmed with anger that they were still alive. Although this part of the story seems farfetched to many, Chris explained that this was why the cause of death of the girls in the autopsy report was smothering. In my opinion, this is one of the most believable parts of the story. I believe this moment really shows who he always was. *He was angry his children were still alive.*

The girls watched in confusion as Chris tried to lift Shanann and carry her out of the bedroom. He lost his balance, stumbled, and then dropped Shanann's body to the ground. He wasn't going to be able to physically carry her down the stairs, so he began to drag her down them. The sound of her body hitting the stairs made loud thumps. Bella began to cry, and CeCe began to whimper.

Chris knew he had to move quickly. The sun was coming up, and people would be waking up. Chris left the girls inside the house and backed his truck into the garage. He carried Shanann's body out and loaded it in the back cab of his truck on the floor. Then, he went back in the house and grabbed the lunch he had packed earlier, a gas can, a rake and a shovel.

It's quite astonishing to think that he was planning to eat only a few hours after murdering his family, and that he even remembered to bring lunch to work.

On his way back out, he spotted the self-help book, *Hold Me Tight* that Shanann had sent him. He grabbed it and callously tossed it in the trashcan in the garage. This could be another way to insinuate Shanann was done and leaving him. He grabbed some garbage bags to cover her face and feet.

In the house, CeCe was carrying her favorite NY Yankees blanket while Bella was clutching her pink blanket she took everywhere with her. Chris put the garbage bags on Shanann's head and feet before he put the girls in the car. He picked up the girls one by one and put them on the bench in the cab with their feet dangling over their mother's body on the floor below them. They cuddled up together, trying to console each other, confused and tired.

Chris started the engine and pulled away from the dream home he and Shanann had built. A home that held so much hope and promise for the future. A home and family that represented the American dream.

Chris began the forty-five-minute drive to Cervi 319, the very same oil tank site that he had texted Kodi Roberts about less than twenty-four hours earlier. He told Kodi he could go out there by himself. Chris knew he would be alone, at least for a short while, and he had planned for it. He had to act quickly to cover his tracks.

"Daddy, it smells," Bella complained.

Chris caught a whiff of a skunk-like smell that was

coming from Shanann's dead body.

In the rearview mirror, he watched Bella and CeCe doze off as the steady movement of the truck in the early morning lulled them into an on-and-off sleep. Occasionally, they would open their eyes and then close them again.

When Chris pulled the truck into the Cervi 319 oil site, no one was there, just as he had anticipated. He stopped the truck, pulled out Shanann's body, and coldly tossed her body to the side of the truck. Without much hesitation or thought, he reached inside the truck and grabbed CeCe's beloved Yankee blanket from her hands. CeCe, too young to comprehend what her father was about to do, did not put up a struggle as Chris placed the blanket over her head and simultaneously put his hand over her neck. He strangled her until he felt her body go limp and lifeless in his hands.

Bella sat silently and in shock next to her sister, watching the unthinkable as it happened. She watched as Chris took CeCe's limp body and carried her up the stairs that led to the top of the oil tanks. He opened the hatch to one of the tanks, only around 8-inches wide, and dropped CeCe into the dark, viscous oil. He waited until he heard the splash her body made as it hit the thick liquid. Then he closed the hatch and went back to the truck for Bella. In his letter to Cadle, he recalled the details in the most detached way, saying, "I couldn't believe how easy it was to just let her drop through the hole and let her go. I heard the splash as she hit the oil."

She was still sitting silently in the truck, her mother's lifeless body outside it, and her beloved sister and best friend, now dead and discarded in a tank of crude oil. Bella looked at Chris with fear and anxiety in her eyes.

"Daddy, is the same thing going to happen to me that happened to CeCe?" Bella asked.

Chris did not remember if he said, "Yes" or said nothing. He took the Yankees blanket and moved toward Bella.

"Daddy, no!" Bella pleaded her soft, quiet voice full of terror.

She did her best to try to fight her father off as she struggled for her life. Chris felt her head moving back and forth as she grunted under the blanket. She was no match for the strength of her father who lifted weights religiously. Chris seemed surprised that out of all three, Bella seemed to put up the biggest fight. He told Cadle, again, completely detached and clinical that, "Out of all three, Bella is the only one that put up a fight. I will hear her soft little voice for the rest of my life, saying, 'Daddy, NO!!! She knew what I was doing to her. She may not have understood death, but she knew I was killing her."

After Chris killed Bella, he took her back up to the top of the oil tanks and opened the hatch to the other one. Larger in stature than CeCe, Bella was harder to fit through the opening, and he had to do some maneuvering to push her body fully through. After hearing her body hit the oil below, he closed the hatch and made his way back to Shanann's body.

He found a spot where he could bury her and shoveled the dirt away as quickly as he could. It was a shallow grave, and in a final act of disrespect, he shoved her in the hole he had dug face down. He noticed that Shanann had given birth, and baby Nico was no longer in her womb. In his letter to Cadle, he mentioned that he was so angry with Shanann he had no intention of "changing how she landed." He used a rake to smooth some weeds over the grave and stood there for a minute. His entire family was gone. No one had arrived at Cervi 319 yet, so he could breathe a sigh of relief for now. He had successfully hidden the bodies of his family. He felt no remorse, only relief that he was finally free of them. Soon, his co-workers would show up, and it would be another normal day at work, except now he could go home to his girlfriend instead of his family. Later in the day, he would text Nikki and tell her, *"My family is gone."*

CHAPTER 17

"Chris Watts is an enigma to many"

"If we do not transform our pain, we will most assuredly transmit it– usually to those closest to us: our family, our neighbors, our co-workers and, invariably, the most vulnerable, our children." —Richard Rohr

Chris Watts is an enigma to many. That is one reason I felt so compelled to write about him. I could not think of another criminal case in the public eye where the perpetrator had displayed so few warning signs. In fact, Chris seemed to fit a profile that was the opposite of a family annihilator, murderer, or psychopath. He lived a life that was defined by low conflict, a sense of calm, and being helpful to others. He was not controlling, angry, dominant, or jealous. Based on interviews with everyone close to him, there were *zero* red flags. Chris never displayed rage or violent episodes toward anyone, and he tried to avoid conflict and violence at all costs. He de-escalated conflict rather than instigating it. He seemed happy to let Shanann direct him and tell him what to do. The way he talked about his daughters was always with joy and affection. Anyone who knew him thought being a father and husband was his happiness and purpose in life.

Chris's adult behavior was consistent with his behavior throughout his life. How did someone who was always so agreeable, likeable, kind, and conflict averse turn into a man who could violently obliterate his family and ultimately end up in the same maximum-security prison as infamous serial killer Ed Gein?

The other fascinating aspect of Chris is that up until those few months before he murdered his family, from a diagnostic perspective, he did not outwardly fit the profile of any diagnosis available in the DSM-5 (the *Diagnostic and Statistical Manual of Mental Disorders*, 5th Edition).[8] Mental health professionals use the DSM to diagnose their patients with mental illness and personality disorders.

Based on interviews, public information, and documents from the investigation, I will construct a theory based on *all* the factors that came together in the perfect storm to create the murderer that Chris Watts ended up becoming. Simply labeling him as a psychopath, family annihilator, or narcissist isn't enough. Understanding how a person becomes a violent murderer can be much more complex than that. Understanding violence and how one becomes violent help

---

8. Black, Donald W., and Jon E. Grant. *DSM-5 Guidebook: The Essential Companion to the Diagnostic and Statistical Manual of Mental Disorders, Fifth Edition.* Washington, DC: American Psychiatric Publishing, 2014.

us understand how we can prevent these types of sense-less and horrific events from happening in the future. It is impossible to spot and avoid every tragedy, but with more understanding of how they come to happen, I hope we can learn to prevent some.

• • •

After research, interviews, and my own professional experience, I surmised that there were multiple factors that all came together at once in a perfect storm that culminated in the heartrending result. In the psychology world, we study a lot of theory, but for this book, I also wanted to look at science, specifically the brain. Messages in childhood, complicated relationships, unique personality traits, environmental factors, and life stressors all seemed to play a role in why Chris Watts ended up making the violent and catastrophic decisions that he did. Ultimately, every-thing that happened was Chris's fault, and the accountability lies fully with him.

It is important to again state up front that I am not for-mally diagnosing or pathologizing anyone related to this case. As far as Chris and a "diagnosis," I, of course, cannot say with 100 percent certainty, what condition he may or may not have. The Goldwater Rule is in the American Psychiat-ric Association's Principles of Medical Ethics, and it states that it is unethical (for a psychiatrist) to give a professional opinion on a public figure whom they have not examined in person and without their consent.[9] I am not a psychiatrist, and the Goldwater Rule is mostly cited when speaking about prominent political figures. Many mental health professionals feel the Goldwater Rule is outdated and that the mental health profession has a "duty to inform" or "duty to warn."[10] Some mental health professionals use "duty to warn" or "duty to inform" as a reason for breaking the Goldwater Rule. Although Chris is not a threat to the general public and is incarcerated for the rest of his life, I still feel it is my duty to inform the public about the profile and traits of people like him. Sometimes, the most dangerous people are the ones we least expect, and it is important to know how to spot them. However, I do not intend to give Chris any definitive diagnosis. I will discuss the personality traits and disorders that Chris has displayed that people have speculated about. To my knowledge, no one has discussed communal narcissism regarding this case, and I believe that understanding all the subtypes of narcissism is important so that we can protect ourselves from its harm.

I also hope that there are lessons to be learned, and I feel relationship education is a good place to start. I have always believed that learning how to communicate feelings and resolve conflict in a healthy way are important skills that

---

9. *Ethics Primer of the American Psychiatric Association.* Washington, D.C.: American Psychiatric Association, 2001.

10. Lilienfeld, Scott, Josh Miller, and Donald Lynam. "The Goldwater Rule: Perspectives From, and Implications for, Psychological Science," 2017. https://doi.org/10.31234/osf.io/j3gmf.

everyone needs to know. I wish they taught these things in school. Sometimes, I wonder if this tragedy could have been avoided if Chris had healthier coping mechanisms, and if he knew there were pro-social ways to get what he wanted, instead of using anti-social ones. At the end of the day, it may be wishful thinking to believe we could stop someone as determined and dark as he has proven himself.

Based on my education, professional work as a psychotherapist, and my extensive training in psychotherapy, relational therapy, and Imago Relationship Theory, I intend to make educated guesses based on all the information made available to me in the discovery documents released by Colorado Law Enforcement and other sources. These are my opinions, and what I have written here does not mean I have all the answers. Ideally, I would like you to look at the information presented and make your own decisions about what you believe to be true.

This analysis is not intended to blame *anyone* except Chris Watts for these murders. Although other relationships and dynamics may have contributed to his ultimate decision to kill his family, Chris Watts has free will, and every decision he made that ended up in the violent murders of his pregnant wife and daughters should be attributed to him and him alone.

I find his story, from birth to adulthood, a fascinating psychological profile. Beyond the morbid fascination many people have with stories like this, it is also a cautionary tale. There are lessons to learn, and hopefully those who read this can learn to spot even the most subtle red flags in their relationships or learn how to deal with their problems in a healthy way, so they don't spiral out of control.

If you've followed this case, you may have heard experts such as criminal profilers and psychologists diagnose Chris in the media. Similarly, in social media groups focused on this case, armchair psychologists also speculate on a possible clinical diagnosis for Chris. The desire to diagnose someone makes sense because most people want to understand human behavior. If we can understand or make sense of a person and their actions, it seems less scary to us. If we can't understand something or make sense of it, the world can feel very scary, unsafe, and unpredictable. Human beings hate feeling out of control. When that happens, we experience anxiety and chaos. We all want the world to make sense. For example, the cliché "Good things happen to good people" is an idea we want to believe in because then it feels as if we have an element of control.

Shanann Watts was a smart, capable, and savvy woman. She made many good choices in life. With the information she had at the time, choosing Chris as her husband seemed like a very smart decision. The way he presented himself to Shanann and the way he acted through most of their relationship made him appear to possess all the traits of what we think a "good" husband and father should be.

If Chris could fool everyone—including his own wife and family—into thinking he was the perfect husband and father, then couldn't Shanann be any of us who believe we have made smart and logical decisions in our lives? In fact, many people who have closely followed this case have commented that they don't know whom to trust anymore. Some women have looked at their gentle and loving husbands with a side eye and thought to themselves, *Do we ever really know someone else?* That question, at its core, is the most chilling part of this story. Do we ever truly know anyone? Even the people we live with day in and day out and think we know inside out?

Some people assume that there must have been *some* red flags with Chris, and it's just that we didn't know about them, or, Shanann didn't tell anyone about some things that could have gone on behind closed doors. I've thought about this myself, especially at the beginning of the case. As a psychotherapist, I know more than anyone that people do a great job of painting an impeccable façade, especially on social media. Often the people who post the most glowing statements about their romantic partners have the darkest secrets. When I was on Facebook at one point in my life, I noticed that the people who were the most enthusiastic about their partners publicly were messaging me privately asking for recommendations for a couples' therapist.

I don't believe Shanann was hiding problems in her relationship with Chris and overcompensating on social media for it. She seemed to truly believe she had a great relationship with him, and he was very good to her for most of their time together. Months before her death, she recorded a video of appreciation for Chris from their home in Colorado and said, "I had some health challenges and then I met Chris. I met Chris because of those health challenges. My friend sent me a friend suggestion for him. It was actually his cousin's wife and I deleted it. I was like, I'm not interested, I don't wanna meet a guy! Buh bye! So, I deleted her friend suggestion for him. I was diagnosed two months later, and I went through one of the, I would say, darkest times of my life because things just got scarier, worse. I thought my life was crumbling underneath me and I didn't know which way to turn…and I got a friend request from Chris. I was in a really, really, really bad place and I got a friend request from Chris on Facebook. And I was like, ah what the heck I'm never gonna meet him. Accept. Well, one thing led to another and eight years later, we have two kids, we live in Colorado and he's the best thing that has *ever* happened to me…At that time he knew me at my worst, and he accepted me. And because of my health challenges, because I got so sick, I let him in. and he only knew me at that time. He knew me at my worst, and he accepted me, and you know, through your vows, through sickness and everything, he's been there. He was the one that let me lay on him and fall asleep for three and a half hours on his lap while he had to pee. He is the best thing that has ever, *ever* happened to me. I'm telling you, when I met Chris, I pushed him away. I gave every excuse for him to run. I mean, every…I gave him an out every single day. And if you guys knew my story with Chris, you know I gave him an out. He went to my colonoscopy, I tortured him, I rejected him. I pushed him away time and time and time again, but when I canceled dates last minute, because that's how life is with my health challenges. You cancel things last minute and it's hard for people to get. It's hard for me to understand. But he stuck around, and he stuck around because he was the one for me and he is amazing, and I can't tell you how wonderful he is".

One month before he started the affair with Nikki, Chris surprised Shanann with thoughtful Mother's Day gifts, as he always had since she became a mother. This particular year, Chris framed all the important dates in their lives: their wedding day and the respective birthdays of their family. He included homemade picture frames decorated by the girls: Bella's was a photo of Chris and the girls, and CeCe's frame had a photo of Shanann and CeCe in it. Both photos were full of embraces and smiles.

When Chris started his affair with Nikki, Shanann's posts about her relationship on social media gradually diminished until they were practically nonexistent. The time she stopped posting lovey-dovey messages about Chris coincided with the time of the affair and when Chris did a total 180 on her. Shanann really believed she had a great marriage until she went to North Carolina for the summer. And why wouldn't she? Her husband doted on her, showed her constant affection, and he never fought with her.

Shanann was a very open and vulnerable person with those closest to her. As soon as problems with Chris began to emerge, she confided in her closest friends about it, and many of them were aware that the marriage was in trouble at the time of Shanann's disappearance. If Shanann was having problems in her marriage before this, it's likely she would have told someone, considering she told so many friends once things got bad with Chris. When she was confiding in close friend Addy over text message, she said, "*We've never had problems like this in our marriage, ever!*"

Shanann relied heavily on her relationships with family and friends for her well-being. She had very intimate bonds with people. Intimacy is when you can share your vulnerabilities with others, and Shanann was never afraid of doing that. Part of her job as a Le-Vel promoter was to portray a fabulous life, because success in multi-level marketing companies is dependent on not only sales, but recruiting others to join your team. Shanann wasn't going to air all her dirty laundry on social media, but those closest to her were very aware when things took a turn for the worst.

People want to believe there were "red flags" with Chris because everyone wants to think that if they were in this situation, they would be able to spot someone capable of doing what he did and get out before it was too late. This is most likely a situation where if there were any "red flags" before he met Nikki, they would be incredibly subtle, and nothing that would suggest someone capable of murdering his pregnant wife, let alone his own children.

Abby Ellin, author of "*Duped: Double Lives, False Identities and the Con Man I Almost Married*"[11] who did extensive

---

11. Ellin, Abby. *Duped: Double Lives, False Identities, and the Con Man I Almost Married*. New York: PublicAffairs, 2019.

research on pathological liars said, "Some people are just really good at lying, and there aren't going to be any signs." Ellin goes on to say that our need to have a "modicum of control" and to think we're smarter than we are leads us to believe that we would know if someone is deceiving us.

Diagnosis helps people make sense of "abnormal" behavior. Although there isn't always a "normal" way of acting and behaving, abnormal behavior or pathology can be thought of as something that significantly interferes with relationships and functioning in life. However, any experienced clinician understands that diagnosis is not always that simple, and you can't always put people in neat little boxes. Furthermore, there are issues with diagnosis and our current healthcare system, and that could be a whole other book!

CHAPTER 18

"Exploitation. Entitlement. Empathy Impairments."

Some of the media experts such as Dr. Phil and well-regarded former FBI criminal profiler Candice DeLong believe that Chris Watts is a "psychopath" and/or a "malignant narcissist." It is certainly possible that he is, based on all the available information, but first let's examine all the possible diagnoses that have discussed.

Psychopath? Sociopath?

The words "psychopath" and "sociopath" are often thrown around interchangeably. William Hirstein, a philosopher and scientist, described the history of psychopaths and sociopaths and how they differ: "In the early 1800s, doctors who worked with mental patients began to notice that some of their patients who appeared outwardly normal had what they termed 'moral depravity' or 'moral insanity,' in what they seemed to possess no sense of ethics or of the rights of other people. The term 'psychopath' was first applied to these people around 1900. The term was changed to 'sociopath' in the 1930s to emphasize the damage they do to society. Currently, researchers have returned to using the term 'psychopath.' Some of them use that term to refer to a more serious disorder, linked to genetic traits, which produces more dangerous individuals, while continuing to use 'sociopath' to refer to less dangerous people who are seen more as products of their environment, including their upbringing. Some people like to make a distinction between 'primary psychopaths,' who are thought to be genetically caused, and 'secondary psychopaths,' seen more as a product of their environments."[12]

Although there has been a lot of debate about the distinction between sociopathic and psychopathic behavior, sociopathy can be thought of as something severely wrong with one's conscience; psychopathy is characterized as a complete lack of conscience regarding others. [13] "Psychopath" and "sociopath" are not technical diagnoses in the DSM-5 but are under the umbrella of a personality disorder known as "antisocial personality disorder." Some mental health professionals believe there is a distinction between a psychopath and a sociopath, while others argue that they are essentially the same thing.

In order to be diagnosed with a personality disorder as

12. Antisocial Personality Disorder." Psychology Today. Sussex Publishers. Accessed October 25, 2019. https://www.psychologytoday.com/us/conditions/antisocial-personality-disorder.

classified by the DSM, one must have impairments in personality both self and interpersonal. Symptoms often start in adolescence or early adulthood and span the course of a lifetime. Personality disorders cause difficulty in interpersonal relationships (conflicts, diffuse or lack of relationships) and significant interference in social situations and the person's life. The technical criteria for diagnosing a personality disorder in the DSM-5 is:

- Significant impairment in self and interpersonal (empathy or intimacy) functioning.

- One or more pathological personality traits.

- Impairments in personality stable across time and consistent in situations.

- Personality impairments not better understood as a normative part of a developmental stage or social environment.

- Impairments not caused only by substance use or a medical condition.

The DSM 5 defines antisocial personality disorder (ASPD) as someone having three or more of the following traits: 1. Regularly breaks or flouts the law, 2. Constantly lies and deceives others, 3. Is impulsive and doesn't plan ahead, 4. Can be prone to fighting and aggressiveness, 5. Has little regard for the safety of others, 6. Irresponsible, can't meet financial obligations, 7. Doesn't feel remorse or guilt.

In the DSM 5, conduct disorder is very much like ASPD, but ASPD is considered a diagnosis for ages eighteen and older, and conduct disorder needs to be present before the age of eighteen in order to meet the criteria for diagnosis. conduct disorder is defined by the following: Aggression to people and animals (uses bullying, initiates physical fights, has a weapon that can cause physical harm, physically cruel to people and animals, has stolen while confronting a person, has forced someone into sexual activity), Destruction of property, Deceitfulness or theft, Serious violations of rules. There are varying degrees of severity to conduct disorder and can be classified as mild, moderate, or severe. Some of the infamous serial killers showed these signs before the age of eighteen and therefore could potentially be classified as having antisocial personality disorder preceded by conduct disorder. For example, Jeffrey Dahmer, Dennis Rader (aka BTK), and Lee Boyd Malvo (one of the DC Snipers) all had a history of killing and torturing animals in their childhood.

Robert Hare, a researcher in the field of criminal psychology, developed the *Hare Psychopathy Checklist* after working with psychopaths over many years. On the checklist, there are twenty traits that each have a score between 0-2. The highest mark someone can achieve is 40. If someone rates over 30 in the test, they are said to be "psychopathic." The traits are pathological lying, glib and superficial charm, grandiose sense of self, need for stimulation, cunning and manipulative, lack of remorse or guilt, shallow emotional response, callousness and lack of empathy, parasitic lifestyle, poor behavioral controls, sexual promiscuity, early behavior problems, lack of realistic long-term goals, impulsivity, irresponsibility, failure to accept responsibility, many short-term marital relationships, juvenile delinquency, revocation of conditional release, and criminal versatility.

What is a narcissist?

The word "narcissist" has been used liberally in the media and with many different definitions. Generally, when people think of narcissism, they think of someone unhealthily obsessed with themselves. In the world of social media, narcissism can be thought of as a person who takes tons of selfies and is preoccupied with their appearance. People also equate narcissism with self-obsession and selfishness. All these things are true, but they do not mean one qualifies for a diagnosis of narcissistic personality disorder (NPD), which is an official personality disorder in the DSM. According to the DSM, between 0.5 and 1 percent of the general population meet the criteria for NPD and 50-75 percent diagnosed are men. If you've heard someone labeled as a "narcissist," it doesn't necessarily mean they have NPD, but they could fall on a spectrum of narcissism.

In order to meet the criteria for NPD, a person must demonstrate grandiosity, lack of empathy for others, and a need for admiration. They often believe they are superior or special. Their self-esteem is incredibly fragile, and they do not take even the slightest criticism well. If they experience any *perceived* criticism, they fly off the handle, which is referred to as "narcissistic rage." In order to be diagnosed with the disorder, a person must have five or more of the following symptoms: 1. Exaggerates own importance, 2. Is preoccupied with fantasies of success, power, beauty, intelligence, or ideal romance, 3. Believes he or she is special and can only be understood by other special people or institutions, 4. Requires constant attention and admiration from others, 5. Has unreasonable expectations of favorable treatment, 6. Takes advantage of others to reach his or her own goals, 7. Disregards the feelings of others, lacks empathy, 8. Is often envious of others or believes other people are envious of him or her, 9. Shows arrogant behaviors and attitudes. Many people with NPD are thought to be in positions of power and fame, such as actors, politicians, CEOs, doctors, and lawyers.

Covert, communal and malignant narcissists

Several professionals in the mental health field identify different types of narcissists that deviate from the criteria of someone with classic NPD. Another type of narcissist is commonly referred to as a "covert" or "introverted/passive aggressive narcissist." These types of narcissists do not seek the type of outward admiration and attention as those with classic NPD do, but they do share some of the hallmark traits of NPD, such as lack of empathy and taking advantage of others.

Dr. Craig Malkin in his *Psychology Today* article, "What's the Single Greatest Danger of Covert Narcissism?"[14] describes covert narcissism as follows: "They may be quiet or shy, and often are, but inside, in other words—covertly—they still harbor overblown visions of themselves and their future: dreams for example of one day being discovered for their remarkable creativity, intelligence, or insight. What's different about covert narcissists is that because they're introverted, they don't advertise their inflated egos. They agree with statements like 'I feel I'm temperamentally different from most people,' and 'Even when I'm in a group of friends, I often feel very alone and uneasy.'" These two statements seem like things Chris might agree with about himself based on his interviews.

Malkin also describes another sub-type of narcissism, what he refers to as "communal narcissism." Because all narcissists are addicted to feeling special and unique, they are willing to do whatever it takes to get their "high." A communal narcissist is often described as the most helpful, caring person in the room. The difference between an authentically caring person and a communal narcissist is the communal narcissist is doing nice things only to get affirmation and admiration, and these are the things a true narcissist wants the most. Communal narcissists are those who give generously to

---

14. What's the Single Greatest Danger of Covert Narcissism?" Psychology Today. Sussex Publishers. Accessed October 25, 2019. https://www.psychology today.com/us/blog/romance-redux/201712/what-s-the-single-greatest-danger-covert-narcissism.

charity, work in nonprofits, are presidents of the PTA, or religious leaders. They always do good deeds for others. They are martyrs.

The communal types may boast about all their generosity and let you know about all the selfless work they have done, but it is also possible that they are covert and won't brag about their good deeds. The bottom line is this: They thrive off approval and being helpful to others, and those behaviors are what elicits praise from others.

Some of the criteria on the Communal Narcissism inventory list (on a scale of 1-7) are statements about how one may feel about themselves: "I am the most helpful person I know," "I am the best friend someone can have," "I am (going to be) the best parent on this planet," "I am the most caring person in my social surrounding," "I greatly enrich others' lives," "I am an amazing listener," "I have a very positive influence on others," "I am generally the most understanding person," "I am extraordinarily trustworthy." There are other statements on the inventory checklist that are more grandiose and relate to saving the world or being famous for good deeds, but all the traits are focused on aspects of themselves that make them feel special and unique. The higher the score, the more likely someone is a communal narcissist.

In Peg Streep's article in *Psychology Today* "The Communal Narcissist: Another Wolf Wearing a Sheep Outfit,"[15] she

---

15. "The Communal Narcissist: Another Wolf Wearing a Sheep Outfit." Psychology Today. Sussex Publishers. Accessed October 25, 2019. https://www.psychologytoday.com/us/blog/tech-support/201605/the-communal-narcissist-another-wolf-wearing-sheep-outfit.

sums up the communal narcissist perfectly when she says: "The reality is that he or she lacks the ability to empathize, is still a game-player, and carries all the other traits generally associated with narcissism. He or she is involved in community *only* as a validation of self."

Again, in "What's the Single Greatest Danger of Covert Narcissism?", Dr. Malkin describes the traits of narcissism and how there is a spectrum on how pathological the narcissist is:

"The more addicted a narcissist is to feeling special, the more likely they are to become disordered, displaying the core of pathological narcissism, or Triple E, as I call it:

Exploitation: Doing whatever it takes to feel special, regardless of the cost to those around them

Entitlement: Acting as the world owes them and should bend to their will

Empathy Impairments: Becoming so fixated on the need to feel special that other people's feelings cease to matter. At this end of the spectrum, we find narcissistic personality disorder.

And herein lies the answer to the question: Built into the definition of NPD is manipulation (exploitation). The more severe the disorder, the more likely the exploitative style is to become abusive. That means *anyone* with NPD can become abusive *over time*. And abuse is dangerous. Disordered narcissists (those with NPD) can be calculating about hiding their abusive side, whether they're extroverted, introverted, or communal, because *all* disordered narcissists are, manipulative."

Toward the end of his wife's and daughter's lives, Chris not only seemed addicted to feeling special, but he also met the criteria for "Triple E." Keep this in your mind when we revisit these traits later in this book.

Finally, there is the "malignant narcissist." Dr. Phil has repeatedly referred to Chris Watts as a malignant narcissist. Malignant narcissism is not in the DSM. Malignant narcissists are thought to be the extreme version of NPD, mixing narcissism and antisocial personality disorder, and often displaying paranoia. Pathological lying, violence, extreme lack of empathy and manipulation are other traits of a malignant narcissist.[16]

Born with a "bad brain"

Psychopathy, sociopathy, and narcissism and how they arise are not entirely understood. Is it nature, nurture, or a combination of both?

Interesting studies done on the brains of psychopaths and narcissists have come up with some intriguing findings and similarities between the disorders. Likely, issues in the psychopathic brain are related to empathy and social emotional abilities, which would make sense, considering psychopaths and narcissists are not able to feel authentic empathy.

One neuroimaging study found those with NPD to have problems with the right anterior insular cortex-region of the

---

16. Lee, Rebecca. "The Ties Between Crime and Malignant Narcissism." World of Psychology, July 8, 2018. https://psychcentral.com/blog/the-ties-between-crime-and-malignant-narcissism/.

brain suspected to be associated with empathy.[17]

Another 2013 study from the University of Germany examined the brain patterns of individuals with NPD. The group that met criteria for the condition demonstrated smaller gray matter volume within areas of the brain associated with emotional empathy that could suggest the brains of those with clinical NPD have empathy deficits in the brain.[18]

As for psychopathy and brain studies, neuroscientist Dr. Kent Kiehl has been using fMRIs (functional MRIs) to detect brain abnormalities in people with psychopathy. He has found defects in the paralimbic system that he believes relate to psychopathy. The paralimbic system is a network of brain regions, stretching from the orbital frontal cortex to the posterior cingulate cortex, that are involved in processing emotion, inhibition and attentional control as the causes for psychopathy.[19]

A few studies on genetic traits of narcissists include one where 304 pairs of twins from Beijing China participated in

17. "The Narcissistic Self and Its Psychological and Neural ..." Accessed October 25, 2019. https://pdfs.semanticscholar.org/111b/26029454e95bf730494dd f88e920a6d93fff.pdf.

18. Schulze, Lars, Isabel Dziobek, Aline Vater, Hauke R. Heekeren, Malek Bajbouj, Babette Renneberg, Isabella Heuser, and Stefan Roepke. "Gray Matter Abnormalities in Patients with Narcissistic Personality Disorder." Journal of Psychiatric Research. Pergamon, June 15, 2013. https://www.sciencedirect. com/science/article/pii/S002239561300157X.

19. McAleer, Kelly. "The Brain of a Psychopath: Using FMRI Technology to Detect Brain Abnormalities, Part I." Psych Central.com, March 27, 2019. https://blogs.psychcentral.com/forensic-focus/2010/03/the-brain-of-a-psy-chopath-using-fmri-technology-to-detect-brain-abnormalities-part-i/.

a study to explore the idea that narcissism is potentially heritable. The study found that narcissistic traits, intrapersonal grandiosity, and interpersonal entitlement are moderately heritable. The study also found that "Intrapersonal grandiosity and interpersonal entitlement have different genetic and environmental bases. About 92-93% of their genetic and environmental contributions can be explained by unique genetic and unique environmental factors, respectively."[20]

Nature, nurture, or both?

There have also been longstanding debates about the nature versus nurture topic among scientists and psychologists. In reference to genes versus parenting, in an interview with *Psychology Today*,[21] Robert Plomin, a behavioral geneticist, says, "What looks like the effects of the environment in which one grows up is often largely a reflection of genetic differences. For example, the best predictor of whether you'll get divorced is whether your parents did, and people say, "Sure, if your parents were divorced, you had bad role models for married life.' But research with adoptees shows that your parents' divorce would predict yours even if you were adopted at birth and raised in a different family. The problem is that

---

20. Luo, Yu L, Huajian Cai, and Hairong Song. "A Behavioral Genetic Study of Intrapersonal and Interpersonal Dimensions of Narcissism." PloS one. Public Library of Science, April 2, 2014. https://www.ncbi.nlm.nih.gov/pmc/articles/PMC3973692/.

21. "What We Get Wrong About the Influence of Parents." Psychology Today. Sussex Publishers. Accessed October 25, 2019. https://www.psychologytoday.com/us/articles/201811/what-we-get-wrong-about-the-influence-parents.

the environment is out there—you can see it and feel it—and you never see genetics. Parents can make a difference, obviously, to some extent. But if you're having kids because you think they're a block of clay to mold into what you want them to be, it's really important to know that although you may be able to control their behavior, you're not changing who they fundamentally are."

This particular quote makes a lot of sense when you look at siblings from the same family. It explains how children can be raised in the exact same environment and turn out totally different from each other. This is one of the reasons it is important not to jump to place blame on parents when their child does something awful.

Genetics and the brain seem to have an obvious influence on criminal behavior and personality pathology, but environmental factors can certainly contribute, influence, and exacerbate issues that are already there.

The origins of narcissism

NPD has its roots in ancient Greek mythology. Although the story varies, the basic idea of it goes something like this. Narcissus was a very handsome, self-absorbed man who, one day, saw his reflection in the water and could not stop staring at it. He became so enamored with himself that he was unable to leave. Disappointed that the love for himself could not be reciprocated, he melted away and turned into a flower.

The psychoanalytic theory posits that the core of narcissism is thought to be the exact opposite of its definition:

narcissism is more about insecurity and low self-worth as opposed to high self-esteem and an abundance of self-love. Narcissism as a personality disorder is a defense mechanism developed at some point in childhood that is in place to help protect the child from feeling the pain of having a vague sense of self, low self-esteem and often feeling unaccepted, unloved, and unwanted.

If a parenting style is neglectful, authoritarian, or abusive, a child can develop a grandiose sense of self to cope with those feelings of inferiority and abandonment. Every child has a deep need for validation, affirmation, and approval. They can get it from others, or they learn that they can give it to themselves if their caregivers didn't provide it for them. Many believe that narcissistic defenses are a way for the child to keep themselves feeling unique and special as they go throughout life to cope with severe feelings of inadequacy or neglect.

Parents also model behaviors for their children. Often, parents are the only models a child has. If a child has never felt unconditionally loved, then usually they won't know what unconditional love means or how it feels. If there is low empathy in the family of origin, a child can either mimic the low empathy or go in the complete opposite direction and over empathize because they understand the pain of having their needs and feelings neglected.

Many times, narcissists aren't even aware that they are deeply insecure and self-hating at their core. The mask they have constructed to protect themselves from these wounds is on so tightly that their deepest longings are locked in their subconscious, often impenetrable.

Otto Kernberg, a psychoanalyst who is most known for his work on narcissistic pathology believed that, "NPD is rooted in the child's defense against a cold and unempathetic parent, usually the mother. Emotionally hungry and angry at the depriving parent(s), the child withdraws into a part of the self that the parents value, whether looks, intellectual ability, or some other skill or talent. This part of the self becomes hyperinflated and grandiose. Any perceived weaknesses are 'split off' into a hidden part of the self. Splitting gives rise to a lifelong tendency to swing between extremes of grandiosity and feelings of emptiness and worthlessness."[22]

Heinz Kohut, another psychoanalyst who focused on narcissism, also believed that a narcissist is made when he/she is deprived of sufficient attention from the mother and then falls in love with him/herself in order to compensate for the lack of attention and love from the mother.

The social learning theory of narcissism is one that makes more obvious sense, focusing on the over-indulgent parent. When parents over-value their children and act as if their child can do no wrong, the child develops an over-inflated sense of self-worth. The child may internalize the belief that they are "special" or that they deserve privileges over others. When children are taught to think they are the center of the universe and not to consider other people's feelings and

---

22. "Narcissistic Personality Disorder." Encyclopedia of Mental Disorders. Accessed October 25, 2019. http://www.minddisorders.com/Kau-Nu/Narcissistic-personality-disorder.html.

needs, they will grow into adults who act on those beliefs.

In an interesting study about the origins of narcissism in children, researchers found that healthy self-esteem was predicted by *parental warmth* and not parental overvaluation.[23] This means that a lack of parental warmth is more of a risk factor for a child to develop narcissistic traits than for a child who is overvalued by the caretakers. There is also a stark difference between parental warmth and parental overvaluation. Just because a parent is over-indulgent and over-complimentary of the child does not mean the child is receiving warmth or receiving the feeling that they are unconditionally loved. They may instead feel that love is conditional because, in some families, it often is. If the child steps out of the image the parent has constructed for them, they know they will not be accepted and therefore develop the belief that love has strings attached.

Are psychopathy, sociopathy, and narcissism treatable? The concept of psychopathy, sociopathy, and narcissism and whether they are treatable disorders is a controversial topic. Some theorists believe these disorders are not curable but treatable, and others believe personality disorders are not treatable, depending on how extreme the pathology is.

One of the reasons narcissism is so hard to treat is because narcissists almost never come to psychotherapy. Narcissists

---

23. Brummelman, Eddie, Sander Thomaes, Stefanie A. Nelemans, Bram Orobio de Castro, Geertjan Overbeek, and Brad J. Bushman. "Origins of Narcissism in Children." PNAS. National Academy of Sciences, March 24, 2015. https://www.pnas.org/content/112/12/3659.

don't think they have a problem, and they certainly think they know better than everyone else anyway. Usually, if a narcissist seeks therapy, it is either because they have hit rock bottom and have no other options, or they are going for couples' therapy. In couples' therapy, a narcissist believes they can convince the therapist to collude with them and tell their partner that the partner is the problem. A traditional narcissist blames his or her partner for all the problems and will agree to go to couples' therapy *if* they believe the therapist will also see the partner as a problem. Narcissistic people have their defenses locked in place. They are almost impenetrable, and self-reflection or self-awareness is almost non-existent. You will never get accountability from them, and if you do, it's usually self-serving and will benefit them in some way. As you may recall, Chris refused to go to counseling with Shanann, and he has not yet received any form of psychological evaluation or counseling in prison.

In my work with couples, the classic narcissistic types have vocalized that they believe they are smarter or know more about my field than I do. They have also convinced themselves that they have won me over with their charm. The narcissist believes in their own charm and manipulation and think they can work their magic on everyone. They don't believe that someone can see through their manipulation because they believe they are the smartest and most convincing person on the planet. This is their downfall because overconfidence is the easiest way they make mistakes. People with high levels of pathological narcissism have little self-awareness, and their relationships are laden with conflict because they don't see how they contribute to problems.

More rarely, I have seen a few covert narcissists in my practice, and these are the ones that shock me the most. The covert types are often very likeable and humble on the surface. They work hard in therapy and seem like they really want to improve their relationship. Later, I might come to find out that they were lying the entire time and engaging in manipulative and destructive behaviors, most often, infidelity, behind their partner's back.

Treating narcissism is possible, depending on the severity of the disorder, but doing so is not easy. Some ways to work with narcissists include trying to help change their ways of relating to others, helping them see their vulnerabilities as strengths rather than weaknesses, and attempting to teach them empathy. Some studies have shown that narcissists are capable of empathy but do not put in the effort to take another's perspective.[24]

Treating psychopathy, given the limitations for empathy in the psychopathic brain, often involves teaching the psychopathic person that there are pro-social ways to deal with their problems and get what they want out of life, instead of resorting to anti-social tactics.

---

24. Sedikides, Constantine, and Erica Hepper. "Moving Narcissus: Can Narcissists Be Empathic?" Personality and Social Psychology Bulletin. Accessed October 25, 2019. https://www.academia.edu/6853822/Moving_Narcissus_Can_narcissists_be_empathic.

The narcissist in a romantic relationship

When a narcissist pursues and enters a romantic relationship, a unique pattern and dynamic exist. Countless articles and books have been written about the emotional turmoil and abuse that narcissists inflict on those who love them.

One of the most important things to know about what a narcissist looks for in any relationship is what is referred to as "narcissistic supply." In her *Psych Central* article, "What is Narcissistic Supply?"[25] Dr. Sharie Stines says, "Narcissists are all about protecting the self—at the expense of the other. Because of the narcissist's inability to connect in a healthy way with another person, he uses a system of relating that is created in order for the narcissist to take care of himself. Instead of healthy connection, a narcissist seeks for *'narcissistic supply.'*"

Dr. Stines states that some forms of narcissistic supply are as follows: attention, compliments/praise, sex, a feeling of power and control, accomplishments, an addictive substance or activity, and emotional energy (positive or negative). The narcissist is fueled by narcissistic supply and finds value in people only when they are giving them supply. The supply further reinforces the narcissist's pathological need to be validated, admired, needed, wanted, and adored. Without narcissistic supply, the narcissist is nothing. You are useful to a narcissist only if you are providing them with the supply

---

25. Stines, Sharie. "What Is Narcissistic Supply?" The Recovery Expert, July 8, 2019. https://pro.psychcentral.com/recovery-expert/2019/02/what-is-narcissistic-supply/.

they need. When you think of narcissists, don't think of them as people with real attachments. If they have people close to them in their lives, it's because they are giving the narcissist the supply that he/she craves and thrives off.

A narcissist (psychopaths and sociopaths as well) does not have depth of real emotion or empathy to truly relate to other human beings, but they are great mimics. They understand exactly what to say and do to win people over. They can also parrot empathy, which can make them seem like caring and kind individuals.

In the initial pursuit phase of a romantic relationship, a narcissist will find their "target." This is usually someone who will provide them with the type of supply they are looking for, probably someone they perceive as having high amounts of empathy. This is because highly empathic people are usually more forgiving once a narcissist lets the mask slip. Narcissists also prey upon those they perceive as weak or in moments of weakness. The weakness in the person gives the narcissist the upper hand, and the narcissist can swoop in and act as the savior, gaining the supply they need to fuel them. As you may recall, Chris pursued Shanann when she was at a very low point in her life.

The first phase of a narcissistic relationship is the "love bombing" phase. Love bombing is when someone makes overwhelming and extreme "romantic" gestures in order to win someone over. Love bombing can include things we may see in romantic movies. In fact, romantic comedies can be problematic because they reinforce the idea that the over-the-top gestures early on in a relationship are "normal" and play into the fantasy of what many people believe a romantic relationship should look like.

The truth is, that love bombing is often a huge red flag. If someone you don't know well seems certain about you being the one for them, that may be reason to give you pause. It takes a long time to get to know a person well, which is why we date before we commit. A narcissist will act as if you are "the one" right away and will tell you so. They may say things like: "You're the one for me," "What we have is unique and special," "I can't see my life without you," and other similar statements. They can engage in stalker-like behavior, but because of romantic comedies and the deep need most of us have to feel loved, appreciated, and special, we may be drawn in by these gestures instead of skeptical.

At first, a narcissist may wine and dine you at the fanciest restaurants, shower you with gifts, or show up unexpectedly at your home or place of work. Not everyone who makes romantic gestures in the beginning of a relationship is a narcissist, but sometimes, you will have a gut sense and feel creeped out by the attention. Other people may feel they have finally found someone who treats them right and conclude that this is the way they should be treated. Of course, you should feel adored and prioritized in a relationship, but also try to be discerning about what feels "normal" versus what could be a manipulative agenda.

The second stage of a narcissistic relationship is called the "devaluing phase." Once a narcissistic person feels more comfortable and that they've won you over, they will enter the devaluing phase. All the sudden, the person you are in a relationship with starts to show signs that they aren't the person you thought they were. I refer to this as the "Jekyll and Hyde" phase. This is when the narcissist's mask starts to slip. They may make a subtle underhanded comment, or they may say something outright mean and cruel. They may withdraw emotionally and not speak to you or grow cold and distant for a few days for no reason. The devaluing can consist of cruelty, all types of abuse, and withdrawal.

With the flip of a switch, the person who once adored you so much is treating you with contempt and hostility. This can be incredibly confusing, especially for those who have never experienced this type of behavior before. What makes it even more confusing is the narcissist can revert to the ideal partner you fell in love with very quickly. You breathe a sigh of relief because you think the partner you fell in love with is back. You may rationalize or make excuses that they were just having a bad day or a bad week. However, this cycle of emotional abuse continues, often with the dark side becoming more of the norm with few glimpses of the "nice" person. When the "nice" person shows up, it is to keep you around and to give you the glimmer of hope so you will stay.

Part of the agenda in the love bombing phase is that it is another way the narcissist gets supply. If the person the narcissist is pursuing is the most attractive, alluring, and special person, the fact that the narcissist has won this amazing person over affirms to them that they are uniquely special by association. I think this is one of the reasons Chris was so drawn to Shanann in the beginning. In his conversations with Cadle, he describes looking at Shanann's photo for the first time and thinking she was the most beautiful woman he had ever seen.

In Craig Malkin's book, *Rethinking Narcissism*,[26] he describes how love bombing can turn to devaluing. "They stop thinking that their partners are the best or most important people in the room because they need to claim that distinction for themselves. And they lose the capacity to see the world from any point of view other than their own. These are the true narcissists, and at their worst, they also display two other traits of a so-called "dark triad": a complete lack of remorse and a penchant for manipulation."

A narcissistic person may also play the victim. They may give a sob story of how they were unwanted or unloved as a child or with previous romantic partners. A narcissist will often act like a martyr. Highly empathic people may feel sorry for a narcissist and want to swoop in and save them. Empathic people will think that all the narcissist needs is unconditional love, and then they will be cured. The sad truth is, no amount of unconditional love will be enough for a narcissistic person because they view people as objects that are only there to fulfill their needs. No one else's needs matter, and a narcissist is almost always incapable of real love.

The final phase in the narcissistic relationship is the

---

26. Malkin, Craig. *Rethinking Narcissism: The Secret to Recognizing and Coping with Narcissists*. New York: Harper Perennial, 2016.

"discard" phase. Some people stay in relationships with narcissists for their lifetimes, but many have experienced the discard phase, which feels like the ultimate rejection. When the narcissist no longer has any need for you, or you no longer give them the narcissistic supply they need, they will discard you and want nothing to do with you anymore. The rejection will be completely cold and heartless, and you will be left feeling as if you meant nothing to them. A narcissist may also find a new person from whom they can get supply, and that person will seem more exciting because he or she comes with the thrill of a new relationship. If you're thinking this sounds like exactly what Chris did to Shanann, Bella, CeCe, and Nico, you're correct. "Discard" doesn't even seem to fully describe the enormity of what he did to them.

Most people describe the discard phase as feeling like the rug was pulled out from under them. The narcissist may dump you or leave you, and you may never hear from them again. They often leave their partners for a new relationship and show no remorse or empathy. The combination of years of devaluing and ultimately being discarded cause very serious psychological and emotional damage to the person on the receiving end. When a narcissist is done with you, they truly do not care anymore. It's almost as if you have the same value as garbage, and you can be discarded as such. People on the receiving end of this take it very personally and believe something is wrong with them. This couldn't be farther from the truth. Something is wrong with the narcissist, and they are incapable of depth of emotion or love.

What can be very confusing about a narcissistic type is that they *seem* as if they have emotion and empathy. Often, it's because their displayed kindness and adoration is what attracted you to them in the first place! They seemed more caring and warmer than anyone you had ever met before. This is because narcissists, sociopaths, and psychopaths are great mimics. Because a narcissist has little self-awareness and sense of self, they must mimic other people's behaviors and emotions to fit in. Psychopaths can seem even more genuine than "normal" people.[27] This is partly because normal people don't fake emotions all the time, but psychopaths must constantly practice portraying emotions, and they can get really good at it. If you are a person void of empathy, in order to manipulate people and get them to like you, you must become really good at convincing people you are nice, kind, and generous.

What is Chris Watts?

Now that we have taken a deeper look at the pathology of narcissists, sociopaths, and psychopaths, can we determine if Chris Watts actually is any of these things? Looking at his behavior *after* the crimes he committed, he certainly had the traits of a psychopathic person: impaired empathy and remorse, criminal behavior (at its worst because he murdered his entire family), pathological lying, manipulative, shallow

---

27. "Psychopaths Mimic Emotions Very Accurately: Brock Study." The Brock News, a news source for Brock University. Accessed October 26, 2019. https://brocku.ca/brock-news/2015/03/psychopaths-mimic-emotions-very-accurately-brock-study/.

emotional response, need for stimulation, sexual promiscuity, impulsivity, and failure to accept responsibility. Chris displayed a lot of these traits based on the information that has been made public *after the crime occurred*. What's interesting and terrifying about Chris Watts is, arguably he displayed almost *none* of these traits up until right before he murdered his wife and children.

It's unlikely we will ever get a functional MRI (fMRI) of Chris Watts's brain. It is certainly possible that he may have areas in the brain where empathy and emotion are compromised. If that is the case, and he has a brain that makes it difficult for him to empathize or experience genuine human emotion or connection, his environment and circumstances still would have likely played a smaller role in his becoming a murderer. It is important to say that environment and upbringing are not the reasons Chris killed his family. There are many people who have had far worse childhoods than Chris, and none of them resorted to killing their families. This is strong evidence that, although stressful situations and environmental factors could have helped fuel Chris's murderous tendencies, they are not the reason for it. You must be a deeply disturbed individual to murder your own children, especially in the way Chris chose to do it.

In order to try to make sense of the most senseless crime one can imagine, I will try to construct a theory on what could have potentially gone wrong. First, we need to start in childhood.

CHAPTER 19

"Was I born that way?"

Attachment Theory and Imago

I am a certified Imago Relationship Therapist, and one of the things I pay close attention to is attachment and development in childhood, because it clearly plays a role in how we choose our romantic partners in adulthood. In short, the Imago theory looks closely at the connection between our unmet needs and frustrations in our adult romantic relationships and how they are connected to our childhood experiences with primary caregivers. More on that later.

Before I discuss the Imago theory in depth and how it relates to Chris and Shanann, I want to highlight some key points of what is known as, "attachment theory."

Attachment theory was born out of the work of psychiatrist John Bowlby and developmental psychologist Mary Ainsworth, who theorized that there is significant importance placed on the child's relationship with the mother that affects social, emotional, and cognitive development of the child.

Bowlby's work with James Robertson observed that, as infants, children experienced *intense* distress when separated from their mothers. Even if the infant was fed by an alternate caregiver, the infant still experienced anxiety. Of course, this makes sense because for the infant to survive, they need to have an attachment to their mother, the source of food and security.

Bowlby's theory also believes that all children are born with an innate desire to form attachment to others for survival. He suggests that infants initially form only one primary attachment and need that attachment figure as their secure base for exploring the world. This plays a part in the future of the child, as this primary relationship influences all future social relationships. If things go wrong during the most critical years in attaching (0-5 years old), then serious consequences in relationships can show up later in life.

Most important, a securely attached child will have received warmth, nurturing, attention, and comfort from their primary caregiver. Children who are securely attached feel protected and seen by their caregivers. They know they can rely and depend on them to meet their needs. As children get older, their need to separate from their caregivers intensifies, but they still need the reassurance that they can come back to a reliable caregiver if need be.

In Imago Relationship Theory, no matter how ideal one's childhood is, no one comes out completely unscathed. In childhood we all eventually develop something called "early wounding." It is impossible for a child to get all their needs met in childhood, and no matter how great a parent is, all parents are imperfect and cannot meet *all* the needs of a child. When a child starts to learn that a certain need of theirs cannot be met, they develop adaptations and defenses that are put in place to help them block hurt and "survive." "Surviving" in our family of origin means developing ways to make life as easy as possible given our circumstances.

Children can develop early wounding at any age. Even babies, as shown by attachment theory, can learn from birth that a primary caregiver cannot meet all their needs. In early childhood, for example, if there is a high conflict household, a child may learn if they stay quiet and do as they are told, they can avoid at least some conflict or punishment.

When we adapt to our environment, we also learn to shut off parts of ourselves we believe are shameful. The messages we receive about ourselves are both overt and subtle, and don't just come from primary caregivers. They come from everywhere: peers, teachers, people in our community, and the media. Everywhere we turn, we see messages about who we are, how we should act, and how we need to adapt to fit in. For example, if we are told we talk too much, we may become reserved in order to hide the part that we are being told is unacceptable and needs to be repressed. If the family dynamic is to constantly brush problems under the rug and not address them, then the child learns that problems should never be discussed, and they do not learn how to deal with issues in productive ways. The child may not have received these specific messages in verbal words, but the messages are implied and absorbed in actions, nevertheless. Sometimes the subtle and covert messages are more powerful than the explicit ones.

These messages and adaptations carry with us all the way into our adulthood. When we become adults, we don't remember or can't access the parts of us that we cut off in childhood. Those parts of ourselves are often connected to our unmet needs and re-accessing them in adulthood is important to our growth and healing. When we are born, we come into the world feeling fully alive. When we can't fully be ourselves, we lose part of that aliveness and authenticity. Part of our well-being and successful development relies on the extent in which we could be most like our authentic selves in childhood.

Chris Watts in childhood

Chris Watts was described as a quiet, shy, and socially awkward child by those who knew him. From interviews with him, Chris described his childhood as good, and he seemed to believe his needs were generally met by his family of origin. In his prison confession to Grahm Coder, Tammy Lee, and Dave Baumhover, he said his mother Cindy was the more "aggressive" partner in her marriage with his father Ronnie. He described his sister Jamie as a mother figure to him, which makes sense considering she was seven years older. Jamie was always open with him, curious about him, and wanted to know how he felt. Chris said his mother Cindy told him he was "hard to read" as a child, which may point to who he has always fundamentally been since birth. He knew he was different than others, in the sense that he didn't feel emotions in the same ways as others around him.

Chris looked up to Ronnie and trusted him more than anyone else in the family. Ronnie was an attentive father in the sense that he showed a genuine interest in Chris and his life. Ronnie would show up at all Chris's sports games, even when Chris wasn't playing, and they would do bonding activities together, such as going to the racetracks. Chris and Ronnie shared a love of cars, and that was meaningful and important to Chris. His relationship with Ronnie seemed to be the most authentic out of all his relationships and where he felt he could be most like his "real" self. Ronnie was, and still is Chris's hero.

From Shanann's perspective, as relayed from her friend in the police discovery documents (and it is unclear whether Chris had explicitly said this to her), it was alleged that Cindy was not a nurturing mother during Chris's childhood and teen years. Also, in police discovery, Shanann told her friend that Cindy was possessive and controlling of Chris, and that when they moved to Colorado, he was "so ready to get far away from the negativity they place in his life."

From Chris's perspective, emotion and dealing with conflict in a healthy way were not modeled for him in childhood. Chris, in his prison confession, stated, "I just don't show emotion as much as other people do. Even when the girls left North Carolina, Shanann's brother, dad were all crying when I left. I never saw my parents get like that when I left. Was I born that way? My dad couldn't speak at the sentencing hearing because he was going to lose it. It hit me because I've never seen him like that. No one has ever seen me that way either. I never saw my dad cry, so maybe it imprinted in my brain that I should never cry... even if something was wrong, I probably would never say anything because I would just deal with it myself. I don't know if growing up that way kept me that way. You deal with things on your own until they build up so much, and you can't deal with them. They take a hold of you in a way you never thought."

These are important insights into Chris's early childhood messages he internalized, and they speak to the importance of allowing children to have space to access all their emotions. Culturally, there has been an epidemic of teaching boys to cut themselves off from important emotions. Universal messages many boys receive include, "Don't cry," "Crying is weakness," "Don't show emotion," and "Don't be a pussy." But boys and men are deeply sensitive humans, and these messages encourage them to repress their basic needs and feelings. The issue I see with men consistently in my psychotherapy practice is like what Chris describes. They cut off from their emotions for so long that, when they finally come to the surface and erupt, they manifest in extreme anxiety, depression, relationship issues, rage, alcoholism, and more. When children grow up with parents who don't express much emotion and don't allow them to express their feelings, they can feel as if they can't depend on anyone, and that increases their risk for becoming adults with narcissistic traits.

I think it's important to say that I do not blame Cindy or Ronnie for Chris's lack of ability to deal with his emotions properly. The only information I have heard about Cindy's relationships with her family of origin was in Cadle's book, which referenced Cindy's relationship with her mother. In the book, it says, "Cindy and her mother did not get along; living just down the street her mother tried to control Cindy, tell her how to raise her children. Although his grandmother was extremely negative, that didn't rub off on Christopher."

Other than that, I have no idea what Ronnie's or Cindy's childhoods were like, but if they grew up in homes where emotion was not outwardly expressed and where problems were not discussed, then I wouldn't expect them to have an open family dynamic in their own family.

As one of my mentors likes to say, "No one teaches us how to be in relationships." If we don't have the right models, then we all just do the best we can without much guidance. Only in recent years, have trends in parenting advice been focused on helping children become emotionally vulnerable and process their feelings. In many families, there are messages that whenever there are problems, you suck it up and keep going.

Apparently, Cindy and Jamie did try to get Chris to open up as a child, so it does sound as if they wanted him to talk about his feelings and open up to them. My speculation is that, from the day he was born, he probably already had emotional vacancies and an inability to authentically connect with others or empathize. However, a "brush-things-under-the-rug" type household could have contributed to his lack of ability to deal with his relational issues in his marriage with Shanann and the other issues he was suppressing and not dealing with in a mature way.

From some of his comments, it seems that Chris almost felt jealous of Shanann's relationship with her family. He saw her parents cry when she left North Carolina, and he thought, "*I never saw my parents get like that when I left.*" He expresses what seems like a longing for someone to outwardly express those feelings toward him, to help him feel special. That was what Chris seemed to crave, and he may have started to resent Shanann for having what he didn't. In fact, in her *Daily Mail* exclusive, Cadle said that Chris was "mesmerized by Nikki. She showed him respect that he didn't feel like he'd ever been shown before."[28] It sounds like Chris felt he had a life-long pattern of feeling disrespected by the people in his life. Whether or not this was real or perceived by Chris, any feelings of disrespect over the years most likely fueled his anger and entitlement.

When Chris was older and in college, and Ronnie developed a cocaine addiction, Chris was as detached as ever. Remembering that time in his life, Chris says: "I don't think

---

28. Boyle, Louise. "Chris Watts Claims Obsession with Mistress Led to Him Murdering Family." Daily Mail Online. Associated Newspapers, October 4, 2019. https://www.dailymail.co.uk/news/article-7534027/Chris-Watts-claims-hadnt-met-mistress-wouldnt-murdered-family.html.

it affected me. It didn't deep down really hurt as much as I thought it would. It was kind of weird. When my mom and sister tried to talk to him about it, he would change the subject, and when I tried to talk to him about it, he would immediately change the subject. He was just coping with…I never came back home. I never really knew why he was doing it. After the fact, I knew he was coping with that. My mom thought he was having an affair because the money was going somewhere. I tried to talk to him about it. You could see it in his face, what drugs do to your face. His skin was loose, nose was bleeding all the time. You could see it in his eyes."

This is another example of the secrecy and shutting down in the family. Ronnie was turning to very unhealthy coping mechanisms to deal with his inability to deal with the difficult emotions of "losing" his son when Chris left the house for college. The secrecy and lack of communication fueled further anxiety in the family. Cindy knew the money was going somewhere and assumed he was having an affair. When we don't have enough information, we create stories, and our minds run away with those stories, creating anxiety. This example also shows Chris's potential lack of empathy and feelings. He expected to feel hurt, but he didn't because he doesn't seem capable of feeling the depth of what is expected with normal human emotions.

Childhood messages
As Chris said in his prison confession, he believed that he

would have to rely on himself for emotional support, and
he would have to deal with his problems by himself. It's not
that Cindy or Ronnie necessarily ever blatantly told him
that, but it's the story he may have told himself based on his
perception. In his childhood, some of his needs may have
been overlooked, partially because he couldn't vocalize them,
either because he didn't know what they were or didn't have
the emotional landscape. Or, he may have also interpreted
the unspoken family dynamic as a message that his emotional needs would not be met by his family and therefore,
he never vocalized them. The focus on emotional needs may
have been placed on the stronger personality types in the
family, such as Cindy and Jamie. Chris may have just faded
into the background and went about his business quietly.

In order for Chris to get his needs met, he believed he
would have to rely on himself to deal with issues as they
came up, but he would also have to find a way to get positive
attention given his personality limitations. He didn't have
the vivacious personality that attracted people to Jamie, so
he would have to figure out other ways to get people to like
him. Jamie was described as outgoing, extroverted, and popular, and Chris figured out those are often the types of people
who command attention. But Chris wasn't that type of
person. He remembers going with his grandmother to pick
up Jamie up from school, knowing that she would always be
the last one out of the building because she stopped to talk
to everybody. That was just her personality. Chris wasn't like
that and said somewhat defiantly that he never wanted to

be like Jamie anyway.

Somewhere along the way in his childhood, he learned that in order to get positive attention, he should assume the role of the "good boy." If he was kind, helpful, and quiet, he could be seen by others and could elicit praise for himself. When Chris remembers the type of child he was, he describes himself as the person who was always trying to "coax people down." One fight in third grade was the only trouble he ever had at school.

According to him, "I never really talked to many people. People knew who I was. I never spoke to many people. I didn't have a girlfriend in high school. I was under the radar. I didn't want to be part of a group or a clique. I didn't want a whole lot of friends."

This comment is particularly interesting because it shows Chris is trying to differentiate himself from Jamie. As she took the role of the likable, popular one, Chris would be in her shadow. Understanding that he was not the one to get the attention he secretly might have craved, he put up a defense by telling himself he didn't want to be like Jamie. He even said, "I was the opposite of her. Maybe I drew on that. I didn't want to be the popular one."

He certainly did an excellent job of constructing his identity as a person everyone liked, respected, and admired. Not one person in his past had anything bad to say about him. The unspeakable acts of violence he inflicted on his family shocked everyone who knew him because of his persona of perfection and goodness. One of his former teachers, Joe

Duty, told the *Fayetteville Observer*,[29] "Oh my God. This is a shock. He was one of the best students I ever had." Duty also spoke to the *Daily Beast*,[30] saying that he told Chris before he graduated, "If I ever have a student who was going to be tremendously successful, it's you."

"That's one of the smartest students I ever had," Duty said. "The guy had a photographic memory."

When the news first broke of the crime, one of Chris's high-school friends, Brandi Smith, told the *Daily Beast* that girls always had crushes on Chris and said, "Most of our conversations that I recall were about music and things like that. I was a bit of an outcast, and he kinda just seemed to understand me. Everyone liked him. It's actually amazing how many people that knew him completely turned on him and think he's this monster when he hasn't even been convicted." She went on to say, "Chris found himself as a father. Those girls brought him to life and out of his shell. He's not a crazy person. He's not a violent, abusive, or mean person. I'll be broken if he's convicted, and it was a lie, but there's a chance...and it's not fair that he's being crucified." Currently, with verbal and written confessions from Chris, it is

---

29. Futch, Michael. "Chris Watts, Accused of Killing Pregnant Wife, kids in Colorado, Has Fayetteville Ties." The Fayetteville Observer. The Fayetteville Observer, August 17, 2018. https://www.fayobserver.com/news/20180816/chris-watts-accused-of-killing-pregnant-wife-kids-in-colorado-has-fayetteville-ties.

30. Briquelet, Kate. "'Everyone Liked Him': Did Colorado Dad Chris Watts Lead a Double Life?" The Daily Beast. The Daily Beast Company, September 1, 2018. https://www.thedailybeast.com/everyone-liked-him-did-colorado-dad-chris-watts-lead-a-double-life.

true that he is a violent, abusive, and dangerous person. This quote from Brandi Smith shows just how skilled he was at portraying the complete opposite of the reality, and that is really quite frightening.

Lance Alfonso, another person from Chris's past who spoke to the *Daily Beast*, played recreational football with him when they were kids. He said Chris "was someone who wouldn't hurt a fly." Again, the contrast here is stark. The man who is described as someone who wouldn't hurt a fly plotted the murders of his family and was relentless about following through with his plan. He's even said in his letters to Cadle that he felt no remorse for his family. All he felt was that he was free to finally be with Nikki. All he cares about is himself.

Chris clearly loved feeling that people thought so highly of him. It's why he played the part of the nice guy so perfectly. It brought him the type of attention he needed. He enjoyed being different from the stereotypical male. He discovered that people liked him if he showed interest in them first, and if he was agreeable and bent over backward for others. In other words, he wanted to come across as a "people pleaser," and the likable Chris that everyone loved carried on into his adulthood. He was the friend, husband, and co-worker everyone wanted. All his coworkers had great things to say about him and fondly referred to him as "Rainman" because of his uncanny memory. After he dropped a lot of weight, they called him the "Silver Fox" for his gray hair and handsome features.

Chris, unlike a person with textbook psychopathic traits, seemed to care deeply about what other people thought of him, and he did not want anyone to see cracks in his carefully constructed mask. This is more in line with traits of a narcissist because narcissists rely heavily on the approval of others for their self-worth. In Cadle's book, one of the things she keeps repeating is how important it is for Chris to maintain a good image for others. She says, "It has been very important for Christopher what people think of him. He says he has always tried to be good to people, always be kind and helpful, and what people thought of him made a difference. It bothers him that people hate him, and, as he puts it, 'judge' him."

Chris felt a sense of pride when he talked about being "different" than the other guys Shanann had dated before him, including her ex-husband. He boasted about how Shanann's father liked him when he and Shanann first started dating.

"I think he really liked me the first time he met me because I was helping Shanann with this car from the dealership, and the wheel was about to fall off. I tried to fit it, and he (Frank) said, 'every other guy she dated would have let me do it.' I always wanted to help people, not hurt anyone. I would always do whatever I could to help. I didn't try to change her (Shanann). I let her be who she is. She knows what she wants, and she goes and gets it. Her first husband tried to control everything. He tried to be Sandi (Shanann's mother), and it didn't work. And she turned into... almost me. She was almost laid back and let him do what he was doing, and then learned she could be herself, and with me she could definitely be herself... and that's how it worked." In these comments, Chris feels good about being liked by being the guy who allows people to be themselves.

I believe that, in many situations in his life, Chris felt he could never be himself (whatever being himself meant to him), so it's interesting that part of his persona was to give the space to allow others to be themselves around him, often at the expense of himself. Chris also mentioned in the prison confession that he could never be himself around Shanann and was always nervous around her. Part of his desire to enter a relationship with Nikki was that he supposedly felt he could be more himself with her, even though he let her control much of their relationship and relied on her advice on everything, from counting calories, to a protein eating plan, to apartment hunting.

In one part of Chris's confession, Colorado Bureau of Investigation agent Tammy Lee tells Chris in reference to his texting coworker Kodi Roberts a day before the murders (to tell him he would go to the Cervi 319 location by himself), "There's a lot of people who said you normally wouldn't do that."

Chris, not understanding what Tammy meant, seemed shocked and aghast and replied,

"Said *I* wouldn't help somebody?" Chris seemed more upset to think that someone said he wouldn't be helpful than he did discussing Bella's post-mortem injuries. All of Chris's identity is wrapped up in being helpful. Even in prison with a life sentence, he is concerned about his

carefully constructed identity having holes poked in it. Cadle, in her visits with Chris relayed that he "feels famous. He's very careful, he wants people to think good of him. It's very hard for him to be called a monster or to be called a murderer. He doesn't like that."

• • •

Deep inside of him, there was an inner conflict brewing between the two opposing parts. There was his construct of "perfect" Chris, and then there was the "repressed rage" Chris. Chris needed to be "good" to fill his need to be admired and liked, but the other part of him resented always having to wear a mask and always having to do things for others.

This inner conflict can, in part, be attributed to the "Nice Guy Syndrome," coined by Dr. Robert Glover who describes these "nice guys" as men who try too hard to please others, neglect their own needs, and end up resentful, unhappy, and angry. In his book, *No More Mr. Nice Guy*,[31] he says the term "Nice Guy" is a misnomer because these "Nice Guys" aren't so nice after all.

In the book, Dr. Glover describes some of the not nice traits of Nice Guys as: 1. Dishonesty. This is because they avoid conflict at all costs and repress their feelings, which actually makes them dishonest with themselves and others.

---

31. Glover, Robert A. *No More Mr. Nice Guy: A Proven Plan for Getting What You Want in Love, Sex, and Life.*

2. Secretive. Because they need so much approval, they hide things that they think might upset others. 3. Manipulative. They use manipulation to get their needs met because they don't know how to ask for their needs in clear and direct ways. 4. Give to get. They give only to get something in return, and they become angry and resentful because they feel they give so much and don't get much back in return. 5. Passive-aggressive. They express their frustration and resentment in indirect ways. 6. Full of rage. "Though nice guys frequently deny ever getting angry, a lifetime of frustration and resentment creates a pressure cooker of repressed rage deep inside these men. This rage tends to erupt at some of the most unexpected and seemingly inappropriate times." 7. Addictive. Because the nice guy represses so much, he needs to relieve his stress, often through addictive behaviors. The most common is sexual compulsiveness.[32]. Difficulty with boundaries. Nice guys have a hard time saying no. They see others as the cause of their problems instead of self-reflecting.

Dr. Glover also notes in his book that nice guys are often mistaken for healthy males, when in fact, they have very unhealthy behaviors in relationships. Many of the women who end up in relationships with these men feel they have met a "real catch," like the way Shanann felt when Chris won her heart. But Glover remarks that, "Unfortunately the negative traits listed above find a way to ooze out into Nice Guys' lives and personal relationships. As a result, these men tend

---

32. [1] Glover, Robert A. No More Mr. Nice Guy: A Proven Plan for Getting What You Want in Love, Sex, and Life. Philadelphia: Running Press, 2017.

to swing back and forth between being nice and not-so-nice. I have listened to countless wives, partners and girlfriends describe the Dr. Jekyll and Mr. Hyde qualities of Nice Guys."

Dr. Glover also believes that the Nice Guy Syndrome arises in childhood. "Becoming a Nice Guy is a way of coping with situations where it does not feel safe or acceptable for a boy or a man to just be who he is," he writes. "Further, the only thing that would make a child or an adult sacrifice one's self by trying to become something different is a belief that being just who he is must be a bad and/or dangerous thing."

Nice Guy Syndrome applies to Chris because it was a way for him to feel valued, respected, and adored. It made him feel special, but it also made him feel resentful. It was the identity he created to adapt to a world and fit in when he felt different from the others around him. Every single human being has needs, and the people who deprive themselves of their needs are almost always deeply resentful inside. In Cadle's book, Chris says he couldn't say no to his wife, he didn't make any decisions, and he swallowed his own needs in order to keep the peace. He admits it was his fault that he kept quiet and never expressed any of his grievances, so Shanann never knew what was bothering him and simmering inside. Clearly, the Nice Guy Syndrome was a ticking time bomb for him that could last only so long.

Shanann, the scapegoat

It's no surprise that Shanann became a scapegoat for Chris.

Even after Shanann died, some people on social media were blaming her for her own death. Some insinuated that Shanann drove Chris to this by being "controlling," but that takes all accountability off Chris. How does it make sense to excuse a man for killing his family because his wife was dominant? In a world where women and children are physically harmed by men way more than they are by other women, this is another way that validates violence against women and children. In fact, according to *Jezebel*, "A 2017 study conducted by the Centers for Disease Control showed that out of 100,000 women killed in the United States, over half were killed by an intimate partner, usually current or former husbands and boyfriends; 15 percent of them were pregnant."[33] Violence against women by an intimate partner is more common than one would think, and there is never any excuse for it.

Chris was cheating on his pregnant wife, he murdered his wife and children, pleaded guilty to all charges, and yet some people were trying to find a way to blame Shanann for everything that had happened.

As for the Watts family, at first, denial was a strong defense mechanism for them. In the beginning it was very hard for them to accept what Chris did. It makes sense that they would have an incredibly difficult time accepting what their son was capable of. They were shocked that their son did

---

33. Reese, Ashley. "Shanann Watts's Murder Is a Grim Reminder of How Vulnerable Pregnant Women Are to Intimate Partner Violence." Jezebel. Jezebel, August 22, 2018. https://jezebel.com/shanann-wattss-murder-is-a-grim-reminder-of-how-vulnera-1828519548

something so opposite from everything they knew him to be. This was not the person they knew and I'm sure that they never could have imagined something like this happening to them.

When Cindy spoke at his sentencing, where he pleaded guilty and received four consecutive life sentences, she spent most of the time telling her son she forgave him and loved him. The Watts family victim statement did say they did not condone what Chris did, and their lives were irreparably damaged, but even as Chris sat in prison in the first few months, they were looking for ways to exonerate him. It makes sense a parent would want to fight for their child and would have a hard time confronting the idea that their child could commit such horrific acts, but they were having an exceptionally hard time accepting what Chris had done.

Cindy's initial interviews with the press (which she later came to regret) consisted of finger pointing at Shanann and trying to fight for Chris, even after he told his parents there was a reason he pleaded guilty. After Chris was sitting in jail, he said, "On the phone they (Cindy and Ronnie) still think there's a chance I could get out. They tell me to fight it. Not every day, on their bad days. My mom loses it a lot. My dad says don't talk about it. They still believe Shanann killed the girls. They think I was railroaded. I don't feel like I was pressured." Cadle has also publicly stated in her exclusive video with *The Daily Mail* that, "I believe that Cindy Watts hated Shanann so much…that she can't get past thinking that Shanann killed her own daughters."

Although both Chris and Cadle have shared that Cindy may believe Shanann killed her daughters, Cindy has not publicly stated that she holds any of these opinions since Chris' sentencing. At Chris' sentencing, the victims advocate on behalf of Ronnie and Cindy stated that they believed Chris needed to take responsibility for his actions. The Watts family will have a long and complicated journey with their grieving process. I do believe that the Watts family, at least on some level, has finally accepted what Chris has done. It must be exceptionally painful to have to live with that.

In Cadle's book, she says, "His (Chris's) mother doted on him, she was used to having a lot of control in Christopher's life." When Chris made his choice to plead guilty and give full confessions to what he had done, it may have been one of the few times Chris controlled his own narrative. It was his decision to plead guilty and his alone. In this case, he would not let anyone else tell him what to do.

Although he has admitted to killing his family in his confessions, he also has a lot of excuses for why he did what he did. Those excuses range from demonic possession, to if he never met Nikki, to if he hadn't gone to the baseball game with her the night before he killed his family, to if his family hadn't gone to North Carolina for five weeks, leaving him alone—if these things hadn't happened, then maybe his family would still be alive, and he wouldn't be sitting in prison. This is placing the blame on absolutely everyone and everything but himself. Spouses should be able to separate physically for periods of time without having to worry about infidelity and murder.

Ultimately, most of these factors probably contributed to the murders, but Chris alone killed his wife and children and made those choices with his own free will. He drove his children for forty-five minutes in a truck with his dead wife in the vehicle and still chose to violently end their lives and dump their bodies in crude oil tanks.

It is also not surprising that Chris blamed Shanann for everything from an Imago theoretical perspective. Earlier, I discussed how no child emerges from childhood without wounding. Because of our unmet needs and shame about the parts of ourselves that we are told are unacceptable, we develop adaptations and defenses to protect us from feeling the hurt and pain associated with those parts.

Imago theorizes that we are *subconsciously* drawn to our romantic partners because they possess both the best and worst traits of our primary caregivers who gave us our wounds (this does not necessarily have to be our parents). When we get into conflict with our romantic partners, they are reminding us of our unmet needs *and* of our primary caregivers. That's because we are subconsciously trying to heal our childhood wounds through our partners. Finding our "Imago" is finding a person whom we believe can make us "whole" again and restore us to our state of natural aliveness before we experienced our wounding.

For example, one couple I worked with, "Adam" and "Veronica" (I have changed their names to protect anonymity) had deep issues with their primary caretakers that was coming out in a very negative way in their adult relationship together. Adam grew up with a very overbearing mother who was constantly telling him what to feel instead of asking him how he felt. Adam found it easier to just become agreeable and quiet around his mother because it was easier than asserting his needs and opinions with her. Adam admittedly said in therapy that he didn't even know what he wanted as an adult because he was never given the space to figure out what he wanted for himself as a child. Veronica grew up with a very cold and distant father. He rarely gave her attention and could be very critical toward her. When her parents divorced, her father became even more distant to the point where she barely ever saw him. Veronica developed a deep fear of abandonment, and even the slightest criticism from Adam would trigger that fear.

When Adam and Veronica fought, Adam would shut down and become cold and critical, reminding Veronica of her father. She would become desperately anxious, fearful Adam would abandon her. Her way of dealing with the anxiety was to try to force Adam to connect with her through meltdowns and tears. Because Adam was so unemotional, especially in conflict, she hoped if she showed extreme emotions, she could cause him to react. All she wanted was a reaction from him, because in her mind, that would show her he cared.

However, the meltdowns and tears would remind Adam of his mother and would cause him to shut down and resent Veronica further. Adam was seeking healing in a partner who would give him space and allow him to be himself, and Veronica was always seeking someone unconditionally accepting and available to her. Therapy was a way for them to recognize their power struggle and find ways to work on their relationship. They realized they could be there for each other in a way that would not trigger their deepest childhood wounds and fears but connect them instead.

In the partners we choose, we are also seeking qualities that we don't have, or the things we lost access to during socialization when we learned to bury parts of ourselves that were once part of our true authentic selves. For example, subdued, laid-back, and introverted Chris was attracted to vibrant, extroverted, and emotional Shanann. In the honeymoon phase of the relationship, Shanann's qualities were very attractive to Chris, but as the relationship went on, those qualities in Shanann would trigger Chris and his repressed self. Eventually, he would come to resent Shanann for being *too* vibrant, extroverted, and emotional. In fact, in Cadle's book, he seems to criticize Shanann for the dinner parties she liked to throw, and her strong personality, among other things. He ended up feeling inadequate with her, saying, "I felt beneath her. She seemed more accomplished than I am and smarter somehow." This was a sign that Chris was threatened by her and had a weak ego and sense of self.

As for Shanann, she apparently had told Chris she wanted a man that could take control of things. Although she was attracted to Chris' laid-back personality in the beginning, she became annoyed with his inability to make decisions as the relationship progressed. She still appreciated Chris' easy-going personality. It made things easier for her as a wife and a mother. However, there were also parts of that aspect of Chris that had the potential to frustrate Shanann.

It is possible that Chris always let other people take control in his life, which could have led to years of repressed resentment and anger. As stated above, it was said that his mother was "used to having control with him," and Shanann had told a friend that Chris's childhood lacked nurturing and Chris couldn't wait to get far away so he could remove himself from the negativity and possessiveness. Cindy's mother, with whom Chris spent a lot of time as a child, apparently had a controlling and negative personality. She looked after Chris while his mother worked, and she could have had a larger influence on him than he realized. Chris possibly felt that he didn't have a lot of autonomy or control in his life, and when he married Shanann he let her take control. However, it is obvious that he didn't like having other people in control of him, even though he made it seem to everyone else that was what he wanted.

In Imago, we want our partner to make everything better. We teach couples that our partner is not deliberately trying to hurt us, rather they are just stirring up old stuff that we are seeking to heal. Chris wouldn't have realized if he were subconsciously wrestling with some of his childhood stuff, hoping to one day feel a sense of control over his life.

In Cadle's book, Chris said he felt like he was able to be himself as a child. In his own words, "My parents never gave me a hard time about being myself." Maybe he was able to be himself to an extent in childhood. However, it seemed that he developed these people-pleasing traits from a young age and therefore was never stating his needs (if he even knew what his needs were). He thrived off approval and what others thought of him. A lot of the good things he did was probably in hopes of receiving praise from others. He may have also felt invisible and inferior next to vibrant and extroverted Jamie and wished he could feel special and important as well.

Chris has said on multiple occasions that he could never be himself around Shanann and was always nervous around her, even after many years in a relationship with her. Yet he was also drawn to her warm personality and her independent self-sufficiency. Where he was indecisive and "go with the flow," she was decisive and knew exactly what she wanted. Chris said he was happy to take the role of the laid-back partner while Shanann made the decisions and steered the ship. But despite how he appeared or what he claimed, he wasn't really happy to do that, and it's been made abundantly clear by the resentment he had for his wife over the years they were together. Happy or not, their dynamic was what he was used to; he was comfortable with it. Shanann's opposite personality traits were familiar to him. He was comfortable letting other people call all the shots. With Shanann, he could continue existing the only way he knew how, as a nice guy who never rocked the boat.

The marriage served Chris because he could be the "good

guy," the perfect husband and father, and he could continue to get the validation he was constantly seeking by being useful and helpful. He was also viewed by others as a supportive partner by letting Shanann dominate the relationship. He viewed himself as giving her the ultimate gift of letting her be herself. All the validation he received by being such a great guy could potentially be his "narcissistic supply." Chris learned that being a people pleaser would give him all the affirmation he felt he deserved. All human behavior serves a purpose. If it didn't, we wouldn't do it. Every behavior of Chris's served a purpose for him. Even if it was maladaptive, it was a means to getting what he wanted.

In his relationship with Shanann, each time Chris felt as if he had to hold himself back or suppress a part of himself, it could have subconsciously triggered the anger that he may have repressed from not acknowledging his needs throughout his lifetime. That was less about Shanann and more about his own issues, but Shanann was the one he was interacting with on a constant basis. She was easy to blame. He wasn't aware of it, but Chris was most likely angry at everyone he felt had controlled him over the years, and Shanann would bear the brunt of it.

This is probably why his perception of Nikki being the first person to truly respect him made her so alluring to him. He may have subconsciously felt his childhood wounds could be healed, and he could be made whole again with Nikki.

Chris and Nikki were having a lot of sex, and self-professed "Nice Guys" often say that sex is the ultimate validation for them, because it is an area where they feel the most wanted. Chris has said that Nikki pursued him and showed a strong sexual desire for him. This was the first time in his life that a woman pursued him and made him feel wanted and desired in a way he claims he hadn't felt before. This was intoxicating for him and could have filled him with narcissistic supply.

Eventually, if the relationship with Nikki continued, he would most likely come to resent her as well. Chris's infatuation with Nikki was shallow. They wouldn't have ridden off into the sunset happily ever after, even if they had ended up together. Chris had been dating Nikki for a short while. He didn't know her. There are people who meet and "fall in love" instantly, get married without knowing each other well, and live a long, happy life together. This is pure luck, and it's awesome when it happens, but it's not the reality for most people. Romantic love is an illusion, and there is a biological purpose to it.

Helen Fisher, a brilliant anthropologist, has written about the concept of romantic love many times. Her paper, "The Nature of Romantic Love,"[34] discusses the work of psychologist Dorothy Tennov, who uses the term, "limerence," meaning, when another person takes on "special meaning." In her paper, Fisher says, "Infatuation (the term I often use for attraction, limerence, or 'being in love') then develops in specific psychobiological pattern, according to Tennov,

---

34. Fisher, Helen. "The Nature of Romantic Love." The Journal of NH Research, volume 6, April 1994. http://helenfisher.com/downloads/articles/04natofrl.pdf

beginning with 'intrusive thinking.' As the obsession grows, many of Tennov's informants claimed that they spent from 85-100% of their waking hours thinking about their 'love object.' They doted on tiny details of the time they spent together, and they aggrandized trivial aspects of the adored one in a process Tennov calls 'crystallization.' Crystallization is different from idealization in that the infatuated person can list the faults of their love object. But the limerent casts these flaws aside and fixates on those characteristics that he or she finds unique and charming."

What we are doing in the romantic love phase, is projecting what we want the other person to be, not necessarily who they really are. In an interview with Helen Fisher on Elsevier.com,[35] she says, "Our brain scanning studies (using fMRI) show that when a person is in love, they exhibit activity in the same brain regions that become active when one is addicted to cocaine and other drugs, including the nucleus accumbens and the ventral tegmental area (VTA), two primitive parts of the brain involved in the production and distribution of dopamine."

Eventually romantic love wears off, and people are disappointed. It is thought there is an evolutionary purpose to sexual attraction and romantic love. If we are sexually attracted to someone, and then we become obsessed with them, we have a desire to procreate. Romantic love doesn't

---

35. Elsevier. "Anthropologist and Love Expert Helen Fisher on the Mysteries of Love." Elsevier Connect. Accessed October 26, 2019. https://www.elsevier.com/connect/anthropologist-and-love-expert-helen-fisher-on-the-mysteries-of-love.

last too long in the grand scheme of things, and if you're lucky, the romantic love phase turns into partner attachment, which can be much more rewarding and fulfilling. Partner attachment is the deep love you feel for your mate, not the butterflies, but a safe, warm, and content feeling.

Chris clearly didn't have real attachments to people if all it took was a brief affair for him to decide to murder his pregnant wife and children. Any attachment he was feeling with Nikki would have eventually faded as well, and he would have soon found excuses to start blaming her for his problems. Again, she had replaced his family because she was a new and more intoxicating form of supply for him. He went from devaluing his family to discarding them because of his lack of real attachment to them.

In defense of Shanann

Some people have found Shanann to be controlling and domineering based on videos they have seen of her on Facebook. However, Shanann was merely reacting to Chris and the role he was playing with her since the day they met. He was a grown man and capable of putting his foot down if he felt he was being treated unfairly. If he repressed parts of himself with her, he needed to take charge of that and express what wasn't working for him. Shanann believed that this was his personality and that he didn't mind her taking the lead. When Chris flipped the script on her, she didn't know what to do or think because she only knew one side of him. Their dynamic changed only when he did.

It is also important to note that Chris pursued Shanann relentlessly in the beginning of their relationship. She was sick and in a bad place mentally and physically when they met. There has even been a study that revealed people with psychopathic traits are particularly adept at detecting vulnerability.[36] Shanann still tried to push Chris away, but he won her over by showing her he was not like other men she had known. He acted kind, selfless, giving, willing to please, and he put her on a pedestal. He made her feel like a queen, and she hadn't had that in her previous relationships, especially not in her first marriage. The relationship started with Chris's deferring to her and giving her control. He started the dynamic between them with the role that he played with her.

If Chris had come to Shanann and told her that teasing on social media made him uncomfortable or upset, I believe she would have taken that seriously, if he had been firm with her. When she saw he was serious about leaving the marriage, she was very ready to look at her flaws and change what she could for the greater good of the relationship, which says a lot about her good qualities. Again, because Chris played a certain role with her, she probably thought that the dynamic between them was playful and loving. Perhaps she even enjoyed being in control in the relationship, but by every indication, Chris willingly gave her control. In the prison confession, he blatantly said he never felt belittled by

36. Chivers, Tom. "How to Spot a Psychopath." The Telegraph. Telegraph Media Group, August 29, 2017. https://www.telegraph.co.uk/books/non-fiction/spot-psychopath/.

Shanann. "If she did belittle me, I can't complain. I always knew I was the introvert and she took control of most situations."

Chris insisted that if he hadn't met Nikki, he never would have thought he had a "bad" relationship with Shanann. "We took care of each other for years," he said. "It was a good relationship. I mean, it's just like, if I never met Nikki, would I ever have thought our relationship was bad? Probably not. That's one thing I always thought about. Even Nikki said, 'I don't want you to leave your wife just because of me.' And I'm just like, what do you mean? Nikki [said], 'If you hadn't met me, would you have known?' And I'm like, nope. I never thought I would have strayed away from her (Shanann) at all. I've never tried to follow anybody."

Speaking from my professional perspective, I will be the first to say that most problems with couples is the dynamic between the couple. No one is perfect, and we are all flawed. That means every single one of us will make mistakes in our relationships. In this case, Shanann was 100 percent a victim, and Chris was 100 percent a violent and ruthless perpetrator. That does not mean Shanann didn't contribute to the dynamic in the relationship, but she is not at fault or to blame for anything regarding this entire situation.

Shanann was earnest and would have done anything to save her marriage. Looking through her text messages to her friends, she was trying to heal the relationship by taking accountability. She was asking Chris what she could do or what she could change to make him happier. She was willing to go to couples counseling, to read books, and essentially do whatever it would take to keep her family together.

Chris showed the opposite attitude of Shanann when it came to his cavalier attitude toward his family. He was willing to throw away his family and destroy his marriage and relationship of eight years—even murder his wife and children—for a woman he had been seeing for six weeks. Shanann and her daughters were disposable to him. For the sake of his unborn child and his daughters, a decent man would have at least tried counseling, but Chris selfishly thought only of himself. He continued to lie and emotionally torture a loyal and devoted wife. It is heart wrenching to look at a selfie Shanann sent to a friend, eyes puffy from crying because of the emotional pain and confusion she was enduring because of Chris. Her normally beautiful and radiant face looked completely drained and hopeless with worry and deep sadness. It's just incomprehensible to think that he was plotting her murder during that time, and she was totally in the dark about whom she had married.

Shanann possessed all the qualities Chris never seemed to have fully developed: warmth, empathy, and a strong sense of self. As much as Chris needed her to take charge, make decisions, and take care of him, she was also inevitably going to trigger his deep need to feel respected and the loss of control he felt in his life. As Chris put on his mask and played a role in his relationship with Shanann, he would always be reminded of the story he was telling himself, that he "couldn't be [himself]" in order to be validated and loved.

Early on in his relationship with Shanann, Chris may have blamed his family for the issues and rebelled against them, specifically when he swore at them before his wedding.

As time went by, he couldn't handle the disapproval from his family and the deterioration of the relationship with his father. Eventually Chris would come to see Shanann as the problem, blaming her for his issues with Cindy and Jamie, and specifically for driving a wedge between him and his beloved father.

Usually, when there is a power struggle in a couple, and old childhood wounds are reopening, people tend to blame their partner for all the problems because blame is easier. If we blame others, we never have to look inward and take responsibility for our own stuff, which is exhausting and uncomfortable. Blame is easy because it means we don't have to admit "failure." For many of us, failure equates to unworthy, a feeling most people want to avoid at all costs.

Although Chris was having an affair and lying and manipulating Shanann, causing her extreme emotional distress, he still had the audacity to blame her for their problems. He never once looked at himself and how he was contributing to the issues in the relationship. Instead of trying to work out his issues for the sake of his children and his family, he used an affair as a way out of his own unhappiness or boredom. Needless to say, these are all extremely selfish, narcissistic, and emotionally immature ways of dealing with relational issues. Furthermore, murder is an extremely psychopathic and antisocial way of dealing with problems.

CHAPTER 20

"A failed psychopath"

My theory is that Chris was possibly born with empathy deficits. He could potentially be both a psychopath and a communal narcissist. He certainly has traits of both. What I believe made him violent and sent him over the edge was a perfect storm of psychopathic and narcissistic traits combined with relational stress, outside influences, and the propensity that the human brain has toward violence, something we will explore shortly.

Chris possesses many traits of psychopathy, although most of them weren't obvious until his thirties. The average person thinks of psychopathy/sociopathy and narcissism in quite simplistic terms when it is actually more complex. When most people think of a "psychopath," they think of someone like the famous serial killer Ted Bundy. Meaning, they think all psychopaths commit violent crimes. People also believe that in order to be a psychopath, the person must have some history of violence, such as torturing small animals or other classic warning signs. Although this is true for some psychopaths who start out with conduct disorder that later becomes antisocial personality disorder, not all psychopaths display signs of violence or abusive behavior. In fact, plenty of psychopathic people are wandering around among us, and can be referred to as "community psychopaths."

I spoke to Kim Gorgens, a Clinical Professor in the Graduate School of Professional Psychology at the University of Denver. An expert on criminal behavior, she did her doctoral research on community psychopaths and teaches The Psychology of Criminal Behavior at the University of Denver. She told me: "I think of psychopathy as a trait that confers some advantages for leadership and politics and relationships, none of which includes murder, obviously. We study psychopathy in incarcerated populations, and those are the folks that aren't very good at it. Chris Watts is a failed psychopath like many others in prison for the same kinds of crimes."

Gorgens made an important point. The only psychopaths we study are the ones who are incarcerated and couldn't use their psychopathy to their advantage. Because Chris Watts didn't show signs of conduct disorder or antisocial personality disorder, it is easy to assume that he's not a psychopath, but we aren't considering the psychopaths among us who aren't in prison and never will be. Many of these people are non-violent psychopaths, but all have the same thing in common: lack of typical human emotion and empathy.

Upon further investigation, completely fascinated by this idea of the psychopaths among us, I stumbled across an article on Talkspace.com, "I Am A Psychopath,"[37] by Athena Walker. Walker argues that psychopaths are mythologized and demonized based on the psychopaths who are incarcerated and studied, which she says only make up a fraction of the total population of psychopaths. She goes on to say the following:

"Our difference is obvious to us as children. The world operates on a construct of emotion that we lack. I have often called emotions temperamental cheat codes to the neurotypical experience. It cuts out a great deal of the weighing information and deciding on actions based on social outcome. Most people act as their internal directional emotions tell them to, and it makes human interaction much easier; everyone is on the same page.

We aren't. Psychopathy is a variant structure of the brain that won't be evident until after the person reaches twenty-five, and at that time, provided the circumstances are present to allow for it, they can be diagnosed as psychopathic. We lack empathy, we lack fear, sadness, anxiety, remorse, we lack many of the things that explain to you in silent code how to behave around others of your kind, and the world in general.

Instead we must either be taught or figure it out on our own. Nothing neurotypicals do makes sense to us. It's like trying to figure out a foreign film without subtitles and no

---

37. Beyla, Chaya, Wisner, Wendy Wisner, byReina Gattuso, Reina Gattuso, Christina Vanvuren, Joseph Rauch, Samantha Rodman, Samantha Rodman, and Athena Walker. "I Am A Psychopath." Talkspace, May 1, 2019. https://www.talkspace.com/blog/i-am-a-psychopath/.

scene context. We just begin to mimic. As we get older, our skill increases and we do better, but in the beginning, we are bad at it. Another issue we face is having to learn the value that neurotypicals place on certain behaviors that to us seem worthless. We must develop cognitive empathy, and use this to guide our interactions...

As we age the differences between us and those around us dictate that we craft a mask that allows us to seem like everyone else. Neurotypicals develop social masks, a presentation of self that presents the best light possible. Psychopathic masks are far more involved and detailed. These masks are a different person entirely, and the more honed the mask, the more obvious it is to us that we are very different from those around us. However, most of us will never think for a moment that we are psychopathic....

When people formed groups, I never cared to belong. When others sought each other out in times of trouble, I saw no need. Problems in the family, which at times were plentiful, simply never fazed me or made an impact on me in any way. This alarmed my parents enough that they assumed I was dangerously suppressing things."

After reading Walker's article I was stunned at how much her self-description sounded exactly like Chris Watts. Chris seems to be exactly what Gorgens stated: a failed psychopath. It is his complete lack of empathy, remorse, and normal human emotion that made him capable of murdering his entire family. Shanann Watts could have been married to a psychopath and had no idea because the mask he crafted was just that good. Just as Athena Walker says, most psychopaths won't think they're psychopathic, and I think it's a safe bet to say Chris never did and still doesn't. In the information we have based on interviews with Chris, his own descriptions of self eerily match Athena Walker's to a tee. If you recall, Chris was very detached when his father was dealing with a drug issue, he said he never cared to have a bunch of friends or belong to any type of group, and he kept all his problems to himself. He never sought others out in times of trouble. Most striking is his lack of emotions. The difference between Athena Walker and Chris Watts is that Chris Watts is a failed psychopath.

Asperger's Syndrome

I am aware that people have speculated that Chris could have Asperger's Syndrome, which is a condition on the autism spectrum. Usually, those with Asperger's are higher functioning on the spectrum. People with Asperger's are known to be quite socially awkward. They miss social cues, they don't show much emotion, they like to focus on a single subject, they repeat things a lot, and they dislike change. Could Chris have Asperger's? Of course, it is possible, and there are some overlaps with psychopathy, but I believe he leans more toward a psychopathic and/or narcissistic type. Although people with Asperger's can have problems with empathy, they are generally not thought to be violent. In fact, they rarely are.

There are some academic journals on Asperger's and

violence, and there are a few case studies in these journals that look at those with Asperger's who have murdered. In the Web MD article, "Asperger's and Violence: Experts Weigh In,"[38] it says, "psychologists and psychiatrists agree that people with autism or Asperger's are not more likely to commit violent crimes than members of the general population, but they say in very rare cases, it can happen." Furthermore, Dr. Marianne Kristiansson, a professor in Forensic Psychiatry in Stockholm, Sweden, who was interviewed for the article distinguishes between the crimes someone with Asperger's may commit versus a psychopath's crimes, saying, " a psychopath commits crimes that he receives some benefit from, and he would not commit suicide after a crime." This sentence describes Chris's crime: He killed his family to receive personal benefit for himself, and he had no intention of committing suicide afterward. His motive was to continue his life with Nikki without his family to hold him back from her.

While people with Asperger's are socially awkward and have trouble with emotions and communication, they are not necessarily manipulative in nature or lacking in remorse. In the *Psychology Today* article, "Asperger's Disorder vs. Psychopathy,"[39] it says the main factor that makes someone with Asperger's potentially become violent is comorbidity with another

---

38. Goodman, Brenda. "Asperger's and Violence: Experts Weigh In." Web-MD. WebMD, December 19, 2012. https://www.webmd.com/brain/autism/news/20121218/aspergers-violence.

39. "Asperger's Disorder vs. Psychopathy." Psychology Today. Sussex Publishers. Accessed October 26, 2019. https://www.psychologytoday.com/us/blog/shadow-boxing/201402/aspergers-disorder-vs-psychopathy.

psychiatric disorder. There are also people with Asperger's who show a lot of remorse, compassion, and empathy, unlike psychopaths. The article says with Asperger's and psychopathy, "the most significant difference is the lack of remorse in psychopaths, along with their propensity to manipulate, blame others, and exploit situations and people." Chris has now blatantly stated he felt no remorse for his family after he killed them, he certainly blamed others, starting with Shanann when he falsely accused her of killing the children. He has also manipulated and exploited people. These things are more in line with psychopathic traits than with Asperger's.

Mimicking and muted emotions

An interesting comment from Chris's prison confession where he indicates he may have a predisposition to psychopathy is his muted emotions. He was able to disguise his lack of empathy because people were mistaking his lack of emotion as being laid back, non-violent, and calm. People often equate these qualities with kindness, but that isn't necessarily true. Chris appeared to be kind and empathic, attentive, and caring because, as an adult, he was able to put on a convincing mask.

So many people close to him described him as never showing emotion, but none of this registered for them as anything potentially sinister until they looked at it in hindsight. Just as Walker said in her article, "The world operates on a construct of emotion that we lack."

When he was a child, Chris's mother and sister constantly

asked how he felt because they had no clue. His mother looks back and clearly remembers Chris being a very quiet child. He was quiet because he was likely observing others so he could mimic them. He knew he was different than other people, and he didn't know how to relate to them.

When Chris was an adult, people thought he was socially awkward, which is another clue that he couldn't relate to others. Someone who had met him at one of the more recent Thrive conferences had said that although Shanann was warm and bubbly, something about Chris was very odd, to her. His face was described as empty with no expressions. She felt something was off with him. It was something that went beyond someone who was just socially awkward, and she couldn't put her finger on it.

Chris learned how to mimic love and emotion by watching others, a common trait of psychopathy. As Walker mentioned in her article, "Nothing neurotypicals do makes sense to us. It's like trying to figure out a foreign film without subtitles and no scene context. We just begin to mimic. As we get older, our skill increases and we do better, but in the beginning, we are bad at it."

In retrospect, we can see that Chris mimicked Shanann. She was exuberant with her feelings, and that came through in her writing on her social media posts. She often posted using multiple exclamation points to convey excitement, something she felt often. I noticed that Chris often used multiple exclamation points as well. He wrote like Shanann, in both his text messages to her (even when he was blatantly lying to her) and in his love letters to Nikki. In a birthday card to Nikki, he wrote ecstatically: "You are truly an amazing, inspirational, and electric woman that takes my breath away every time I see you! You are Wonderful! Don't EVER stop being you!!!! HAPPY BIRTHDAY!!!"

As discussed previously, on Facebook, Shanann posted a picture of a text message exchange with Chris about a picture of the ultrasound of baby Nico. Chris responded, "Little peanut!! Love her/him already!!!" Chris never wanted Nico, so this proclamation of love was a lie. If you didn't know Chris in person, you would believe, based on his writing style, that he was an exuberant, over-the-top, emotional person—just like his wife. Yet those who knew him in person said he never showed emotion. Did he learn to mimic Shanann just so he could fit into her world? Perhaps he was always nervous around her because he was acting the whole time and knew it wasn't genuine.

If Chris was indeed a psychopath, he was able to hide his true self for so long because he probably mastered the art of mimicking others. As self-professed psychopath, Athena Walker said above, the masks of psychopaths are way more detailed than those of the average person. The reason he felt he couldn't be himself around Shanann and always had to think about what he was going to say to her was because he was mirroring her personality. He had to think about what she would say or want from him in order to have a functional relationship with her.

When Chris was writing his love letters to Nikki, he was

telling her what he believed she wanted to hear, and instead of using his own words and feelings, he was using song lyrics, which is again, a form of mimicking.

Chris also appears to have psychopathic traits because he was confused about what he thought he was supposed to feel as a father. He said the following in his prison confession: "No father would ever do anything to hurt his blood and flesh and I did that ... and I just don't understand how it happened. I've even read books that said no dad would ever do anything to hurt his children. So, I always think to myself: was I even a dad at one point? I don't know." Chris had to read a book to understand that a father has a natural instinct to protect his children. He didn't have the normal feeling of wanting to protect your children from harm at all costs. He wasn't like other fathers because it was easy for him to hurt his children when they got in his way of getting what he wanted.

Of course, Chris had some feelings, and he wasn't totally void of emotion. We know, for example, that he felt rage and anger. Beyond his feelings of rage, anger, and sexual desire, his emotional landscape seemed to be a mystery to him. This is common when children don't learn how to identify and label feelings in childhood, or when bigger personalities take up space in the home. The child then learns that their emotions are not the important ones and should be suppressed.

Boys are also universally socialized to receive the message that anger, and sexual desire are the only feelings that are socially acceptable. Add empathy deficits and an inability to understand emotions, and it's clear that Chris didn't know what love really was. He certainly said the words "I love you" and acted as if he loved other people, but it's clear that he didn't experience love for other people in a real and genuine way. He had to search, "what do you feel when someone says I love you" because he really had no idea.

Just because someone is psychopathic doesn't mean they are aware they are one. In fact, some psychopaths may believe they feel love and experience some emotions that are typical to the human experience. The article, "The Scientific Signs You Are in a Relationship with a Psychopath" in *Neuroscience News*,[40] states, "psychopaths do appreciate their relationships in their own way. They do suffer pain, feel loneliness, have desires and feel sadness if they do not receive affection." If Chris is a psychopath, or has traits on the spectrum of psychopathy, that would help explain why his relationships worked for as long as they did. It also explains why he may believe he loved and still loves his family, regardless of his actions.

Chris would eventually end up explaining to the investigators that he doesn't feel things the way "normal" people do. He said his attorneys told him he needed to show more emotion. In his confession, he told investigators, "I don't show emotion. I hold it in as much as I can. I don't want to know what I looked like or sounded like on the TV interview. People said I looked soulless. Everything was harbored

---

40. Neuroscience News. "The Scientific Signs You Are in a Relationship with a Psychopath." Neuroscience News, December 2, 2018. https://neuroscience-news.com/psychopath-npd-abuse-relationship-120187/.

deep down, and one night in my cell it hit me. That everybody was gone. In my head it didn't register, and now it feels real every day. It's weird how emotions process differently with me than everybody else. If I lost my kids at a grocery store, I wouldn't panic. I'd walk around and look for them, but I wouldn't cry. I don't wanna think I'm a cold-hearted person. I just don't show emotion as much as other people do."

It's clear that Chris does not want to think or believe he is on the spectrum of psychopathy and narcissism. He says he doesn't show emotion as much as other people do and processes things differently than "everybody else." However, he gives insight to the fact that he doesn't feel universal human emotions like panic or anxiety. Again, back to Athena Walker's article: "We lack empathy, we lack fear, sadness, anxiety, remorse, we lack many of the things that explain to you in silent code how to behave around others of your kind, and the world in general."

The latest research from a Dutch university[41] found evidence that "psychopathic individuals have deficits in threat detection and responsivity, but that the evidence for reduced subjective experience of fear in psychopathy is far less compelling." Sylco Hoppenbrouwers, one of the people behind this study told *Forensic Magazine*,[42] "We now show that psychopathic individuals mainly have deficits in assessing

---

41. "Parsing Fear: A Reassessment of the Evidence for Fear ..." Accessed October 25, 2019. https://www.apa.org/pubs/journals/features/bul-bul0000040.pdf.

42. Augenstein, Seth. "Psychopaths Feel Fear, But Not Danger." Forensic Magazine, September 1, 2016. https://www.forensicmag.com/article/2016/09/psychopaths-feel-fear-not-danger.

threats and risks but may in fact feel fear." This could explain why Chris felt he could get away with murdering his family, because it's obvious he has deficits in assessing threat and risk.

In describing how he might react if he lost his children in a grocery store, Chris Watts is a perfect example of such a psychopathic individual. He said if he lost his children, he wouldn't panic. The image of him calmly walking through a grocery store and not experiencing panic or concern is an example of a deficit in threat detection and responsivity. Most parents know the immediate glimmer of panic and fear that instinctually kicks in when they are at a playground or store and can't find their child. Chris does not experience this.

However, there are moments where he does feel fear and panic. This seems obvious from the bodycam footage from Nate Trinastich's house as he is watching the security footage. As Chris puts his hands on his head and rocks back and forth, you can see he is in complete panic over the idea that he's probably going to get caught. There are several other moments in the bodycam footage where you can detect alarm and fear on his face, but again, those moments are related to the possibility that he is going to get caught for his actions. Hoppenbrouwers' study would explain how Chris could be a psychopathic individual and still feel fear.

One of the most obvious signs of Chris' empathy deficits was his ability to drive a car for forty-five minutes with his daughters' feet dangling above their dead mother. Then after all that, subjecting his daughters to horrific fear as he killed them with his bare hands. Perhaps out of all the cruel acts he carried out, the most incomprehensible is subjecting Bella to watch her beloved CeCe die in front of her, and then watching her sister's lifeless body dropped in the oil tank. All at the hands of the father she once joyfully sang about as her hero. As any average person with normal levels of empathy knows, the idea of killing your own child and putting that child through the hell Bella endured is beyond unfathomable and impossible to relate to on any level. Furthermore, for most people, the idea of killing *any* child is the most incomprehensible thing imaginable.

Another clue Chris gives in his confession with investigators is a story from grade school about the time he wrote an entirely made-up essay about having spent the summer in China. He seems to brag and takes delight in his ability to be convincing, even when making up a totally fabricated story. "When I was a kid, I convinced my teacher I went to Japan or China over the summer…I said oh, I went to China. She actually believed it! I was really convincing."

One of the investigators prompts him more by saying, "So you're a smart dude?"

Chris responds with, "Yeah. At the parent teacher conference, she said, oh how was China?"

A person with psychopathic and narcissistic traits is charming and deceptive. They can lie very easily and take delight in it. In fact, a phenomenon called "dupers delight" is the feeling of excitement, like a rush of endorphins when conning or manipulating someone else. In this case, you get a glimpse into the fact that not only does Chris feel proud of himself for conning another person, but he also thinks quite highly of himself and his intellectual capabilities. Of course, all children lie, and this incident on its own wouldn't be a red flag, but it is worth noting as we look back at Chris's life and the traits that empowered him to commit such unspeakable acts.

His state of mind is also reflected in his internet searches directly after the murders. Chris did tell Cadle that Nikki was the one who told him to look up the lyrics to "Battery" that morning, but who knows if this is true? His family had been dead only a few hours when he searched the lyrics to Metallica's song "Battery" at 10:10 am. In the song, the lyrics illustrate themes such as the following: hypnotizing power, a hungry violence seeker feeding off the weaker, lunacy, pounding out aggression, and several times the lyrics use the phrase, "cannot kill the family."

Even though Metallica's meaning behind the song has nothing to do with killing a family, the lyrics discuss the intoxicating feelings of aggression, lunacy, power, and violence. Based on these lyrics, it almost seems that he got a euphoric rush after killing his family. The "hypnotizing power" speaks to the narcissistic and psychopathic desire to have power and control over others. If he did, in fact, feel a euphoria and connection to the song regarding "hungry violence seeker, feeding off the weaker," this would be very indicative of someone with psychopathic traits.

For example, serial killer David Berkowitz described what he felt after the first time he killed someone: "I was literally singing to myself on my way home, after the killing. The tension, the desire to kill a woman had built up in such explosive proportions that when I finally pulled the trigger, all the pressures, all the tensions, all the hatred, had just vanished, dissipated but only for a short time."[43]

The ability Chris had to go about his life as normal after he had murdered his family is the most chilling part of this case to some people. Calling the school to tell them the girls would not be coming back, texting the real estate agent about selling the house, supposedly texting Nikki to tell her his family was gone, and discussing pawning Shanann's ring—all these behaviors show signs of someone with absolutely no remorse. Chris would say he wasn't thinking, was in shock, and couldn't logically explain his behavior at that time. In prison, he has had time to reflect that if he were not so selfish and caught up in his own needs and desires, then he would still have the great life he always had. He feels remorse now because he is in prison for the rest of his life. He was coddled and spoiled by Shanann but couldn't see it until, through his own actions, he lost it. This again just reflects his own selfishness and lack of regard for others. Hindsight is 20/20. Had he gotten away with this crime; he would have most likely lived his life guilt-free. Maybe Bella's pleading "Daddy no!" before he snuffed out her life would come and haunt him in his dreams from time to time. However, his ultimate remorse, shame, and the few tears he has managed to shed seem like

43. Shelton, Jacob. "Serial Killers Describe What It Feels Like to Kill." Ranker. Accessed October 26, 2019. https://www.ranker.com/list/serial-killers-describe-killing/jacob-shelton.

they are only coming from self-pity.

The communal narcissist

In addition to psychopathic traits, Chris also seems to have some traits of a communal narcissist, as he thrived off being helpful and good to others. He enjoyed being a martyr. He appeared to secretly harbor feelings of grandiosity around his helpfulness. He also cares, to an excessive degree, about what other people think of him. He wants people to think he was always good and is still good. His good deeds and his kind identity now seem disingenuous because it appears he only did them to make himself feel good and feel important. As a refresher, "communal narcissism may be understood as an agency-communion characteristic; that is, communal narcissists' agentic core motives (i.e., grandiosity, esteem, entitlement, and power) are expressed through communal means (e.g., helpfulness and trustworthiness)."[44]

When investigators told Chris in prison that "they (Shanann's family) still love you," he perked up excitedly and said, "That's amazing to hear that! I figured they would have hated me." His deep need for approval from others—including the parents of the woman he murdered—is constantly present. I think this is where people get tripped up in this case, and this is exactly why people like Chris Watts are so dangerous. Because he seems so nice and cares so much about what others think, people reason that he must be a good person

---

44. Naderi, Iman. "Communal Narcissists 'Go Green' to Enhance Their Social Status: An Abstract." SpringerLink. Springer, Cham, June 27, 2018. https://link.springer.com/chapter/10.1007/978-3-030-02568-7_160.

who loved his family and made a mistake, snapped, or was possessed by an evil spirit. By looking at Chris through the lens of a good person who made a mistake, we diminish the lives of the people he killed and how severe his actions were. He killed his pregnant wife and children in cold blood. He wasn't on drugs, and he wasn't mentally ill with psychosis. Remember that psychopathic and narcissistic people are incredibly charming and know how to appeal to people. Just because someone cares what others think about them does not necessarily make them humble, empathic, or a good person.

Chris exhibits detachment from reality about the magnitude of his crimes. In prison, he says, "Back when I was in Weld County [his first prison in Colorado], I didn't feel like myself anymore. Some of my friends would say good things, but I was thinking, 'how could anyone say those things about me now?' Maybe that was what they would say back in the day. Now, they will say 'Chris Watts the guy who did that horrible stuff to his family.' I know I shouldn't take to heart what other people think about me. It's just a matter of what God thinks about me...what he thinks about me, not anybody else. Everybody's gonna have their opinions about me. Before I got in trouble... I mean, there's that somebody on TV, that guy killed somebody, that guy's horrible. Now, when something comes out on the 6 o'clock news I don't even pay attention to it. I don't want to be in that position where I'm judging somebody else because that's what people were doing to me. I don't want to be that person anymore. I'm hoping I can step back and look at everything I've done in my life… and I did some good things but the most important thing, I screwed up the worst."

Chris continues to show major detachment from what he has done. He apparently has photos of his family in prison, and there was a petition circulating trying to get the prison to take them down. The petition argued he shouldn't be able to have photos of the wife and children he killed. Chris was angry and unable to comprehend why people would want him to suffer. He also doesn't consider himself a murderer and thinks he should get out of prison and live his life as an ordained minister because, in his mind, this was just a one-time occurrence. In his words to Cadle, "Yes that petition really blew my mind that people really want to make me suffer like that. Even if they did ever take my pictures, they can't take my memories…Do I feel like I should be incarcerated? For the act I committed, I most definitely think so. Do I imagine myself ever doing anything like this or be a danger to society? I most definitely think NOT! If I were to ever be released, I know I would go straight to a ministry and start going to jails/prisons and help inmates."

Chris also hinted in his letter that he hopes he could eventually be released for "good behavior." Chris clearly believes he doesn't deserve to live his life in prison, acts as if he made a small mistake that can easily be forgiven, and should go on to live his life in service to God and others. That's not a luxury that Shanann, Bella, CeCe, and Nico were given. Lives were destroyed, even beyond Shanann, Nico, Bella, and

CeCe. There was a ripple effect that extended to the families and everyone else who was touched or had their life permanently altered because of this senseless tragedy.

Steve Wrenn, the Deputy District Attorney for Weld County told Fox News regarding the Chris Watts case, "Police officers, first responders, prosecutors, defense attorneys—we operate in a world where we see bad people do bad things on a somewhat daily basis. This took it to a level that I don't think a lot of people are still able to get their heads around. It's impacted the way we go about our daily lives and how we interact with our families, how we are able to do our job sometimes." Wrenn continues, "The ripple of one crime like this has been phenomenal. The first responders that had to remove the children from the oil tanks—they'll never be the same. Some of the investigators I know had struggled to return to their jobs and go about investigations the same way."[45]

...

Detective Baumhover, one of the lead investigators may never return to work because of his trauma from the Watts case. When you look at Chris in comparison, he wants people to know he is content in prison, talks about the murders in a detached way, and only delivered an apology to everyone

45. Nolasco, Stephanie. "Chris Watts' Horrific Killings of Wife, Daughters Still Haunt Investigators, New Doc Reveals." Fox News. FOX News Network, June 1, 2019. https://www.foxnews.com/entertainment/chris-watts-murders-documentary-tell-all.

he had hurt after Cadle mentioned he never apologized to them. The opposing reactions of Baumhover and Chris are like night and day. Baumhover never knew Shanann and her children personally and he is so emotionally affected that he can barely go out in public He lives in fear of seeing little girls because it may trigger a traumatic response.[46] Chris is sitting in prison, writing letters to people and fantasizing about his story of redemption. He seems like he is enjoying the attention.

Chris agreed to have Cadle write the book if it was a story of his path to redemption and his journey to finding God in prison. He chose Cadle, probably in part, because he wanted to control the narrative. She is a religious woman and not a journalist, and so he might have felt she would paint him in a more favorable light. He was also able to share his newest version of "why." Chris now claims he was possessed by something evil. He wants everyone to know that the murderer who stood on the porch with a smirk on his face while his family was left to decompose at his workplace wasn't really him. He was just possessed for a short time, and now he's good again. It will be hard to convince the majority of people that this is the case.

Chris is still seeking approval and praise, even from prison. He was aware that everything he wrote to Cadle would be published, and when he writes his acknowledgments in the

46. Schmelzer, Elise. "'This Changed All of Us': A Year after Watts Murders Shook Colorado, Investigators on the Case Continue Grappling with Trauma." Lamar Ledger, August 13, 2019. https://www.lamarledger.com/2019/08/11/christopher-shanann-watts-murders-colorado-ptsd-trauma/.

book, it's almost like he thinks he's a celebrity and not a murderer. It truly is odd that a man who slaughtered his family for a girlfriend he had known for a few months would have an acknowledgment section in a book. The last paragraph appears as if he is imagining he is writing to his fans (and he does have fans and people who write him in prison, so maybe his perspective is somewhat accurate). He closes his acknowledgments with: "Ok, I think that's all I got for now! I pray the Lord keep guiding us, protecting us and correcting us so we stay on His path. I will leave you with a few verses that the Lord brought to my attention. Take care and God Bless! In Christ, Chris."

His delusions of becoming a martyr and helping people are even more fully realized for him now that he is internationally known. Chris has been thinking a lot about finding his "purpose" and talks about his view of what he believes is his unique and special purpose in life. "Honestly, when I was sitting in the cell, I was listening to everybody tell me, if you do this, you could hang yourself, drown yourself in the toilet. At one point, I was listening to them. I felt maybe there was a different purpose for me somewhere else. Maybe it's here (the current Wisconsin prison where he is being held). I prayed to God to move me away from Colorado. There was a hit on me! God moved me here for a reason."

When pressed further about his desire to help people, he said, "This one girl is in an abusive relationship and can't find a relationship with God. I never read the Bible before this. In Weld County, I read it. That was the only book I got.

I read it cover to cover. It stuck with me. I've been reading more and more here, writing a couple scriptures a day and giving it to my mom and dad. My Uncle Johnny and his wife are missionaries, and one of my cousins as well, and they are helping my mom and dad. They're amazed with how mature I am with the Bible. I have a good memory. I've memorized a lot of scripture and can help people that way. There are inmates that have left and gone to a different place who have written me and asked, 'Hey can you give me a couple scriptures? Help me through this?' Maybe I can help somebody that way."

As far as traits of communal narcissism, Chris seems to have strong feelings around his new purpose and possibly has some traits on the communal narcissist checklist, such as: "I will be well known for the good deeds I have done," "I have a very positive influence on others," "I greatly enrich others' lives," "I will be famous for increasing people's well-being" and, "I'll make the world a much better place." I would like to think Chris found God and wants to help people, but it's also hard to take him seriously after all his lies and all the pain he has caused so many people.

As he sits in prison, people in contact with him continue to talk to the press about Chris as a self-professed "changed man." These people are spreading the message that Chris wants the world to know: He is now a man of God and should be forgiven for his transgressions. Forgiveness doesn't always mean that you accept or condone what someone has done, rather, you don't hold anger in your heart towards them.

Forgiveness is a personal thing and those who want to forgive Chris for what he has done absolutely should, but it also makes complete sense as to why people wouldn't feel very charitable towards him. Chris's mom, Cindy, shared a letter he wrote to her from prison with the television station, HLN. In it, he writes, "I'm still a Dad! I'm still a son! No matter what... Now, I can add servant of God to that mix! He has shown me peace, love, and forgiveness, and that's how I live every day."

The truth is, Chris lost his "dad privileges" when he killed his children. Even if he sincerely found God, this still feels like a way to absolve himself of blame and guilt for what he did. Only Chris knows if his new life as a servant of God is real or genuine, but of course people are going to be very skeptical that his remorse only came about after his realization that he will be in prison for the rest of his life.

Chris also told Cadle that he believes if he maintains his good behavior, one day he may be able to get out of prison, even though he was sentenced to life with no parole. Given that he is still on his very best behavior in prison, he is hopeful he can one day be released, and is trying to convince others that he won't be a danger to the public if he does get out. How are we supposed to think he is genuine after everything he has done and lied about? It just comes off hollow, like he's trying to manipulate the public. This tactic is to push his agenda, and hopefully get what he wants, a life outside of prison.

Can someone be both a narcissist and psychopath? Of

course, it is possible that Chris could be a primary psychopath with other comorbid conditions, such as communal narcissism. I personally do not believe that most people fit into neat little boxes of diagnosis, and Chris may not either. Human beings are very complex, and there is still so much we don't understand about many of these conditions. It's going to be impossible to know definitively what's going on, but knowledge is power. Hopefully a better understanding of these conditions and how they manifest will push the discussion on how we can spot red flags and use appropriate treatments for people who may have a propensity toward violence.

Classic narcissistic abuse

Continuing with the theme of narcissism, Chris' relationship with Shanann followed the path that all abusive narcissistic relationships do, but theirs was a bit different from the norm. This is perhaps one of the reasons that made this case so psychologically compelling. Many people who have been in relationships with narcissists see that the mask of the narcissist can slip fairly quickly. People in relationships with covert narcissists (those who are not overly grandiose and may seem nice and normal to the outside world) may suffer from abuse behind closed doors, but the rest of the world may see their partner as great. From all the public evidence documented of Chris's and Shanann's relationship, if there was any abuse coming from Chris, it must have been so subtle that it was unnoticeable.

As Shanann stated in shocked texts with her friends, these problems came out of left field when she and the girls went to North Carolina. Shanann was baffled because she and Chris had never had any significant problems in their relationship before. Even if they had disagreements or scuffles, they were no more than what any normal couple deals with. For the entire eight years she had spent with Chris, he had acted one way with her and only up until six weeks before he killed her, did he turn from Mr. Hyde to Dr. Jekyll. Shanann stated she didn't know who he was anymore. She was crying for days out of confusion, shock, and fear of losing her marriage and family.

In the beginning, Chris went through the typical motions of how a narcissistic type of person would pursue someone. As stated earlier, when he first met Shanann, she was at rock bottom in her life because of circumstances around her health and divorce. In the Facebook video earlier mentioned in this book, she describes her attempts to push him away as he unremittingly pursued her. Chris stuck around until he won her over. Narcissistic and psychopathic types prey on weaker people because they need to feel a sense of control and power. Chris made himself valuable in the way only he knew how, by making himself helpful and special by differentiating himself from the stereotypical guy.

He accompanied her to a colonoscopy after only two months. He took pride in the fact that he helped her with a car from the dealership with a wheel that was about to fall off. He liked the fact that he was helpful "just like her dad."

All this praise made him think that he was the special one. This is what narcissistic types need: fuel that makes them feel that they are more special than everyone else. This is also how Chris won people over and got people to like him so much. Sandi told Shanann that Chris was sent to her from God after Shanann called her early in the relationship and told her that Chris let her sleep on his lap for hours and didn't disturb her, even though he had to pee. We know now that that type of praise was what Chris likely needed to further validate his belief of his uniqueness.

It would have been almost impossible to predict that Chris would have turned out to be the murderer he became, but after eight years, the "devalue" phase emerged. At this point, the narcissistic person has already won you over, and they start to become cruel and abusive: mentally, emotionally, physically, sexually, or all four.

Chris started devaluing Shanann as his affair with Nikki grew more serious. Imagine Shanann's surprise and confusion to see such a radical change in the person she thought she knew so well. And he had been so consistent the entire time she had known him.

In the beginning of his relationship with Nikki, he was still telling Shanann what she wanted to hear. An example of this was shown in text messages between Chris and Shanann on July 10, 2018: "You OK? It's like you don't want to talk. I kept trying to talk and I had to dig it out of you?" Shanann said. Chris responded: "I'm fine baby. The last few days at work have put a lot of responsibility on me with new people.

I didn't mean to seem short Boo. I love you to the moon and back." Even though Shanann knows something was different and didn't feel right, Chris was making her think that everything was fine. This was frustrating for Shanann because she knew something was wrong, but she wasn't sure what. Chris was making her feel like she was crazy, gaslighting her.

Because it seems that Chris had no real attachments to his family besides whatever value they provided to him, when he no longer had use for them, he found it easy to throw everything away.

When Chris shifted to the devalue phase with Shanann, he made her feel the worst she had ever felt in her life. During the weeks he was devaluing Shanann and the girls, numerous text messages showed Shanann's distraught state of mind, which was directly related to how quickly Chris flipped the switch and became a cold and distant husband.

For people who have never experienced the devalue phase, it is incredibly confusing to see a person who once put you on a pedestal suddenly act so cruel, cold, and unfeeling toward you. There is an element of disbelief because you feel that the "old" person, the one who was so kind, sweet, adoring, and giving is still there. The sad truth is, the real person is the cruel one with no empathy for you or your feelings. If you've never experienced something like this, or if the change is so abrupt and shocking, it can be incredibly difficult to process.

Not only would this be difficult for Shanann to understand and process, but she also had other important factors to consider, such as her daughters, unborn son, and finances. They had already filed for bankruptcy, mainly because of all the medical bills from Shanann and the girls along with a hefty mortgage. Even if Shanann had slight inklings that something was very wrong with Chris, she wouldn't have had enough time to fully process everything because of how quickly and suddenly things went downhill.

Shanann was a tough and independent woman. She did consider leaving Chris, and she spoke candidly to friends about the possibility. In text messages, her friend Cassie and her husband Josh even offered to take Shanann and the kids in if they needed a place to live if she left Chris. If she had more time on this earth, I'm sure she would have taken them up on that.

Chris duped Shanann by giving her false hope imminently before he murdered her. She was feeling quite optimistic before she left for her final trip to Arizona by the sound of her text to Chris, which is reprinted in its entirety earlier: "*Good morning, honey… We are checked in and everything… Enjoy the girls…I told Bella I was leaving for work with Nicki and assured her I was always coming home… Give them lots of kisses for me… I miss and love you so much…Love you baby. Send me pics.*"

The discard phase and in this case, "the final discard," is when the narcissistic person is finished with you for good. It is when they have no use for you anymore, and you can no longer provide them with the supply they need.

Chris had found a new source of supply and admiration

for himself in Nikki, and his old life no longer served a purpose for him. In, fact, his life of the last eight years had become an obstruction to getting what he wanted. This is also where the blame and rage toward Shanann came in the picture. Shanann, and by extension, the children, became the reason he couldn't get what he wanted. Thus, he reasoned that the only way to get what he wanted was to just annihilate the old life, literally. Discard is the most accurate word for what Chris did to his family and how he did it. He dumped his daughters' bodies in crude oil and threw his pregnant wife face-down in a shallow grave. It's as if they were garbage taken out to the landfill, not innocent human beings. Looking at how Chris chose to deal with his problems is the biggest indicator of how disordered his mind is. While Shanann was looking to cope with their problems in emotionally healthy ways, by her willingness to go to counseling, read relationship books, and work on herself, Chris was deciding that calculated murder was his best option.

Perhaps in an attempt to absolve himself of all his sins, Chris confessed to Cadle that he had zero remorse after hiding the bodies of his family. It's impossible for a normal person to fathom their own children having the same value as garbage, but this is why it's so important to understand the profile of a person with psychopathic and severe narcissistic traits. They are very dangerous.

When Chris talks about Shanann, Bella, and CeCe, he seems to think of them as objects that were only useful when providing something to him. His interest in other people was all about what they could give him. Even when he says he has remorse for what he's done, it's not about missing his family, losing out on the opportunity to know Nico, and watching his daughters grow up. It is more about his sorrow for having to live the rest of his life in prison: "I look outside every day. What would we be doing right now? Right now, I would have had a 5-year-old 3-year-old, most likely a one-month old son and a beautiful wife, and now it's just me." This statement is yet again, all about him and what he could have had if he had not made the depraved choices that he did. He's feeling sorry for himself, not sorry that his family is gone forever.

When Chris describes his role as a father, he says, "All I wanted all my life was to be a dad and have kids that love *me*." Take notice that he specifically said he wanted to be a dad so he could have kids who would love *him*, as opposed to having children *he* could love. This is because he may not have had the capacity to truly love anyone, although he certainly felt a need to have other people love him. Sadly, the attachment to his children seems to be a narcissistic one. It was all about what they were giving him: love, attention, giving him purpose, or just making him look good to other people.

Chris never talks about his girls in a loving or attached way. After he's killed them, and he's giving interviews to the media pretending to be distraught, his scripted speech about missing them sounds detached and rehearsed. He has no emotion as he says he misses them "throwing chicken nuggets" at him. He makes no mention of missing aspects of them that a parent would long for…snuggling with them, hearing their laughter, and playing with them. Even when being interrogated by investigators, he can't even find nice things to say about his daughters. Instead, he starts to say the girls are "bossy like their…" but cuts himself off before he says "mother." He is so detached from his own children that after he's killed them, he can only think to describe them as "bossy."

It's interesting to hear Chris talk about his memories of Shanann. It's like she was an object to him, perhaps even a trophy. In Cadle's book, he speaks about her captivating beauty and how she looked on their wedding day. In his confession with law enforcement, he acknowledged that she was a good person who took care of people, but any sort of attachment he had to her feels shallow. When he talks about Nikki, he actually says nothing about her personality. What he does is highlight how she made *him* feel. He felt that she treated him with respect, but that was again, about whatever need these women were filling for him; it wasn't about who they were. People with narcissistic traits may actually believe they love other people, but love to them is using others to bring them whatever it is they need.

In "Can Narcissists Change?" in *Psychology Today*, author Craig Malkin says, "Even when they fall for someone who could be more than just an adoring fan—someone who offers the hope of a more authentic, enduring love—narcissists still live with the paralyzing fear they'll somehow be deemed unworthy."[47] This is what appears was happening with Chris. Deep down, he knew that not only was he unworthy, but someone would eventually discover who he really was, and he was the opposite of how he portrayed himself to the world. We know he felt unworthy, as he admitted that he felt beneath Shanann, and that she was smarter than he. He resented her for that. Initially, he was thrilled that Shanann, who was beautiful, smart, and ambitious, would choose him. It made him feel important, but then he just became threatened by her.

Because Chris was so emotionally stunted and immature, any type of positive attention that made him feel exceptional would hook him. Nikki's interest surprised him because he hadn't received that kind of attention before from women. He thrived on praise, attention, and feeling special, so when Nikki wanted sex from him all the time and seemed interested in what he had to say, he thought that whatever was stirred up inside him could be love for the first time.

Shanann adored Chris, but they had been together a long time and weren't in the honeymoon phase where everything is new and exciting. This is common in almost all long-term relationships after the honeymoon phase wears off. Couples may eventually begin to bicker, annoy each other, and unfortunately, sometimes that turns to bitter resentment. Nikki and Chris were in the peak of the honeymoon phase. In that phase, the person you are with can do no wrong, so it

---

47. "Can Narcissists Change?" Psychology Today. Sussex Publishers. Accessed October 26, 2019. https://www.psychologytoday.com/us/blog/romance-re-dux/201309/can-narcissists-change.

was completely unwarranted of Chris to compare the two relationships.

CHAPTER 21

Protect and prevent

The Evidence of Premeditation

For a long time, the question of whether this was premeditated or if Chris just snapped in a fit of rage lingered. It makes sense to want to believe he snapped because the idea of premeditation is so creepy and frightening. To think that a person that you trust, love, and share a bed and a life with could be plotting your murder is unsettling to say the least.

We now know after his letters to Cadle that he was scheming and plotting. His texts to Kodi Roberts making sure he would be at Cervi 319 alone that morning seem like too much of a coincidence to be one. Now it's safe to say that, after his own admission of premeditation, this was part of his plan, and his intention was to dispose of the bodies there.

Observers reported that Chris was not just cold and distant with Shanann, but also irritable and angry with the girls in the week leading up to the murders. Sandi Rzucek noticed Chris driving fast and erratically in North Carolina, exhibiting reckless behavior. She and her husband Frank also noticed Chris having little patience with the girls on the trip. At a trampoline park in North Carolina, a witness noticed him completely disinterested and aloof with his family.[48]

And what about the photo of the life-size doll covered in a sheet that Chris sent to Shanann, and which she posted on Facebook soon after? Some people speculate that Chris may have done that on purpose as a way of taunting or toying with Shanann, already knowing what was going to happen to her.

Now that we know this crime was planned, and Chris sent that photo to Shanann days before he killed her, we can see there was likely major significance to that photo. It's deeply sad to look back and see how Shanann responded to the doll photo with such humor. The picture was a real threat, and she had no clue. This is again why understanding the profile or someone like Chris is so important. He is the most dangerous kind of person because he came across to everyone as one of the least threatening people, when he was the opposite.

Chris started to act is if he were coming around right before he murdered his family. Shanann seemed hopeful in her last few days on this earth. Why would Chris pretend he was open to working out their issues when it was clear he had no intention of doing so? Perhaps Chris was telling her

---

48. Wral. "Fayetteville Mom Captures Slain Watts Family on Camera during Myrtle Beach Trip." WRAL.com, August 22, 2018. https://www.wral.com/fayetteville-mom-captures-slain-family-on-camera-during-myrtle-beach-trip/17786760/.

what she wanted to hear to keep her off his back, knowing that she wouldn't be around much longer to deal with.

It's also curious as to why Chris charged the credit card at The Lazy Dog restaurant the night before he murdered his family, knowing that Shanann would get the alert with the $62 charge. If he knew Shanann would be gone, it didn't matter what he did, so he had no fear of being caught at this point.

His behavior after the crime also has people convinced that these crimes were completely premeditated. His unaffected demeanor after he disposed of the bodies, searching the Metallica lyrics to "Battery," calling the real estate agent about selling the house, responding to an email about fantasy football, talking to Nikki, and calling the girls' school to say they would no longer be attending do not seem to reflect the actions of someone temporarily psychotic or traumatized from what he had just done. If it had all been a shock to him that he was capable of doing this and he was caught off guard, how could he be so calm and "normal?" He was so overjoyed his family was gone that he made some major mistakes by jumping the gun on starting his "new life" and taking the steps to unenroll his daughters from school and sell his house.

One of the biggest clues to premeditation was something very subtle. Shanann and Chris found out they were having a boy only a few days before the murders. Shanann wanted to announce it on Facebook right away, but Chris told her to hold off until Monday until after she was back from her

Arizona trip. Why would he have her wait until Monday? What would happen in those few days between Friday and Monday that would change anything about the announcement? He knew Shanann would be dead by Monday and he wouldn't have to deal with another announcement about the pregnancy. The pregnancy was a thorn in his side from the moment Shanann announced it, and he would disregard any normal human decency to make sure the pregnancy wouldn't interfere with the new life he was looking forward to starting.

Kim Gorgens, the psychologist I interviewed for this book, who believes Chris could be a "failed psychopath," told Fox News that "the murders committed by psychopaths are quite well thought-out in nature, and the deliberate crime is more often than not, committed by someone who wouldn't be ideally suspected."[49]

If Chris is a psychopath, this all makes sense. He was the last person anyone would have suspected until he started acting completely unaffected when his family disappeared. While the crime wasn't very intelligent, he had thought it out and planned it, to at least some extent.

But if he did thoughtfully plan this crime in advance, why would he have made so many stupid mistakes? If he had had a well-thought-out plan, wouldn't he have done a better job of covering his tracks? If he does have narcissistic and psychopathic traits, his belief in his ability to be cunning would cause him to be over-confident and make mistakes. Many

---

49. "Professor: Christopher Watts Could Be a Psychopath." FOX31 Denver, August 22, 2018. https://kdvr.com/2018/08/21/could-chris-watts-be-a-psychopath/.

narcissistic people think they are smarter than everyone else, and that is their downfall. They can't see reality. Chris was very sloppy in the trail he left, but there are several things that could have messed up his pre-meditated plan:

1. Shanann's flight delay: If her flight was several hours behind schedule, and he was determined to go through with his plan, he would have less time to get everything done before his co-workers showed up at Cervi 319.

2. Nicki Atkinson's quick thinking: Atkinson really was a hero in this story because of how quickly she acted. Right away, she picked up on the fact that something was wrong with Shanann and had the police come immediately for a wellness check. Her quick thinking got the ball rolling and ultimately stopped Chris from covering up his tracks because he didn't have time to.

Chris wasn't betting on the police showing up so soon. He wanted people to believe that Shanann had taken the girls and run off to spite him. If he could convince others that story was true, and if he was severely narcissistic, he would think that story would seem plausible to others. As a bonus, he could gain narcissistic supply by playing the victim. He wanted the sympathy of those who would view him as a victim of a spiteful woman who took his children and left him. This would benefit him in multiple ways. He could get rid of his family and start a new life with no baggage, and he could also be perceived as the victim.

Why did Chris Watts kill his family?

The question of "why" is the million-dollar question to which no one will ever know the real answers. As prosecutor Michael Rourke said in *The Coloradoan*, "How can we expect Watts to tell the entire truth about what happened?" His confession may have many truths in it, but Chris is clearly not a reliable source, considering how many lies he has already told. For what it's worth, Rourke and the investigators all believe that Chris's confession is mostly honest. Rourke stated, "I'm assuming what he is telling is truthful. I don't think that everything that came out of his mouth during those interviews was the truth because I honestly don't believe that this monster has the ability to have remorse at all."[50]

In the same interview, Rourke also mentioned that certain evidence from the investigation matched up with Chris' account. The most compelling piece of evidence that matched up with Chris' story is the video footage that Nate Trinastich had of Chris loading the truck the morning of the killings. When looking at the footage very closely, there is a small shadow beside Chris that is obviously one of his daughters. In the video,

---

50. Swanson, Sady. "Colorado District Attorney: Chris Watts' Recent Murder Confession Mostly 'Truthful, Credible'." Coloradoan. Fort Collins Coloradoan, March 8, 2019. https://www.coloradoan.com/story/news/2019/03/07/chris-watts-murder-confession-investigators-mostly-truthful-credible-colorado-says/3093624002/.

Chris bends down and scoops up the small body, putting her in the truck after loading Shanann's body. Rourke also said that video footage "would be consistent with his statements that the girls were alive when they left the house and walked out to the truck."

The walls were closing in on Chris, and the charade of his double life was coming to an end. For him, the ultimate annihilation of himself would be the discovery that this carefully constructed identity and mask he had made for himself over his lifetime was about to crumble. Not only would he lose the new life he was hoping for, but if it got out that he was an adulterer, he would be the villain, and he wouldn't be able to handle that.

But why did he have to kill his family? Why couldn't he just get a divorce? Most people would not resort to murder in this case, but if Chris had narcissistic and psychopathic traits, as I suspect he did and does, his family was an obstacle, and he had no empathy for them. If he wanted a clean start with Nikki and didn't want responsibilities as a father of three, financially or otherwise, then in his twisted mind, the only possible way to get exactly what he wanted was to get rid of his family entirely.

Did Chris have a break from reality?

Because Chris had no history of violence or anything in his past that would predict that he could be capable of any kind of violence, many who followed this case have thought he must have "snapped." By "snapped," it seems they think he had a break in reality, or something sinister took over him. Thus, they believe his actions—murder of a pregnant wife and two young daughters—are not representative of who he really is.

Some look at the happy photos and videos of Chris with his family and believe he loved them and had a momentary lapse in sanity. It's too incomprehensible to think that someone so seemingly normal and nice could do something so awful. We have to rationalize it. We don't want to believe that type of evil exists with no explanation for it. Furthermore, we want to believe that we would at least be able to spot evil if it was lurking in our lives.

Chris initially said that he snapped in a moment of rage. In his confession from prison, he said that Shanann allegedly saying he "would never see the kids again" made him snap. This is an ironic excuse considering that he ensured he would never see his children again by killing them. He has now confessed that he premeditated this and that he wasn't in a rage when he murdered his family. He also says that an evil, dark force had come over him at that time but is no longer present and says he has remorse now.

To help me understand more about the neuroscience of crime, I spoke with Dr. Douglas Fields, a neuroscientist and author of *Why We Snap: Understanding the Rage Circuit in Your Brain*.[51] He has researched this topic extensively and is a wealth of important information on understanding the root causes of violence.

Dr. Fields makes a distinction between "snapping" and

---

51. Fields, Douglas. *Why We Snap: Understanding the Rage Circuit in Your Brain*. New York: Dutton, 2016.

insanity. "Snapping" is something that happens to people without mental illness or psychosis. In other words, they are considered to be mentally healthy people with little to no warning signs for violence. Fields believes that snapping is something that can happen to anyone, provided the right circumstances.

"When somebody snaps, it becomes overwhelming," he told me. "It excludes all other deliberation and consequences and engages in violence."

Fields also explained to me that, "understanding the neuroscience and how the brain operates can be helpful, in addition to knowing the triggers that unleash violence. Life stressors also lower the threshold and almost always contribute to acts of violence. We all have the capacity for violence because, as a species, we need to protect ourselves, our young, and our family. The capacity for this behavior doesn't have to be learned."

It's interesting that in Chris's case, he killed his family instead of protecting them, as most people are hardwired to protect their young and their family.

It is important to understand what happens to the brain when a rage response is triggered, and that a rage response doesn't necessarily happen in an instant. Fields explained to me that recent research in neuroscience points to the hypothalamus—there are distinct neural circuits that are associated with things like hunger and sex, and they respond in a matter of seconds to threats or perceived threats. The brain's threat detection is stored in the hypothalamus. In research experiments with animals, when this part of the hypothalamus is stimulated by electrodes, the animal will immediately become violent and attack and kill another animal in its cage.

The reason we all have aggression wired in our brains, and why we are all capable of violence, as Fields mentioned, is because it's necessary for our survival. When the "fight or flight" response kicks in when we feel a threat, we must make a choice on whether to act. Choosing violence is risky because we could get hurt or killed by making the violent choice, but in certain circumstances, most of us will engage in violence acts if necessary. In Field's article, "Neuroscience, Blind Rage, and the Killing at Carderock," he says, "only a few specific triggers will activate the brain's rage circuits for sudden aggression; but once tripped, the reaction can be overwhelmingly strong."[52]

Once the region in the hypothalamus has been inactivated, the aggressive response fades away. Fields gave me the example of when someone bumps into you in a crowd. Your immediate response is to tense up and feel a twinge of anger or annoyance. However, if the person says, "Oh, I'm sorry," that anger and annoyance melts away almost immediately. This is because you realize that your rage was a misfire. A misfire is when we realize that the perceived threat isn't really a threat, and that the knee-jerk response was our primitive survival mechanisms kicking in. Fields believes that

---

52. Fields, R. Douglas, Troy Farah, and Bryan Walsh. "Neuroscience, Blind Rage, and the Killing at Carderock." Undark Magazine, September 30, 2019. https://undark.org/article/wilo-why-we-snap-killing-carderock/.

understanding your misfires and your triggers are helpful ways for people to deal with rage and could potentially stop violence from occurring.

His book goes into detail about the specific triggers that trip the rage response in humans. He created the mnemonic LIFEMORTS, which includes the nine major triggers of violence. The nine triggers are the following:

> **Life-or-limb**: This is when you feel that your life is threatened, or that you may be at risk to suffer a serious injury.

> **Insult**: It is important to note that it is the *perception* of insult that trigger rage. What was said that was perceived as an insult may not be intended to be one.

> **Family**: If you feel your family is threatened, especially offspring, siblings, and parents, your rage response can be triggered. This is a basic instinct in both animals and people. Family is what carries the genes, and we have an instinct to pass on those genes.

> **Environment**: This is the instinct to protect your home or your property. People and animals are territorial. We need our home or territory for our survival.

Mate: As Fields' book succinctly states, "The Darwinian drive to pass on genes from the fittest individuals is the bedrock underlying the ready willingness to fight to the death over mates."

Order in society: Fields' book explains this as, "Violence is used to enforce the rules of society, to assure fairness, and to correct transgressions…. rage attacks frequently break out in response to a perceived social injustice. The trigger often ignites mob violence."

Resources: This is about protecting our resources. Human beings will react with violence in order to prevent theft of the resources that are crucial to their survival.

Tribe: Protecting the tribe is a form of altruistic behavior, but it also divides and leads to violence. Tribalism is an "us vs. them" attitude. According to Fields, "It is the basis for racism and war. Avoiding this trigger is essential for peace."

Stopped: Fields says, "being restrained, cornered, imprisoned, or impeded from the liberty of pursuing one's desires will trip this trigger of rage." This trigger misfires in certain situations, such as someone cutting you in line at the store. On a much larger scale, this trigger can also happen when someone is experiencing oppression because they are prevented from having the same benefits of society as others.

Because the main motivation for this crime was to start a new life with Nikki, Chris' rage at his wife and children may have been tripped by the S (Stopped) trigger. He wanted to start a new life and felt that Shanann and the girls were impeding him from pursuing his desire.

In his most recent confessions to Cadle, Chris describes overwhelming anger toward his wife and daughters. In his account, when he discovers his daughters are still alive after his initial attempts to kill them, he describes being very angry that they were still alive. When he pushes Shanann's body into the shallow grave face down, he describes being so angry with her that he had no desire to change how she landed. These are clear examples that his brain was tripped by the "S" (stop) trigger. When his girls weren't dead after his first attempt to kill them, he became angrier because they were stopping his plan from going smoothly.

Dr. Fields mentioned it is possible he could have also been tripped by the M (mate) trigger, willing to become violent to ensure he could have a life with his new mate. It is possible to have more than one trigger that activates the violent response.

Chris was also under stress (much of it stress he created for himself) at the time of the murders. Dr. Fields says the presence of stressors contributes to this trigger of rage in the brain almost all the time. Chris was in the middle of a conflict between his parents and wife. When Shanann and the girls got back from North Carolina, he could no longer live the single lifestyle or carry on the double life he was leading with Nikki. There was a third baby on the way, one he didn't want. He wanted out of his marriage, but realistically he knew that leaving the marriage and keeping his new relationship a secret would not be easy at all. A combination of the stress and the LIFEMORTS triggers could have helped take Chris over the edge and tripped his wires for violence.

Remembering that snapping is a break from reality and not insanity, would it even be possible for Chris to have snapped considering he planned the crime for weeks? I asked Dr. Fields if the process of snapping could last hours, days, or even weeks. I personally always had a suspicion that this crime was premeditated over the course of days or weeks, and I was skeptical if snapping could last over prolonged periods of time.

Dr. Fields says that snapping, or a break from reality, can go on for a long time before someone comes out of it and feels remorse. So, according to him, it is possible that Chris could have had a break from reality during the time he premeditated the crime and up until the point he says he started to feel remorse. Dr. Peter Ash, director of the Psychiatry and Law Service at Emory University in Atlanta, Georgia has a similar opinion on snapping. He told CNN, "Although a person's snap into violence may come as a total surprise, in most cases there is a psychological buildup to that point. There's a pathway to violence that starts with some thinking and then fantasizing about a plan. There may be a more explicit planning phase that other people don't particularly notice."

Even though some people who snap may have remorse after the fact, any inkling of remorse from Chris feels disingenuous because it seems it is because he has to live the rest of his life in prison. Of course, in hindsight he has remorse because he is missing the comfortable life he used to have, but that's not necessarily remorse for what he's done. It's hard to say how many people have genuine remorse after they've snapped, or if they are just devastated because they've ruined their lives due to their actions. Dr. Fields does believe that many of these people have genuine remorse, and people write to him from prison, thanking him for his book and helping them make sense of their crimes.

Whether Chris' violent acts are related to psychopathy, narcissism, the phenomenon of snapping, or a combination of all these things would be impossible to fully determine with certainty, but it seems probable that it is a combination of all of them. He could have had psychopathic and/or narcissistic traits to begin with, and then had his "S" trigger tripped in his brain and experienced a break from reality. His break from reality could have given him the delusional mindset that killing his family would be a good option, thinking he could get away with it. Now as he sits in prison, and regardless of whether his remorse is genuine, he can see that killing his family was a horrible idea.

Although we can scientifically explain violent acts committed by otherwise "normal" people, this is in no way an excuse for their behavior. Most people under tremendous amount of stress and who have these same triggers do not commit murder. Dr. Fields stresses that, "we need to understand these incomprehensible situations, but it doesn't excuse them, because we are all responsible for our behavior. It's helpful to understand from the neuroscience what causes violence. I'm often asked to defend people in court because defense attorneys are looking for this kind of excuse that they had no control, and I don't testify in those situations."

Ultimately, it seems that the perfect storm of our genetics (personality traits), environment, and life stressors play a role in why we snap. Many of us know what that feeling of rage is, or we at least know what it's like to be pushed to a point where we feel we could explode. However, we don't commit murder or hurt others. Most of us certainly don't plot the murders of our spouses and children because it goes against our basic human code. There is something in us that stops things from going too far, and only in extreme situations where we may have to defend ourselves from injury or death, would we ever resort to violence. Chris Watts made selfish decisions. In many ways, he was the architect of his own stress. There are people who have had way more stress in their lives than Chris, and they would never make the choices he did.

How do you spot the red flags and protect yourself?

As I researched and wrote this book, I have continued to hold the belief that no one could have ever seen this tragedy coming or stopped it from happening. As I stated before, if Shanann had any inkling her husband was capable of murdering her and her children, she never would have left him alone with the girls. If anyone close to Shanann and Chris thought this was possible, I'm sure they would have done something to try and stop it from happening. Not one person interviewed who knew Chris personally could have fathomed he was capable of murdering his own family.

This case has certainly been one that gives people pause. Some have told me that since this case, they have looked at their husbands and wondered if they are hiding something or wondered if they could be capable of this kind of violence.

Abby Ellin, author of the book *Duped: Double Lives, False Identities and the Con Man I Almost Married*, told me there is often no way to tell who is duping us. "Almost everyone's been duped at some point in their lives, and if they haven't, they know someone who has. No one wants to talk about it because they're so humiliated, but it's part of the human experience. It's nothing to be ashamed of. Even really smart people get duped! Sometimes smart people get duped more because they think they're immune to it. Especially when it comes to love, we want to believe the best in people. We want to believe in the happily ever after, so we give the benefit of the doubt."

Most people who have affairs and devalue their partners

do not commit these types of murders. However, I believe it's important to include some red flags and tips to help you protect yourself and familiarize yourself with the warning signs of potentially dangerous people in hopes that it could help you or your loved ones.

1. They exhibit no empathy for you or your perspective. Empathy is the ability to understand and share the feelings of another person. For example, if you recognize someone is sad, you would also feel sad for them and connect with that feeling of sadness, even if you hadn't experienced the same thing in your life. Chris started to show extreme empathy deficits in the weeks before the killings. It's possible he showed them even earlier, but we can't really know for sure as Shanann is not alive to look back, reflect, and speak from her perspective. We can easily deduce that Chris didn't display any empathy for his wife or children once he started the affair with Nikki. Many people don't outwardly show emotion, but it doesn't mean they don't have empathy, so that is not necessarily a way to tell if someone has empathy deficits.

Some things to look for when looking for someone with genuine empathy include the following.

• **Do they seem to understand other people's**

feelings and perspectives, or do they have a hard time putting themselves in someone else's shoes? Sometimes you can pick up on this by listening to what people say. Are they judgmental and cruel or open to hearing different perspectives?

• **Do they seem to pick up on emotional cues like sadness or vulnerability?** If your partner sees you deeply hurting, do they try to genuinely comfort you? Do they feel bad? Do they have an emotional response? Does it feel genuine to you, or are they just telling you what you want to hear?

2. **They are ready to walk away from you with no good reason or explanation.** Chris was ready to walk away from his family and a pregnant wife with absolutely no remorse or explanation. If somebody is ready to discard you and get rid of you without communicating or trying, it might be best to let them walk. If they are willing to walk away so easily after a deep and meaningful history together, it shows their lack of character and their limits to form real attachments and bonds to people. If someone is ready to leave a relationship so easily, there is most likely something else going on. Let them walk away and take necessary steps to protect yourself.

3. They gaslight you. Gaslighting manipulates someone else into doubting their own sanity. For example, when Shanann asked Chris at the beach in North Carolina if there was someone else, he denied it. Even though she had a feeling that something was off, and she knew something was very wrong, he denied the truth, and that made her doubt her sanity. Shanann was forced to question everything: What happened? How did he fall out of love with her so fast? What did she do? Did he meet someone else? Her gut was telling her something was wrong, but because Chris was being so deceitful and duplicitous, she wasn't getting straightforward answers. Therefore, she wasn't sure what was reality anymore.

When I asked Abby Ellin what she believes is the number one sign of a duper based on her research, she said, "The minute anyone is going on the offense and attacking you and accusing you, they're guilty. If they're making you think you're the one with the problem, something's wrong."

If you are in a relationship, and you start to feel crazy, and you are questioning everything, those are signs that someone is emotionally manipulating you.

4. Your gut is telling you something is very wrong. The most effective and accurate tool any human being has is their "gut" feeling. We are all equipped with survival mechanisms that help us detect threat and danger. Feeling anxiety and a deep sense that something is very wrong usually means something is. Trouble often happens when people go against the gut feelings they have. Shanann knew something was wrong but she just couldn't figure out exactly what it was. That feeling of "knowing" (even if you rationally question it) is your gut feeling and should always be taken seriously. For a much more in-depth look at how we can use our sense of intuition to protect ourselves from danger, read Gavin de Becker's book, *The Gift of Fear*.[53]

Preventing violence

What are some of the things we can do on an individual level to help prevent violence from occurring? What are lessons that can be learned from this story that we can apply to our own lives?

1. Don't brush problems under the rug. It's never a good thing to pretend problems don't exist. While too much conflict can be a bad thing, having no conflict at all can be destructive, and in some cases, deadly. If you or loved ones have

---

53. Becker, Gavin De. *The Gift of Fear: Survival Signals That Protect Us from Violence*. London: Bloomsbury, 2010.

trouble dealing with conflict, there are many professionals that can help you learn healthy ways to communicate. For example, in Imago Relationship Therapy, we teach people how to address concerns and frustrations in a safe and healthy way.

2. Destigmatize mental illness and promote mental health awareness. Unfortunately, there is still a lot of stigma on seeking counseling for issues. If there were less stigma and shame around getting help for mental health issues, I imagine some, but not all tragedies could be avoided. Even destigmatizing disorders like psychopathy and narcissism is important because if there is more public awareness about these disorders and less shame, there may be a way to treat these disorders, by teaching empathy, and showing pro-social solutions to solve problems instead of antisocial ones.

3. Be aware of the misfires in your brain when you become angry. Dr. Fields wrote his book *Why We Snap,* because he thought if people could understand the nine triggers that lead to violence, and recognize when our brain is having a misfire based on how our brain was designed for us to detect threat, we may be able to avoid some violence. If we can identify the right triggers when we feel anger or rage, and understand where it is coming from, we may be able to take a step back and release some of our anger. Help teach others about these triggers.

● ● ●

Chris in prison

Now that Chris is in prison for the rest of his life, his urges to be important, special, and a martyr seem to be coming to the surface. Dr. Robi Ludwig, a psychotherapist, wrote a Fox News article, "How could a man like Chris Watts so callously slaughter his entire family?" In the article, she says, "Chris Watts may not have been able to find his relevance in the real world but seems to have found it in prison. In prison, Chris feels like an important man; the man he always thought he should be. He gets fan mail and love letters. His newly revealed confessions after "finding God" are making him even more of a global star, albeit a notorious one. He is making his mark on history, so he thinks. His egotistical plan and sick need for distinction and recognition are finally being met. Criminality led to his celebrity."[54]

Chris says he now believes that his mission and purpose in life is to help and serve others through God. Whatever demons he had been hiding throughout his life are now exposed, but he refuses to accept that people see him as a

---

54. Ludwig, Robi. "How Could a Man like Chris Watts so Callously Slaughter His Entire Family?" Fox News. FOX News Network, March 9, 2019. https://www.foxnews.com/opinion/how-could-a-man-like-chris-watts-so-callously-slaughter-his-entire-family.

monster. He doesn't want to be judged and wants a second chance. In prison, he believes he has been given another chance. He is oddly grateful for this new beginning and in his own words said, "I never knew I could have a relationship with God like I do now. That's the amazing grace in all this. I wish no one had to pay a price for it. I know everyone has a purpose; I just hope I can find mine. The only thing you can do now is to pray and seek peace and hope everyone can find it too."

According to an article in *The Los Angeles Times*, "Faith in the System: Inmates across the nation are turning to religion in some form. But is it sincere or spin control?" Christian conversion experiences run as high as 150,000 a year among the nation's 1 million inmates, but most "commitments to Christ" don't last and some prisoners convert several times annually, says Rutgers criminal justice professor Todd Clear." The article also says, "Understandably, judges and parole boards rarely put much faith in convict conversions, experts say, "There's such an incentive to fabricate that it's difficult to be convincing," UCLA's Wiley explains. "The problem is that the best evidence of a genuine conversion comes after a person leaves prison."[55] Whether or not Chris' conversion is genuine is anybody's guess, but the damage has been done and there is no reversing the pain he has caused.

Too many people had to pay the price for Chris Watts's

---

55. "Faith in the System: Inmates across the Nation Are Turning to Religion in Some Form. But Is It Sincere or Spin Control?" Los Angeles Times. Los Angeles Times, October 11, 1994. https://www.latimes.com/archives/la-xpm-1994-10-11-ls-49030-story.html.

selfish and inexcusable actions. As said previously in this book, Detective David Baumhover of the Frederick Police has stopped working since March of 2019. *The Denver Post* reported he had to leave because of his severe PTSD from this case. Baumhover suffers flashbacks and is triggered whenever he sees little girls, and it's almost impossible for him to go anywhere because children are everywhere. Baumhover told the *Post*, "I have a hard time dealing with the probability that my career is ended, and not the way I wanted it to."

Other people associated with the case have experienced their own trauma and still have nightmares about things like oil tanks. Chris Watts single handedly destroyed the lives of not only Shanann's friends and family, and his family, but the lives of strangers who had to immerse themselves in the case. Chris doesn't seem to care very much. After all, he's told Cadle that he's content in prison. It's hard to imagine being content after you've ruined so many people's lives.

Chris Watts says he wishes in hindsight that no one had to pay the price for him to have a relationship with God, but Shanann, Bella, CeCe, and Nico paid the ultimate price. They don't have any second chances. They are gone. We will never see their full potential or purpose and what they would have done with their lives.

Is there anything we can learn from this tragedy? I can't help but think if Chris knew how to deal with his emotions or had a clue about how he was unfairly misdirecting his anger at his wife and kids, the outcome might have been different. Even if he is a psychopath or a narcissist (or both), it is still possible he could have gone through life as a non-violent person had he been given the proper tools. We will never know if things could have been different or if Chris was always destined to go down a path like this.

The most terrifying part of all of this is that we will probably never be able to prevent violence. We don't have the control that we would like to in this world. Repeating myself again, I don't believe that there was any way Shanann or anyone else could have seen this coming. Did Chris Watts dupe everyone? According to Abby Ellin, dupers are successful because they believe their own lies. Her takeaway (and mine), is that there's no foolproof way to avoid being duped because, "…we don't really ever know anybody else."

ACKNOWLEDGMENTS

It takes a village to do most things in life, and writing a book is certainly no exception. I would like to thank just some of my little village that made this possible...

To Bonnie: An amazing writer, teacher, mentor, editor, human, and now someone I get to call a dear friend. You were brought to my life for a reason! Your wise advice, no matter how blunt, has been instrumental to my growth. I will be forever grateful to your encouragement, your nurturing, and your sage wisdom. Your belief and faith in me is something that will never leave me. Thank you for pushing me to be the best I can be, and for always being there for me- love you!

To Alan Kaufman: Thank you for your brilliant expertise and legal advice. I so appreciate your counsel, your wisdom, and your help with this project. Thank you for all your guidance.

To Caroline Teagle Johnson. Your talent is unparalleled. Thank you for your professionalism, your vision, your creativity, and for giving me a beautiful book that I am so proud of.

To Dr. Kimberly Gorgens, Dr. Douglas Fields and Abby Ellin: Thank you for granting me interviews in the midst of your busy lives and schedules. I am honored and humbled to have such brilliant and talented people featured in my book. Thank you for the important work that you share with the world, and for sharing it with me.

To my mentors, **Carl S**. and **Rebecca S**: Thank you for teaching me everything Imago related, and then some. It has shaped me as a person and a therapist. The knowledge you have given me helped inform the writing of this book, and I am always grateful to both of you for nurturing me and believing in me.

To **Bob G**: I love being on our podcast journey together. Some of the topics were incredibly helpful with writing this book- especially the "nice guys." I learn and grow from all our conversations. Thanks for keeping my brain stimulated and keeping me laughing!

Thank you to my beta readers: Caryn, Katie D., Hayley and others in different parts of these acknowledgments. It's always scary to share your writing with others. Thanks for letting me feel safe to share it with you all, and for your feedback that gave me the confidence to share it with more people. And Caryn, thank you for helping with the first line in the book!

To **Melissa T.**: You read the entire first draft in a matter of days and gave such thoughtful and helpful feedback that I really took to heart. You went above and beyond for me and I will always appreciate it. Thank you so much for everything.

To **Lisa, Erin and Kim**: You are amazing friends that I cherish, but you have also gone above and beyond in supporting this book and helping me to put it out into the world. I am lucky to have such talented, fierce and inspirational women in my life and I adore and love you all. **Lisa**- Thanks for working so hard on all things marketing and PR and doing all the things I didn't want to do! Thanks for being my unofficial "book" therapist and all the support you've given me over the years. I treasure our friendship and was happy and comforted to work with a good friend on this project. **Kim**- you're one of my favorite people in life. I'm just a better person when I'm around you. Thank you so much for being so reliable and on top of everything. Your support, dedication, and friendship has been instrumental to the launch of the book. **Erin**- you inspire and amaze me every day. I'll never be able to adequately express what your friendship means to me. You're more than a friend, you're family.

To my AMAZING support squad in life: Suzanne, Meg, Jenny HLP, Robyn, Christine, Silvia, Mer, Katy, MB, Khalil, Melissa, Scott K., Dani, Ali, Zan, Dana, Beebs, Summer, Amanda W., Nat, Becky, Kasia, Lila, Tania: Whether I have known you since birth or just in the last few years, thank you for always being by my side and supporting everything I do. It means the world to me and I love you all!

I am blessed with a large and loving extended family that support me in everything I do. For this book, I want to specifically thank **Russ and Marina,** who are always in my corner and cheering me on. I want to thank **Marcella** for always believing in me, wanting the best for me, and always being there for me *at all times*. **Ramsey and Joe**- you're the best cheerleaders. I always feel so supported by you both. **Massi, Hazem, Soud and Sara** you aren't blood related, but you are true family in every sense of the word. You've been supporting me 100% with this book, and I'm so glad I gained the best cousins I could have asked for later in life. I love all of y'all!

Mom and Dad: It goes without saying that you instilled all my best qualities in me. Dad always makes sure to keep me humble and working hard and mom believes I can do anything I put my mind to. You're both my number one fans. Thank you for your unconditional love and giving me the ability to believe in myself. I love you and look up to you both so much. I wouldn't be where I am today without either of you and your unwavering love, guidance, and support. I hope I continue to make you both proud.

To my children and Goddaughter: Everything I do is for you all. I hope I make you proud. There are no words that will ever adequately describe the love I have for you kiddos, so just know you're my reason for everything and I love you very, very much.

And finally, there are three people that I had to save for last:

Sarah Lindsey – Every single day you have been there for me as someone to consistently lean on. Whether you were reading the book, asking me for updates every day, and just being a rock for me in general…you have always been there. I am so grateful for your friendship. I'm filled with gratitude that you were there to "hold my hand" every step of the way. You're one in a million. Thank you for your unconditional support and love, in this book and in life. I love you!

A.Mowle- What can I say? For over 20 years you have

been the most loyal and supportive friend to me. I'm not sure there's anyone out there who believes in me the way you do. Not a day goes by where I don't thank my lucky stars for you. Even in your busy life as an attorney and mother, you offered to transcribe interviews, you thoroughly read my manuscript, you were available at all hours of the day- calling me in the middle of court to answer a silly question or validate a concern I had. You're my best cheerleader in life and the kindest soul on this earth. I will never be able to adequately express how you've impacted my life. Love you forever, and don't you forget it!

Last and certainly not least... **to my husband:** This book exists because of you. You were the one that knew I would write a book one day, and you never let me forget it. Don't think a moment goes by where I don't recognize how you support me in everything I do. You believe in me more than I believe in myself, and I often feel the strength to keep going when I would have otherwise given up because of you. You lift me up and let me dream big. You give me strength, courage, take my fear and anxiety away, and push me outside my comfort zone. With you by my side, I feel like I can do anything. The best decision I have made in life was marrying you. Thank you, literally, for everything. Love you always.

Lena Derhally is a licensed psychotherapist certified in Imago Relationship Therapy. She specializes in relationships and sees individuals and couples with a variety of issues. She has published numerous articles in *The Washington Post* and *Huffington Post*. She has also been interviewed for a variety of publications as an expert, including *Self Magazine* and *Glamour Magazine*. She is the co-host of a psychology podcast, "Sessions with Bob and Lena" and is a public speaker. In her spare time, when she is not spending time with her family and friends, she enjoys being a clinical instructor in the Department of Psychiatry and Behavioral Sciences at the George Washington School of Medicine, where she mentors medical students. She is also very passionate about raising money and awareness for children with trauma who have been afflicted by war. Lena lives in Washington DC with her husband and children.

BIBLIOGRAPHY

Interviews, transcripts, body camera footage and evidence has been taken from the Weld County Colorado District Attorney, Frederick Police Department and Colorado Bureau of Investigation's official Discovery documents, the five-hour confession with Chris Watts from his prison, conducted by CBI and Frederick PD, and Chris Watts' sentencing. All other sources are included below.

"Antisocial Personality Disorder." Psychology Today. Sussex Publishers. Accessed October 25, 2019. https://www.psychologytoday.com/us/conditions/antisocial-personality-disorder.

"Asperger's Disorder vs. Psychopathy." Psychology Today. Sussex Publishers. Accessed October 26, 2019. https://www.psychologytoday.com/us/blog/shadow-boxing/201402/aspergers-disorder-vs-psychopathy.

Augenstein, Seth. "Psychopaths Feel Fear, But Not Danger." Forensic Magazine, September 1, 2016. https://www.forensicmag.com/article/2016/09/psychopaths-feel-fear-not-danger.

Becker, Gavin De. *The Gift of Fear: Survival Signals That Protect Us from Violence*. London: Bloomsbury, 2010.
Beyla, Chaya, Wisner, Wendy Wisner, byReina Gattuso,

Reina Gattuso, Christina Vanvuren, Joseph Rauch, Samantha Rodman, Samantha Rodman, and Athena Walker. "I Am A Psychopath." Talkspace, May 1, 2019. https://www.talkspace.com/blog/i-am-a-psychopath/.

Black, Donald W., and Jon E. Grant. *DSM-5 Guidebook: The Essential Companion to the Diagnostic and Statistical Manual of Mental Disorders, Fifth Edition*. Washington, DC: American Psychiatric Publishing, 2014.

Boyle, Louise. "Book Reveals Chris Watts's Letter Confessing How He Killed His Family." Daily Mail Online. Associated Newspapers, October 4, 2019. https://www.dailymail.co.uk/news/article-7520985/Chris-Watts-chilling-letter-confessing-killed-family.html.

Boyle, Louise. "Chris Watts Claims Obsession with Mistress Led to Him Murdering Family." Daily Mail Online. Associated Newspapers, October 4, 2019. https://www.dailymail.co.uk/news/article-7534027/Chris-Watts-claims-hadnt-met-mistress-wouldnt-murdered-family.html.

Briquelet, Kate. "'Everyone Liked Him': Did Colorado Dad Chris Watts Lead a Double Life?" The Daily Beast. The Daily Beast Company, September 1, 2018. https://www.thedailybeast.com/everyone-liked-him-did-colorado-dad-chris-watts-lead-a-double-life.

Brummelman, Eddie, Sander Thomaes, Stefanie A. Nele-mans, Bram Orobio de Castro, Geertjan Overbeek, and Brad J. Bushman. "Origins of Narcissism in Children." PNAS. National Academy of Sciences, March 24, 2015. https://www.pnas.org/content/112/12/3659.

Cadle, Cheryln. *Letters from Christopher: The Tragic Confessions of the Watts Family Murders*. Pittsburgh, PA: Dorrance Publishing, 2019.

"Can Narcissists Change?" Psychology Today. Sussex Publishers. Accessed October 26, 2019. https://www.psychologytoday.com/us/blog/romance-redux/201309/can-narcissists-change.

Chivers, Tom. "How to Spot a Psychopath." The Telegraph. Telegraph Media Group, August 29, 2017. https://www.telegraph.co.uk/books/non-fiction/spot-psychopath/.

Ellin, Abby. *Duped: Double Lives, False Identities, and the Con Man I Almost Married*. New York: Public Affairs, 2019.

Elsevier. "Anthropologist and Love Expert Helen Fisher on the Mysteries of Love." Elsevier Connect. Accessed October 26, 2019. https://www.elsevier.com/connect/anthropologist-and-love-expert-helen-fisher-on-the-mysteries-of-love.

Ethics Primer of the American Psychiatric Association. Washington, D.C.: American Psychiatric Association, 2001.

"Faith in the System: Inmates across the Nation Are Turning to Religion in Some Form. But Is It Sincere or Spin Control?" Los Angeles Times. Los Angeles Times, October 11, 1994. https://www.latimes.com/archives/la-xpm-1994-10-11-ls-49030-story.html.

Fields, Douglas. *Why We Snap: Understanding the Rage Circuit in Your Brain.* New York: Dutton, 2016.

Fields, R. Douglas, Troy Farah, and Bryan Walsh. "Neuroscience, Blind Rage, and the Killing at Carderock." Undark Magazine, September 30, 2019. https://undark.org/article/wilo-why-we-snap-killing-carderock/.

Fisher, Helen. "The Nature of Romantic Love." The Journal of NH Research, volume 6, April 1994. http://helenfisher.com/downloads/articles/04natofrl.pdf

Futch, Michael. "Chris Watts, Accused of Killing Pregnant Wife, Kids in Colorado, Has Fayetteville Ties." The Fayetteville Observer. The Fayetteville Observer, August 17, 2018. https://www.fayobserver.com/news/20180816/chris-watts-accused-of-killing-pregnant-wife-kids-in-colorado-has-fayetteville-ties.

Glover, Robert A. *No More Mr. Nice Guy: A Proven Plan for Getting What You Want in Love, Sex, and Life.* Philadelphia: Running Press, 2017.

Goodman, Brenda. "Asperger's and Violence: Experts Weigh In." WebMD. WebMD, December 19, 2012. https://www.webmd.com/brain/autism/news/20121218/aspergers-violence.

"Insights on Why People 'Snap' and Kill." CNN. Cable News Network. Accessed November 5, 2019. http://www.cnn.com/2009/HEALTH/05/26/snap.moments/index.html.

Lee, Rebecca. "The Ties Between Crime and Malignant Narcissism." World of Psychology, July 8, 2018. https://psychcentral.com/blog/the-ties-between-crime-and-malignant-narcissism/.

Lilienfeld, Scott, Josh Miller, and Donald Lynam. "The Goldwater Rule: Perspectives From, and Implications for, Psychological Science," 2017. https://doi.org/10.31234/osf.io/j3gmf.

Ludwig, Robi. "How Could a Man like Chris Watts so Callously Slaughter His Entire Family?" Fox News. FOX News Network, March 9, 2019. https://www.foxnews.com/opinion/

how-could-a-man-like-chris-watts-so-callously-slaughter-his-entire-family.

Luo, Yu L L, Huajian Cai, and Hairong Song. "A Behavioral Genetic Study of Intrapersonal and Interpersonal Dimensions of Narcissism." PloS one. Public Library of Science, April 2, 2014. https://www.ncbi.nlm.nih.gov/pmc/articles/PMC3973692/.

Malkin, Craig. *Rethinking Narcissism: The Secret to Recognizing and Coping with Narcissists*. New York: Harper Perennial, 2016.

McAleer, Kelly. "The Brain of a Psychopath: Using FMRI Technology to Detect Brain Abnormalities, Part I." Psych Central.com, March 27, 2019. https://blogs.psychcentral.com/forensic-focus/2010/03/the-brain-of-a-psychopath-using-fmri-technology-to-detect-brain-abnormalities-part-i/.

Naderi, Iman. "Communal Narcissists 'Go Green' to Enhance Their Social Status: An Abstract." SpringerLink. Springer, Cham, June 27, 2018. https://link.springer.com/chapter/10.1007/978-3-030-02568-7_160.

"Narcissistic Personality Disorder." Encyclopedia of Mental Disorders. Accessed October 25, 2019. http://www.minddisorders.com/Kau-Nu/Narcissistic-personality-disorder.html.

Neuroscience News. "The Scientific Signs You Are in a Relationship with a Psychopath." Neuroscience News, December 2, 2018. https://neurosciencenews.com/psychopath-npd-abuse-relationship-120187/.

Nolasco, Stephanie. "Chris Watts' Horrific Killings of Wife, Daughters Still Haunt Investigators, New Doc Reveals." Fox News. FOX News Network, June 1, 2019. https://www.foxnews.com/entertainment/chris-watts-murders-documentary-tell-all.

"Parsing Fear: A Reassessment of the Evidence for Fear ..." Accessed October 25, 2019. https://www.apa.org/pubs/journals/features/bul-bul0000040.pdf.

"Professor: Christopher Watts Could Be a Psycho-path." FOX31 Denver, August 22, 2018. https://kdvr.com/2018/08/21/could-chris-watts-be-a-psychopath/.

"Psychopaths Mimic Emotions Very Accurately: Brock Study." The Brock News, a news source for Brock University. Accessed October 26, 2019. https://brocku.ca/brock-news/2015/03/psychopaths-mimic-emotions-very-accurately-brock-study/.

Schmelzer, Elise. "'This Changed All of Us': A Year after Watts Murders Shook Colorado, Investigators on the Case Continue Grappling with Trauma." Lamar Ledger, August

13, 2019. https://www.lamarledger.com/2019/08/11/chris-topher-shanann-watts-murders-colorado-ptsd-trauma/.

Schulze, Lars, Isabel Dziobek, Aline Vater, Hauke R. Heekeren, Malek Bajbouj, Babette Renneberg, Isabella Heuser, and Stefan Roepke. "Gray Matter Abnormalities in Patients with Narcissistic Personality Disorder." Journal of Psychiatric Research. Pergamon, June 15, 2013. https://www.sciencedirect.com/science/article/pii/S002239561300157X.

Sedikides, Constantine, and Erica Hepper. "Moving Narcissus: Can Narcissists Be Empathic?" Personality and Social Psychology Bulletin. Accessed October 25, 2019. https://www.academia.edu/6853822/Moving_Narcissus_Can_narcissists_be_empathic.

Sethi, Arjun, Eamon Mccrory, Vanessa Puetz, Ferdinand Hoffmann, Annchen R. Knodt, Spenser R. Radtke, Bartholomew D. Brigidi, Ahmad R. Hariri, and Essi Viding. "Primary and Secondary Variants of Psychopathy in a Volunteer Sample Are Associated with Different Neurocognitive Mechanisms." *Biological Psychiatry: Cognitive Neuroscience and Neuroimaging* 3, no. 12 (2018): 1013–21. https://doi.org/10.1016/j.bpsc.2018.04.002.

Shelton, Jacob. "Serial Killers Describe What It Feels Like to Kill." Ranker. https://www.ranker.com/list/

serial-killers-describe-killing/jacob-shelton.

Stines, Sharie. "What Is Narcissistic Supply?" The Recovery Expert, July 8, 2019. https://pro.psychcentral.com/recovery-expert/2019/02/what-is-narcissistic-supply/.

Swanson, Sady. "Colorado District Attorney: Chris Watts' Recent Murder Confession Mostly 'Truthful, Credible'." Coloradoan. Fort Collins Coloradoan, March 8, 2019. https://www.coloradoan.com/story/news/2019/03/07/chris-watts-murder-confession-investigators-mostly-truthful-credible-colorado-says/3093624002/.

"The Communal Narcissist: Another Wolf Wearing a Sheep Outfit." Psychology Today. Sussex Publishers. Accessed October 25, 2019. https://www.psychologytoday.com/us/blog/tech-support/201605/the-communal-narcissist-another-wolf-wearing-sheep-outfit.

"The Narcissistic Self and Its Psychological and Neural ..." Accessed October 25, 2019. https://pdfs.semanticscholar.org/111b/26029454e95bf730494ddf88e920a6d93fff.pdf.

"What We Get Wrong About the Influence of Parents." Psychology Today. Sussex Publishers. Accessed October 25, 2019. https://www.psychologytoday.com/us/articles/201811/what-we-get-wrong-about-the-influence-parents.

"What's the Single Greatest Danger of Covert Narcissism?" Psychology Today. Sussex Publishers. Accessed October 25, 2019. https://www.psychologytoday.com/us/blog/romance-redux/201712/what-s-the-single-greatest-danger-covert-narcissism.

Wral. "Fayetteville Mom Captures Slain Watts Family on Camera during Myrtle Beach Trip." WRAL.com, August 22, 2018. https://www.wral.com/fayetteville-mom-captures-slain-family-on-camera-during-myrtle-beach-trip/17786760/.

Watts, Chris. Interview with Tomas Hoppough. Denver 7 ABC. August 15, 2018.

Watts, Cindy. Interview with *9 Wants to Know*. 9 News.Com, Denver Colorado, November 15, 2018.
Watts. Cindy. Interview with HLN. *Killer Dad: Chris Watts Speaks*. HLN, July 13, 2019.

Made in the USA
Middletown, DE
06 December 2019